THE INCONVENIENT GENERATION

THE INCONVENIENT GENERATION

Migrant Youth Coming of Age

on Shanghai's Edge

MINHUA LING

STANFORD UNIVERSITY PRESS
STANFORD, CALIFORNIA

Stanford University Press
Stanford, California

Printed in the United States of America on acid-free, archival-quality paper

Library of Congress Cataloging-in-Publication Data
Names: Ling, Minhua, 1979– author.
Title: The inconvenient generation: migrant youth coming of age on
    Shanghai's edge / Minhua Ling.
Description: Stanford, California : Stanford University Press, 2019. |
    Includes bibliographical references and index.
Identifiers: LCCN 2019006066 (print) | LCCN 2019007223 (ebook) |
    ISBN 9781503610774 | ISBN 9781503609976 | ISBN 9781503609976 (cloth : alk. paper) |
    ISBN 9781503610767 (pbk. : alk. paper)
Subjects: LCSH: Youth—China—Shanghai—Social conditions. | Children of
    internal migrants—China—Shanghai—Social conditions. | Rural-urban
    migration—Social aspects—China—Shanghai.
Classification: LCC HQ799. C62 (ebook) | LCC HQ799.C62 S44 2019 (print) |
    DDC 305.235—dc23
LC record available at https://lccn.loc.gov/2019006066

Cover design: Kevin Barrett Kane
Cover photo: Minhua Ling

Typeset by Westchester Publishing Services in 10/14 Minion Pro

For my parents

CONTENTS

ACKNOWLEDGMENTS

I am greatly indebted to many people and institutions without whose encouragement and help this book could not have been possible. My warmest gratitude goes to the migrant youth and their families in Shanghai, who welcomed me as an inquisitive researcher and friend and shared their dreams, disappointments, struggles, and successes over the years. I feel honored to witness and even participate in some of their life trajectories, and I hope my work does justice to their experiences. I am also deeply indebted to the teachers, administrators, and social workers who allowed me to conduct research in their schools and organizations.

I would like to thank Helen Siu for introducing to me to anthropology and always supporting me with her unwavering encouragement and constructive vision through many years. I greatly appreciate the generosity, patience, and insightfulness of William Kelly and Erik Harms. I cannot thank Deborah Davis enough for her continuous support and perceptive comments through the years. I am grateful to James Scott for the inspiration he provided in the agrarian studies seminar and the Incubator Breakfast sessions. In a formative stage of this project, the development of my intellectual interest is owed in large part to Karen Nakamura, Mike McGovern, Douglas Rogers, Jonathan Spence, and Pierre Landry.

As I worked on the book manuscript, I benefitted greatly from the comments of many colleagues. Particular thanks go to Jun Zhang for her timely and critical comments and continuous support throughout the whole process. I would also like to thank Matthew Guttman, and Teresa Kuan for reading and commenting on chapter drafts. I very much appreciate the thoughtful comments from Pál Nyíri, Robert Weller, Biao Xiang, and Juan Zhang at different writing stages. I feel much gratitude, moreover, to my colleagues at the Chinese University of Hong Kong for their encouragement and support for my research and writing: the mentorship and friendship of Joseph Bosco, Ju-chen Chen,

Sealing Cheng, Susanne Choi, Denise Ho, Gordon Mathews, and Ka-Ming Wu have meant a lot to me. And I thank Minlei Ye of the Chinese University Press for her valuable comments on my book proposal and insights into academic publishing. I am particularly grateful, furthermore, to Jan Kiely for his dedicated support for the completion of this book project.

A number of friends have helped with the project more than they know. I benefitted greatly from discussions with Amy Zhang and Yu Luo, both of whom also hosted me in New Haven. I would also like to thank Yi Kang, Xiaobo Lu, and Shuping Wang from my writing group. I feel fortunate to have been able to engage regularly in stimulating conversations with my anthropology classmates, including Ryan Sayre, Abigail Dumes, Susanna Fioratta, Radhika Govindrajan, Elizabeth Miles, Lucia Cantero, Luisa Cortesi, Brenda Kombo, Nathaniel Smith, Michael Degani, Vikramaditya Thakur, Aniket Aga, Joseph Hill, and Richard Payne.

I am indebted furthermore to Marcela Maxfield, Jenny Gavacs, and Sunna Juhn of Stanford University Press for their tireless assistance throughout the publishing process. The book, moreover, benefited substantially from the extremely encouraging and helpful comments from two anonymous reviewers. In addition, I would like to thank Gershom Tse for his meticulous editing work and Puzhou Wu for his beautiful map.

For the essential financial support for fieldwork research and writing, I am grateful for a Hong Kong Research Grants Council Early Career Scheme Grant, a Chinese University of Hong Kong Direct Grant for Research, a Yale East Asian Studies Prize Fellowship, a National Science Foundation Grant, two Yale MacMillan Center Research Grants, two Yale Council on East Asian Studies Research Grants, and a Yale Council on East Asian Studies Summer Travel and Research Grant. I appreciate the Universities Service Centre for Chinese Studies' support for my research in Hong Kong.

For their guidance and insightful suggestions in the course of my fieldwork in China, I would like to thank Tianshu Pan, Guoli Dong, Guoyou Song, Yihan Xiong, Jianliang Sun, Hua Liu, Laihai Lou, Yinhou Yu, Zhenlin Zhang, Ruiming Ni, Yichao Zhang, Jianing Zhang, Juan Bai, Jonathan Hursh, and Lusheng Lin.

An earlier version of Chapter 4 appears as "'Bad Students Go to Vocational Schools!': Education, Social Reproduction and Migrant Youth in Urban China," *China Journal* 73 (2015): 108–131, and part of the research for Chapter 5 was also drawn upon for "Returning to No Home: Educational Remigration and Displacement in Rural China," *Anthropological Quarterly* 90, no. 3: 715–742, 2017.

I want to thank the journal editors, especially Andrew Kipnis, and the anonymous reviewers for their valuable comments and suggestions.

Finally, I am deeply indebted to my family—my parents, grandparents, and my son—for their unconditional love and support for me. Thank you, Calvin, for being patient and understanding when your mom was so often absent while completing this book. I especially want to thank my mother, who ignited my interest in this topic, assisted initial data collection, and helped care for Calvin. I cannot imagine finishing this book without her unfailing support.

THE INCONVENIENT
GENERATION

INTRODUCTION

Coming of Age in an Urban Growth Dilemma

WITH OVER TWENTY-FOUR MILLION residents, Shanghai has become one of the world's most populated cities. Discussions of how to curb its population growth and prevent overcrowding and social disorder feature prominently in official documents and the media. At the core of these discussions is the question of how to keep the migrants, who come from different parts of China and account for over a third of the city's total population, under control. Since Shanghai's natural population growth rate among its native residents has been negative over two decades,[1] most of the city's population growth has been driven by internal migration. Migrants also outnumbered native residents in the fertile age groups of seventeen to forty-three by 2010,[2] which means that they will contribute more to the city's population growth by birth in the long run. Migrants are hence seen by city officials and native residents as both an indispensable resource and a burdensome threat. This has been evident now for years in everyday life, even amid many an average school day, as I have witnessed as a participant observer.

In early January 2007, approximately two thousand students and teachers were preparing for the day's lesson at Jianying Hope School, a privately run elementary school for migrant children in northern Shanghai. Suddenly, more than a hundred police officers and security agents cordoned off the school's courtyard. By noon that day, the school had been shut down, and by the following week, the students had supposedly been reallocated to a public school. A spokeswoman for the Shanghai Municipal Education Commission offered almost no explanation for the school's closure, only saying, "We are not kicking them out of Shanghai."[3]

The ambivalence of the spokeswoman's response reflects an urban growth dilemma that is by no means unique to Shanghai. In pursuit of economic growth and urban expansion, the need for human capital often comes with a fear of overpopulation and overstretched social services. On the one hand, cities need a continuous supply of labor to operate factories, run restaurants, build and maintain infrastructure, and care for children and the elderly. On the other hand, city governments and urban elites feel burdened with the cost of labor reproduction—laborers demand housing, schooling, medical care, and social security. The mutually contradictory incentives pulling in and pushing out migrant workers produce such an urban growth dilemma under capitalist urbanization around the world (E. Friedman 2018).

The socialist *hukou* (household registration) system, instituted by the government led by the Chinese Communist Party (CCP) since the 1950s, imposes highly particular conditions and contours to Shanghai's urban growth dilemma. As an "internal passport" system, the *hukou* registers and controls population within national borders. It divides Chinese citizens into two household categories (*huji leibei*): "agricultural [*nongye*]"/rural, and "nonagricultural [*feinongye*]"/urban. The *hukou* system also assigns each household a place of registration (*huji suozaidi*), tying one's legal status and entitlement to welfare to the specific locale. In the Mao era, the *hukou* system served the socialist planned economy by institutionalizing geographic segregation, preventing population movement, and redistributing social wealth based on state plans (F.-L. Wang 2005; Whyte 1995, 2010). In the post-Mao era, the state has loosened its control over the citizens' physical movement to stimulate export-oriented economic development, which demands constant flows of cheap labor comprised mostly of rural-to-urban migrants (K. W. Chan 2010; K. W. Chan and Buckingham 2008; K. W. Chan and Zhang 1999). The largest population movement in human history has thus been unfolding within China's national boundaries since the 1980s. By 2010, over 220 million Chinese were reported to have worked and lived outside of their registered *hukou* place (National Bureau of Statistics of China 2012).[4] The *hukou* system nevertheless remains largely intact and continues to tie individuals' access to public services with their *hukou* places instead of residential places, making migrant workers de facto second-class citizens suffering from discrimination and maltreatment in their adopted cities (Pun 1999; Solinger 1999).

As now one in three children living in Shanghai are nonnative and do not hold Shanghai *hukou*, it is almost impossible and certainly impractical for the municipal government to "kick out" all migrant children, as the official spokeswoman admitted. Coming from all over China, the parents of these children have been working and living in the city for years, if not decades, and have become indispensable to Shanghai's manufacturing and service industries. Meanwhile, as the city faces a rapidly aging local population due to three decades of the "one-child policy," the need for young, skilled labor becomes more urgent than ever. This second generation of migrant youth will be a key source for Shanghai's labor pool, so how these migrant children learn and socialize carries significant implications for Shanghai's socioeconomic transformation.

In addition, for the Shanghai municipal government, escalating conflicts resulting from international migration in developed countries in the West have become cautionary tales about the risks brought on by marginalized migrant youth in cities. In 2008 when the Shanghai municipal government announced plans to close all unqualified migrant schools by 2010 and use its public schools to absorb those migrant students, policy makers referenced the November 2007 Villiers-le-Bel riots in Paris, sparked by the death of two teenagers after they collided with a police car: "The 2007 Paris Riot is an alarm for us. We need to take lessons from those events: we need to care for migrant children. We need to respect them through real and tangible actions, facilitating them to develop a sense of belonging to the city" (Shanghai Municipal Education Commission 2008, 4).

The sudden closure of Jianyin Hope School described above represents the state's harsh response to facilitating urban inclusion of migrant children. By 2010, the Shanghai municipal government closed over 120 migrant schools that had fallen below official standards set by its education bureau. It had reportedly invested 150 million RMB (about $21 million) in 2008 and 2009 to subsidize public elementary and middle schools to accommodate migrant students at no cost, to improve the facilities and management of all remaining migrant schools, and to open public vocational schools to migrant graduates. However, implementation was often volatile and would bring unintended and uneven consequences. How did the city government and its apparatus balance the competing imperatives of inclusion and exclusion in governing the migrants? More importantly, how did migrant children navigate the institutions and discourses that still privilege the native population? And what do their experiences and subjectivities say about the nature of citizenship under the joint forces of the late-socialist state and the global capitalist economy?

Drawing on ethnographic data collected from multisited field research between 2007 and 2017, this book traces the journeys of dozens of migrant students from middle school to the labor market in the years after the Shanghai municipal government partially opened its public school system to them. It offers the first longitudinal account of second-generation migrant youth growing up in Shanghai as the city wrestles with the mandate to "care for migrant children." Through the trajectories of these migrant youth, this research explores the urban growth dilemma and its everyday ramifications. It reveals the contested process of segmented inclusion, during which institutions, discourses, and practices relating to land ownership, family planning, educational eligibility, residential status, and employment structure accommodate migrant youth just enough to guide them through the schooling system toward manual labor but fail to give them the same opportunities enjoyed by their local peers.

This is a story of an inconvenient generation of migrant children coming of age through channels that designate them second-class citizens in a reemergent global Shanghai. Necessary yet burdensome, migrant youth are inconvenient subjects to the local government that must struggle with contradictory imperatives of developing a prosperous and orderly city. Local states readily combine their administrative apparatus with market mechanisms and sociocultural criteria to selectively include or exclude subgroups and to achieve a desired urban population and metropolitan image.

The case of Shanghai exemplifies the intensification, rather than reduction, of inequality against the backdrop of economic growth and urban development. Migrant youth in both international and intranational contexts face bureaucratic and legal restrictions and experience linguistic and cultural discontinuities. Examining these experiences through the lens of Shanghai reveals the everyday politics of citizenship as an ongoing process of inclusion and exclusion in the era of urbanization and globalization.

PEASANT WORKER

The urban growth dilemma in Shanghai manifests itself in the naming practices of its migrants. *Yimin*, the Chinese equivalent for "migrant," is almost never used in official documents and daily conversations. For almost two decades, Chinese rural-to-urban migrants have been referred to as "floating populations" (*liudong renkou*). This term presumes a temporality to China's internal migration: migrants are believed to migrate seasonally to towns and cities and will, it is presumed, ultimately return to the countryside. Coupled with the more derogatory term *mangliu* (literally "blind flow"), "floating population" also suggests the perceived danger associated with the migrants' transience and aimlessness, which potentially threaten the established social order (Dutton 1999; Solinger 1999; L. Zhang 2001a).

Nevertheless, China's internal migration patterns have been changing from seasonal migration to urban settlement. A 2010 survey conducted in China's five major metropolises, including Shanghai, finds that nearly 20 percent of migrant adults stayed in their adopted cities for more than a decade (China Family Planning Committee 2010). Many first-generation migrants have also managed to bring their spouses and children to live with them as they have grown increasingly financially secure. As urban settlement and family unification became more common among rural migrants, the term "floating population" gradually lost its currency in the early 2000s.[5] In its place, "peasant worker" (*nongmingong*, or *mingong* for short) has become the most common way to refer to migrant workers in both state discourse and everyday conversations. The official term for migrant workers' children consequently has changed from "floating children" (*liudong ertong*) to "peasant workers' children" (*mingong zinü*).[6]

In March 2006, the state council issued its "Opinions on Solving Peasant Workers' Problems." For the first time, the Chinese state set forth its official definition of "peasant workers": "peasants who are registered with an agricultural *hukou* but engage mainly in non-agricultural work (especially during off-farm seasons) in urban areas or in township-level enterprises" (State Council 2006, 1). The state council specified two reasons for adopting the term "peasant worker" to define migrant workers: first, the term had already been used in the media; and second and more importantly, the term is an "accurate" way of categorizing this social group. By confirming the official term, the official opinion reifies the binary categorization of the citizenry through the *hukou* system. It refuses to admit, still less to problematize, the arbitrary and artificial nature of a rural-urban divide in face of massive migration and urban settlement. Instead, the state council goes as far as acknowledging that the rural-urban binary is simplistic and arguing for the necessity for space in between. It claims that this social category of "peasant worker" "exists and will remain long-term as China continues to industrialize and urbanize" (State Council 2006, 1). This statement naturalizes the unilineal trajectory of development from an agricultural, rural society to an industrial, urban one (Fabian 1983). The definition readily identifies the group "peasant workers" as symbiotic with the nation's industrialization and urbanization and impresses upon people that such a transitional category caught between the binaries is and should be accepted as a social fact.

However, the official explanation hides the crucial effects of institutional discrimination against the rural population, which has fundamentally shaped China's internal migration, its patterns, and the migrants' livelihood. In the era of Mao's planned economy, the party-state heavily subsidized city-oriented industrialization and provided urban residents a so-called iron rice bowl that came with long-term employment, as well as access to public housing, schooling, and medical care through the *danwei* (work unit) system. In contrast, state investments in irrigation, basic infrastructure, and medical care in the countryside were disproportionally low (Davis and Wang 2009; Whyte 2010). Agricultural households suffered tremendously during the famines of the early 1960s partly because of disastrous policies that collectivized land, prohibited sideline production, and extracted agricultural surplus to subsidize industrialization. Though incrementally improved, the livelihoods of rural people remained meager and strained in most parts of Mao's China.

Although market-oriented economic reforms have opened new ways for "agricultural" people to break out of rural poverty by working and trading in towns and cities, the socialist *hukou* system and its segmented governing logic remain largely intact. Since the late 1990s, even though a series of policy adjustments were introduced to loosen *hukou* restrictions on migrants' physical mobility (K. W. Chan 2012; K. W. Chan and Buckingham 2008; C. Chen and Fan 2016), it remains difficult for rural-to-urban migrants to change their *huji* category or registered *huji* place. Rural-to-urban migrant workers have been subject to widespread discrimination despite their tremendous contribution to the urban economy (K. W. Chan and Zhang 1999; Goldman and Perry 2002; Guang 2010; B. Shi 2005; Solinger 1995, 1999; F.-L. Wang 2005; Whyte 2010; H. Yan 2003; L. Zhang 2002b). Their nonlocal status has prevented them from accessing public provisions, including basic social and medical insurance, in their adopted cities. More importantly, *hukou* status is hereditary. Migrant children who were raised or even born in Shanghai still hold "agricultural" status and are registered as residents of their parents' *hukou* place. Under the label "peasant workers' children," these children continued to be denied urban local residential status and to face numerous obstacles to attending urban public schools.

The "Opinions on Solving Peasant Workers' Problems" interprets the foreseeable continuation of rural-to-urban migration by way of the conventional push-and-pull economic model. Yet it is overt discrimination against the "peasants" that has facilitated China's export-oriented economic growth. China has become the "world's factory" partly by dampening the price of migrant labor and shirking state responsibility to provide them social welfare (E. Friedman 2014; Pun 2005a, 2005b; Pun and Chan 2012; Pun and Lu 2010; Swider 2015). In naturalizing migrants' in-between status as "peasant workers" in the name of developmental necessity, the Chinese state has ignored the institutional injustice embedded in the *hukou* system. The state's definition of "peasant workers" thus reveals its unwillingness to address systematic discrimination against those rural-to-urban migrants. Whether the transitional social category of "peasant workers" will and should exist for long remains more a question of the state's intentions than one of the natural consequences of urbanization.

OUTSIDER

The state council's argument for the necessity of the category "peasant workers" signals the state's intention to maintain the territorialized citizenship regime that has been built upon the *hukou* system. As more and more migrants work and reside longer in cities, the rural-urban divide that has been emphasized by extant studies of the predicaments facing Chinese migrant workers actually becomes less relevant in their everyday lives. It is the inside-outside distinction that intertwines with the local-nonlocal binary in the *hukou* system to continue to differentiate groups and distribute public services and symbolic resources.

The schooling barriers facing migrant children exemplify how China's territorialized citizenship regime renders migrants second-class citizens and even noncitizens once they are on the move. Although China's constitution and its compulsory education laws mandate that every Chinese citizen has the right and obligation to receive nine years' basic education, the legal framework requires local governments to enroll and fund local students whose *hukous* are registered in their vicinity through its public school system. Consequently, migrant children whose *hukou* registrations remain tied to their parents' native places cannot attend public school in their adopted cities for free. They either pay exorbitant fees to buy their seats in urban public schools or attend substandard private migrant schools at a lower cost (Y. P. Chen and Liang 2007; Han 2004; Kwong 2004; Z. Liang and Chen 2007; Yuan 2010; Zhu 2001). Many more are left behind in home villages without parental supervision in order to receive free basic education (C. Liu 2008; Z. Liu 2009; Lü 2007; Y. Lu 2012; K. Wang 2007; Ye 2010; Ye and Pan 2008).[7]

There is a complex relationship between spatial hierarchy and subject formation (L. Zhang 2001c, 2002a). The place of origin listed in the *hukou* register determines one's position in the spatial hierarchy and, to a large extent, shapes one's life chances because public resources highly correlate with the spatial hierarchy of China's political economic structure.[8] Shanghai, as one of China's four municipal cities (*zhixiashi*),[9] enjoys greater administrative autonomy, fiscal power, and resources (educational and more) than other locales. Provincial capital cities and major cities along the east coast are on the next rung of this hierarchy, followed by small cities and counties. Towns and villages in the southwest and northwest hinterlands are at the bottom.[10] Native residents in Shanghai are better positioned by birth, in terms of life chances, than their fellows in remote areas and small towns and villages. Moreover, big cities like Shanghai boast developed consumer markets, entertainment venues, and symbols of modernity. The spatial differentiation applies to cultural and symbolic resources for constructing identities and drawing boundaries.

In everyday conversations, migrants are often referred to as *waidiren* (outsiders) as well. This term *waidiren* carries a particularly derogatory connotation in Shanghai. Because of the city's history of being China's biggest and most prosperous metropolis since the late nineteenth century, being a native Shanghainese often confers on its local residents a sense of superiority over their fellow countrymen, especially those coming from the rural regions. In Shanghai dialect, *waidiren* is often used interchangeably with *xiangxiaren* (people from the countryside, country bumpkins). People from rural China are often considered not only different from but also inferior to local Shanghai residents. Visible socioeconomic deprivation among low-income migrants—partly resulting from *hukou* policies that deny migrants equal access to land use, labor protection, medical insurance, school access, and other rights—reifies the negative connotation of *waidiren* as the poor and uncivil.

Place-based prejudice and identity politics have long been common in Shanghai's modern history. "To be a *Shanghairen* [Shanghai people] was to be urbane and sophisticated like the Jiangnan elite, in contradistinction to the crude, backward natives of Subei," observed Emily Honig (1992, 131) in her study of the social construction of the "Subei people" in Shanghai since the mid-nineteenth century. Even though no place called Subei actually existed, the social category of Subei people was created to give a label to poverty-stricken migrants, mostly from northern Jiangsu, in the nineteenth and early twentieth centuries. The construction of such an inferior Subei people has been instrumental for the Shanghai elites, many of whom were actually migrants from southern Jiangsu, to define themselves and claim their sense of sociocultural superiority in semicolonized Shanghai, a treaty port where "foreigners shaped the city's political and social life in profound ways" and "portrayed all Chinese as uncivilized and backward" (Honig 1992, 131). Identity based on one's native place hence functions similarly to the way racial and ethnic labels do in forming the basis of prejudice and discrimination.

Since the 1950s, the *hukou* system and its place-specific welfare provision schemes have reinforced such spatial-social differentiations and place-based prejudices. In Shanghai, since residents originating from both southern and northern Jiangsu were officially categorized as Shanghai *hukou* holders, the spatially less specific labels of *waidiren* and *xiangxiaren*[11] have been used to index the Others when local residents make dismissive comments about rustic manners or social problems that are believed to be associated with new rural-to-urban migrants. The evocation of *waidiren* maintains an increasingly porous inside-outside boundary amid China's rapid urbanization process and supports state agendas to control population size and protect nativist interests.

SEGMENTED INCLUSION

Because rural-to-urban migrants are indispensable to China's economic development, a series of policy adjustments have been instituted since the 2000s that allow for a certain degree of inclusion. The notorious detention and deportation system, which authorized city governments to arrest, detain, and deport "undocumented" migrants back to their home counties, was scrapped in 2003, ensuring migrants increased personal security and freedom.[12] Changing and transferring *hukou* status have also become easier for migrants living in small towns and cities, and many cities have set up limited social security schemes to cover migrant workers with formal labor contracts.

The focus of local state agents has turned from outright exclusion to the "segmented inclusion" of the migrant population. These gradual and selective policy modifications aim to achieve a desired urban population for national development. Administrative regulations are meant to work in tandem with market mechanisms and cultural criteria to create a new generation of urban citizens who rise to desired thresholds of economic, social, and cultural capital. As the historian Mae Ngai wrote about Mexican immigration to the United States, immigration policies draw "lines of inclusion and exclusion that articulate a desired composition—imagined if not necessarily realized—of the nation" (2004, 5). Chinese cities like Shanghai have adopted the same rationale in dealing with internal migrants to facilitate local economic growth and maintain sociopolitical order as the metropolis intensifies its participation in the global economy.

The Shanghai municipal government offers its privileged local *hukou* status to only a very small number of migrants who have either a large sum of money (enterprise owners and home buyers[13]) or high educational qualifications. Since 2004, the city government has been experimenting with a point accumulation system (*jifenzhi*) modeled after the immigration policies of Western countries like Canada and Australia (L. Zhang 2012). Nicknamed the "internal 'green card' system," the point accumulation system evaluates applicants' qualifications according to the following criteria: age, education, occupation, assets, years of service, contribution to local employment, and so forth. Only those who accumulate a total of 120 points or more are eligible to apply for formal Shanghai residential status in order to enjoy basic public services (*jiben gonggong fuwu*). The point accumulation system helps "formulize and make transparent the highly unequal methods large cities have used for distributing rights to local services for many years" (E. Friedman 2018, 11).

Conditional welfare policies concerning who gains access to local public services result in new forms of inclusion and exclusion, which reflects the neoliberal stance of the municipal government that seeks to align with social groups of economic value and desirable social characteristics. It represents the "rescaling" and "reterritorializing" of citizenship in the globalizing era (Ong 2006; Purcell 2003). T. H. Marshall's (1964) classic definition of citizenship refers to economic, social, and political rights and obligations tied to individual citizens within nation-states. Since Marshall's work, the concept and practice of citizenship have been complicated by the increasing global movement of capital, people, technologies, and ideas across national borders (Appadurai 1996; Clifford 1994; Gupta and Ferguson 1997; Hannerz 1996). The rise of such transnational institutions as the WTO and NAFTA and the international reorganization of production and finance since the 1970s point to the destabilization of such a citizenship framework based on the nation-state. Formal membership in a nation-state has become "neither a necessary nor a sufficient condition for substantive citizenship" (Holston and Appadurai 1999, 4). Elite transnational immigrants with sufficient economic, social, or cultural capital have been shown to exercise a strategically "flexible citizenship" (Ong 1999), with which they are able to maximize personal gains across borders. Meanwhile, immigrants of lower socioeconomic status find themselves shunned or discriminated against.

The processes of negotiating citizenship take place not only between the state and individuals but also among groups and communities. When city governments bestow full urban membership on a select few, they signal a set of values to the society at large. Studies on second-generation immigrants in the United States have shown that not only the contractual state-citizen relations defined by the host government's policies but also concrete interactions and negotiations between individuals, labor markets, and local communities shape how and on what terms migrants become members of the receiving society (Portes and Rumbaut 1990, 2001; Portes and Zhou 1993). Studies of mainland Chinese immigrants to Hong Kong seeking to reunite their families since the handover of the British colony back to China in 1997 also show how the qualities of an ideal citizen defined by the Hong Kong government "become part of the cultural/social landscape of communities" and "define the possibilities for inclusion at local and national levels" (Newendorp 2008, 17).

In mainland China, in addition to the labels "peasant worker" and "outsiders," the prevalent discourse of *suzhi*, or "quality," serves as an amorphous but expedient articulation of certain values desired by the state (Anagnost 2004; Kipnis 2007; Sigley 2009; Sun 2009; Tomba 2009; H. Yan 2003). *Suzhi* plays a central role in the processes of shaping Chinese citizenship by contributing

> to understandings of the responsibilities, obligations, claims, and rights that connect members of society to the state; to determinations of which individuals and social groups are included in this set of rights and responsibilities and which are excluded; to discourses on how to produce the "ideal" citizen as well as what to do about the less-than-ideal citizen; and to processes and institutions that produce and reproduce boundaries and gradations between different types of citizenship and citizen. (Jacka 2009, 524)

The Chinese population has been stratified along a gradated *suzhi* axis, which shapes social perceptions of entitlement and distributions of substantive citizenship among different groups. Elite migrants who are qualified to gain sufficient points and acquire Shanghai's local *hukou* status are deemed to be of "high *suzhi*." The municipal government calls them *rencai* (talents), who are desirable for Shanghai's socioeconomic development and the state's effort to build a cosmopolitan image. In contrast to "talents," "peasant workers" lack *suzhi* (Murphy 2004; Sun 2009; H. Yan 2003). Media representations of migrant workers of lower status often emphasize their crass appearance, lack of education, and the way they congregate in crowded urban enclaves. The fact that a majority of migrant families have two or more children and do not invest as intensively in their children's education as urban single-child families is often framed as evidence of migrants' "low *suzhi*" and lack of civic consciousness. They are undesirable and hence unqualified for full citizenship in Shanghai. Such civilizing *suzhi* discourses define citizenship through "intimate, often embodied, practices that mark individuals and groups as appropriately or insufficiently civilized, thereby establishing their eligibility for inclusion in or exclusion from an ideal body politics" (S. Friedman 2006, 243).

"Segmented inclusion" suggests an open-ended process of gauging and positioning different local and migrant subgroups in Shanghai. I use "inclusion" instead of "assimilation" as the latter suggests a hierarchical relationship between the host communities and (im)migrants while emphasizing cultural integration. The above-mentioned government policies never intended to assimilate migrant youth into Shanghai's local culture. Ethnographic data also show that migrant youth position themselves not only in relation to local Shanghai residents of different socioeconomic backgrounds but also in juxtaposition to their parents' generation and to rural peers in the countryside. Unlike their parents, they are less inclined to embrace regional identities or maintain the dialects, cuisines, and customs shaped by their native places. Nor are they as keen to master the Shanghai dialect and assimilate into the local society to maximize their chances for personal gain from Shanghai's economic restructuring and urban development. I avoid using "assimilation" to predict the life trajectories of second-generation migrants, which are still ongoing processes full of contention and possibility.

LIMINAL SUBJECTS ON SHANGHAI'S EDGE

The segmented inclusion of migrant youth in Shanghai induces and reinforces their in-between status in China's territorialized, dualistic citizenship regime. I borrow Victor Turner's (1967) concept of "liminality" from his study of rituals marking life-stage transitions: migrant youth can be regarded as "liminal subjects" "betwixt and between" fixed structural classifications. Turner defines "liminality" as being "neither here nor there" and being "betwixt and between the positions assigned and arranged by law, custom, convention, and ceremonial" (1969, 95). When China's internal migrants are officially labeled by the state as "peasant workers," they are institutionalized as liminal subjects: neither peasant nor worker, neither living in the country nor belonging to the city. More importantly, the migrants' liminal status translates into lived experiences of, for instance, random detention, wage difference, delayed payment, the absence of a labor contract, makeshift rental housing, and uncompensated forced relocation. Such precarious experiences in turn reinforce migrants' liminal status in urban China.

Examining migrant youth coming of age in Shanghai as "liminal subjects" offers unique insight into the late-socialist mode of urban governance. This ethnographic project departs from the established institutional approach. It explores the effects of *hukou* policies on everyday experiences of migrant children in multiple social realms in light of the Foucauldian notion of governmentality (Burchell, Gordon, and Miller 1991; Foucault 2010; Rabinow 1984; Rose 1999, 2007), which reveals the persuasive, often nonrepressive governing strategies or "conduct of the conduct" that shape people's sense of self and entitlement. This study exposes both the institutional apparatus and the discursive practices through which the late-socialist state constitutes its migrant population as necessary but inconvenient subjects in its avid pursuit of urbanization and modernization. I adopt the term "late socialism" to emphasize the dominance of one-party rule and the legacies of socialist institutions and practices in today's China despite accelerated marketization and privatization, entrenchment of global capital, and integration in global affairs (L. Zhang 2001b).[14]

This research offers a practice-oriented analysis of the making of a new subject—that is, "second-generation migrant workers"—and highlights the temporal and spatial aspects of the mechanisms through which institutions and discourses persuade or compel migrant youth to remain in the liminal status of "peasant worker."[15] Not only the substance of citizen rights but also the challenging conditions under which such rights are conferred matter significantly. For instance, policies regarding migrant children's free access to basic education required their parents to produce proper documents, including residence permit, proof of employment, and record of family planning compliance, which were time-consuming, incurred extra expense, and required basic literacy and social skills to navigate through the local bureaucratic apparatus; also, the municipal education commission distributed policies regarding vocational school subsidies and enrollment quotas to middle school administrators only a few short weeks before school enrolment began, and these administrators were not obliged to publicize the policies to migrant parents. Such practices put people with severe time and income restraints, limited education, and socialization in urban environments at a disadvantage in claiming or even understanding substantive rights.

The segmented inclusion of migrant students in Shanghai's education system deserves particular attention. In modern societies, individuals are expected to move through distinct institutionalized life stages: childhood, youth, adulthood, and old age (Ariès 1962; Cole and Durham 2008). This chronological vision manifests mostly through schooling. In postreform China, particularly, the sociocultural model of upward mobility via formal education from primary school to four-year university has been widely accepted as the proper rite of passage for Chinese urban youth (Woronov 2011, 2015). However, the Shanghai government only offers nine years of basic education in the public schools that have been opened to migrant students. Migrant students are still ineligible to take the high school and university entrance examinations in Shanghai. This significantly reduces their chances for higher education and their competitiveness in the job market. It also renders migrant students liminal as they are forced to remain in middle school only to complete the course without progressing to the next level of education in the normative manner. Unlike their local peers, they are excluded from the *gaokao* rite of passage (i.e., studying hard to pass standardized examinations oriented toward a university education). The inability to receive quality schooling and the lack of equal opportunities has a negative impact on learning incentives and reduces the sense of entitlement.[16] This in turn funnels these young people toward socially stigmatized vocational training and, subsequently, to low-income manufacturing and service jobs.

Nonetheless, liminality entails not only risks but also possibilities. Migrant youth exercise their agency in contesting limits and earning gains. Whereas most China studies portray rural migrants as victims of the *hukou* system, this book rejects a top-down reproduction story and argues that migrant youth, as "liminal subjects" in China's dualistic citizenship regime and its fast-forward modernization project, embody what Erik Harms (2011) calls "social edginess." In his study of social life on the outskirts of Ho Chi Minh City, Harms shows how living in periurban zones is both alienating and empowering to people under rapid urbanization projects. Critical studies of youth agency (Bourgois 1995; Butler 1997; Chatterjee 2004; Gramsci 1991) have also demonstrated how young people are able to transform the operation of "fields," to borrow Bourdieu's notion that describes arenas of practice with distinct sets of rules, knowledges, and forms of capital. They are also able to form identities extraneous to their existing class. By using the term "edginess," in contrast to the more passive term "marginality," I highlight the agency of migrant youth as periurban beings who are moving "into, outside and across the boundaries created by discrete categories" (Harms 2011, 36) of rural and urban, inside and outside, to maximize their access to material and symbolic resources.

The opening up of the public schooling system in Shanghai, though limited and segmented, enables migrant youth to form new subjectivities and social relations that were unavailable to their first-generation migrant parents. Barred from competing in the high school and university entrance examinations regardless of their academic performance and educational desire, migrant students are better positioned to see through China's seemingly meritocratic but highly repressive and unequal examination-oriented education system. They have learned to utilize their abundance of time to gain intimate knowledge of urban living by being consumers, enjoying leisure activities, and working part-time jobs. In the socially stigmatized secondary vocational education system, where migrant students are inevitably concentrated along with underperforming local students, they are able to form friendships, courtships, and social networks across the rural-urban and local-nonlocal boundaries—phenomena rarely reported in studies of adult migrant workers (Guang 2010; Pun 1999; H. Yan 2003, 2008). These cross-boundary interactions and engagements prepare second-generation migrant youth to embrace city living with more ease, confidence, and a greater sense of entitlement than their parents.

Outside of school settings, migrant youth also make use of their liminal status to respond fluidly to Shanghai's changing political-economic conditions. They live on the periurban edge, oscillating "betwixt and between" the city and the countryside, the inside and the outside, spatially, socially, and symbolically. Most migrant families rely on rental housing on the city's outskirts to minimize living costs, maintain native-place networks, avoid state surveillance, and benefit from informal economic activities. Having grown up in Shanghai, migrant youth neither identify with their home villages nor consider themselves "Shanghainese." As the symbolic binary of the country and the city is fluid rather than fixed (Williams 1973), migrant youth may invert the meanings of the ideal categories of the rural and urban, the inside and outside, according to context. In the city, migrant youth often distinguish themselves as the "generous Other" in contrast to the "mean and stingy" local Shanghainese. Back in the countryside, they often talk and act in subtle ways to evoke urban superiority in front of their rural peers. Although most rural-to-urban migrants are by no means on a par in terms of capital and power with those overseas Chinese entrepreneurs who hold multiple passports studied by Ong (1999), they follow the same cultural logic of "flexible citizenship" to maximize their opportunities.

It is hence not surprising when the 2014 *hukou* reform that encouraged *hukou* transfer to towns and small cities was met with lukewarm response among migrants (C. Chen and Fan 2016). Younger-generation migrants are not interested in acquiring the local *hukou*; instead they are keen to make the best of their in-betweenness. They cling to the collective land ownership that their rural *hukou* status bestows on them in hopes they may someday gain a windfall from land expropriation by local governments or private developers. They also take advantage of the state subsidies for vocational education that only agricultural *hukou* holders receive. In the face of postreform China's complex economic and sociocultural reconfigurations, migrant youth act on such shifting possibilities in hopes of mitigating *hukou* barriers amid rapid urbanization.

TRACING THE UNMARKED OUTSIDER IN A GLOBAL CITY

This book grew out of thirty months of multisited ethnographic fieldwork between 2007 and 2017.[17] I chose to focus on Shanghai because the city offers the most intriguing urban space for a critical investigation of the politics of citizenship. The city has seen its number of migrants multiply from over 260,000 in 1981 to over 17 million in 2010 (Shanghai Bureau of Statistics 2011). In retrospect, the making of modern Shanghai centers on the continuous integration of migrants. Once a small market town perched at the mouth of the Yangtze River Delta where it opens into the East China Sea, Shanghai grew rapidly in terms of population and economic power, especially after it was opened as one of the first treaty ports following China's defeat to the British in the First Opium War (1839–42). With the influx of people, money, technology, information, and ideas from all parts of China and the rest of the world, Shanghai became one of the world's metropolitan centers in the early twentieth century (Yeh 2007). Its semicolonial history, through the late nineteenth and early twentieth centuries, makes the city a unique place for studying the politics of difference among social groups (B. Goodman 1995; Hershatter 1989, 1992; Honig 1990, 1992, 1989). Shanghainese identity has never been concrete; it has always been a porous notion constantly being negotiated.

Once again at the forefront of China's socioeconomic transformation, Shanghai represents a critical case for studying the impact of globalization on local labor markets and migrant livelihood through examining social integration and identity formation. With all the challenges it faces with population control, urban planning, and social integration, Shanghai provides a rich site for studying urbanization. Shanghai's renewed ambition to become a global city after 1992's escalated economic reforms has pushed the municipal government to adopt a more outward-looking approach to incorporate migrant populations. By focusing on second-generation migrant youth in Shanghai, *The Inconvenient Generation* contributes a timely and important empirical study to the growing literature on China's migration and urbanization.

For yearlong dissertation research between June 2008 and August 2009, I chose two main field sites on Shanghai's outskirts where migrant families have concentrated (see Map 1). I conducted participant observation in ninth-grade classrooms and teachers' offices throughout the academic year of 2008–09 in the Bridge Middle School ("Bridge School") in Bridge Town in Pudong District. I chose the Bridge School because of its accessibility through family networks and more importantly the demographic change of its student body. The Bridge School is a nonelite full-time public secondary school (*quanrizhi putong zhongxue*) of middle-tier ranking in terms of school size and reputation. Established in 1950, it once educated local students from Bridge Town and nearby villages. Since 1990, Bridge Town has been designated by the municipal government to be one of Shanghai's "strategic towns" for urban development and is at the core of one of Shanghai's special economic zones (SEZs). The physical landscape of the town's surroundings has within two decades been transformed from rice paddies to factories, office buildings, retail stores, and residential complexes. The establishment of the SEZs has also triggered a constant inflow of migrant workers ever since. The town's migrant population grew from 45,000 in 2000 to 92,000 in 2010, making up half of the town's total population of 185,000 (according to the town gazetteer, based on the 2010 national census). The school has consequently enrolled migrant students since the late 1990s and, since 2007, has offered free schooling to migrants who have the required documents.[18] With migrant youth making up half of the student body, the Bridge School represented a great opportunity to study the everyday practices of inclusion and exclusion in public educational institutions. In addition, during weekday evenings and weekends, I volunteered as an English tutor and program facilitator in an activity center run by a local nongovernmental organization ("NGO J"), which had provided free extracurricular learning opportunities and support to migrant children since mid-2000s.

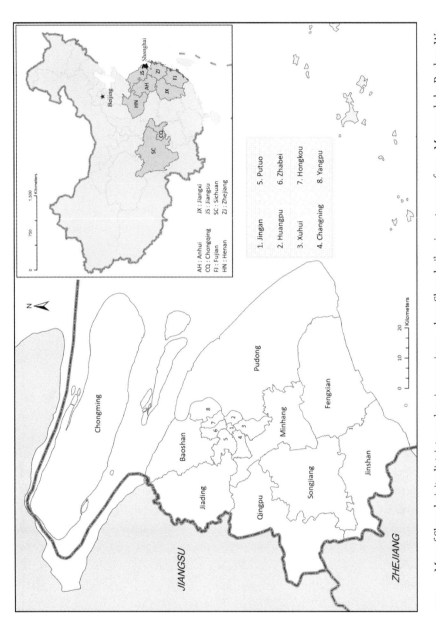

MAP 1. Map of Shanghai, its districts, and major provinces where Shanghai's migrants came from. Map made by Puzhou Wu.

Through these two sites, I established close contact with sixty migrant students, with whom I conducted in-depth interviews, along with numerous informal conversations, group discussions, home visits, and open-ended interviews with the parents. I also went along with them to some of their vocational schools and interviewed dozens of schoolteachers, administrators, social workers, and labor agents. I maintained correspondence with the key interlocutors via email, social media, and follow-up summer fieldtrips between 2012 and 2017. In addition, three field trips in rural Anhui in the summers of 2006 and 2007, one in rural Sichuan in July 2009, and one in rural Henan in June 2011 allowed me to follow some of the interlocutors and observe rural livelihoods and schooling conditions in order to contextualize their migratory experiences and educational trajectories from both the sending and receiving ends.

Without distinct physical, linguistic, and stylistic features that tell them apart from their native peers, second-generation migrant youth in Shanghai are rather unmarked in daily interactions. All the migrant students and their parents in this study are ethnically Han Chinese, which corresponds to the predominance of Han Chinese (about 91.5 percent) nationwide, as well as in Shanghai. Approximately half of the migrant families came from villages in Anhui Province, which is the biggest sending province of migrants to Shanghai. The rest came from rural Sichuan, Jiangsu, Jiangxi, Zhejiang, Henan, and Fujian Provinces (see Map 1). Although there are regional differences in terms of cuisine, dialect, and custom, migrant youth who grew up in Shanghai exhibit few overt cultural differences from each other or their local peers. All the migrant students in this study speak standard Mandarin Chinese in and outside of school most of the time because of the heavy-handed state promotion of Mandarin in Shanghai over the past three decades. Even though some of them are able to converse in their local dialects with their parents at home, they switch between their dialects and Mandarin Chinese and use Mandarin more frequently. Many are unable to converse solely in local dialects back in their home villages. Most migrant students report that they understand a fair amount of the Shanghai dialect but are unable to speak it well, which they do not find to be a significant obstacle in everyday communication because of the dominance of Mandarin in the media and public spaces in Shanghai.[19] Most pick up popular Shanghai expressions through everyday conversations, but not many indicate a strong interest in mastering the Shanghai dialect despite their long-term residence in Shanghai and preference to live there. Of course, this language barrier does occasionally give rise to prejudice.[20] The lack of close contact with local Shanghai residents due to spatial and social distance, especially before vocational training, and the nationwide language standardization campaign reduce both the necessity and incentive for learning Shanghainese.

My approach to getting to know migrant students through the public schools and NGOs before reaching out to their parents allowed me to examine the less-studied but important migrant subgroup of the self-employed and petty businessmen. Over three-quarters of the migrant families in this study have made a living in the informal sectors of the economy, working as subcontractors, small traders, street peddlers, garbage collectors, interior decorators, pedicab drivers, convenience store keepers, and so on. Unlike wage-earning migrant laborers working in factories, restaurants, construction sites, and beauty salons, these self-employed and petty businessmen have more physical and financial independence to bring their young children to their adopted cities. By focusing on this subgroup, I also problematize the homogenization of migrants as "peasant workers" in official documents and public discourse. Discursive measures and cultural ideals are essential to frame and sustain policies and institutions that create not only ideological biases but also very real consequences for the disadvantaged. My ethnographic project emphasizes how the labeling practice regarding rural-to-urban migrants has contributed to the ossification of their subaltern status (Spivak 1988).

This book is divided into seven chapters. Chapters 1 and 2 contextualize these migrant youths' adolescent experiences by examining their living environments and family relations. Chapter 1 describes the predominance of cramped rental housing among migrant households in periurban zones in Shanghai. While such spatial arrangements symbolize migrants' precarious status in the city, they also enable migrants to minimize living costs, maintain native-place networks, and maximize working opportunities. Chapter 2 probes the politics of urban citizenship embedded in the discourses of family planning and child-rearing practices in Shanghai. In the same way that rental housing on the city outskirts is seen as a signal of trespass, migrant parents are often represented and perceived as irresponsible and even uncivil in the state-promoted discourse of *yousheng youyu* (bearing and rearing fewer but better "quality" children).

The subsequent sections unfold according to life stages to trace these migrant youths' coming-of-age experiences in the public education system and the consumer and labor markets. The temporal order reflects the progression of their personal lives under institutional constraints and discursive biases. Chapter 3 examines the everyday practices of segmented inclusion in Shanghai's public middle schools that have taken in qualified migrant students for free. The elimination of school segregation is, nevertheless, far from being sufficient to remove differentiation and discrimination when academic high school and university entrance examinations remain closed to migrant students. Frustrated at the structural denial of opportunities, both migrant students and schoolteachers are compelled to reduce the effort they put toward schoolwork and teaching. For migrant students who want to stay in Shanghai after completing nine years of basic education, they have few schooling alternatives other than secondary vocational education. Chapter 4 examines the anxieties and ambivalence experienced by migrant students before and after enrolling in these public vocational schools. Chapter 5 follows migrant students who left Shanghai for their registered hometowns in hopes of making up for the disadvantage of not being able to attend high school or pursue a university education. The "home" trips undertaken by the migrant students are nevertheless fraught with contradictions and frustrations. Institutional barriers, regional disparities, and sociocultural differences have made it hard for migrant youth to adapt to the rural schooling system.

Migrant youths' estrangement from their registered home villages also results from a hierarchy of consumer citizenship. Chapter 6 examines the consumer desires and behaviors of migrant youth. Despite their socioeconomic disadvantages, they actively engage in mass consumption and construct their sense of belonging through material and cultural goods. Yet China's spatial-cultural hierarchy and the ongoing social stratification embedded in these practices render consumption disfranchising. The feeling of frustration grows as these students enter the labor market and face the gap between job expectations and working experiences. Chapter 7 demonstrates how job placement for migrant youth is undermined by *hukou* restrictions and social bias against outsiders. Segmented inclusion as experienced by migrant youth in Shanghai's public school system has extended to the labor market. Youthful desires for autonomy and wealth come into tension with the state's intention to produce a new generation of cheap manual labor.

The trajectories of these young men and women continue to unfold at a time of competing economic and social imperatives in Shanghai. More than a case study of China's internal migration, this book illuminates processes of contention over entitlement and belonging comparable with those in other rapidly expanding megacities. Not only nation-states but also city governments readily combine their administrative power with market force and socio-cultural bias to selectively include or exclude subgroups, which reflects and reinforces existing differences and hierarchies. The politics of citizenship and its everyday ramifications on individuals' sense of identity, educational outcomes, work opportunities, and citizenship claims often maintain, rather than break, inequality even amid rapid economic growth and high population mobility in an era of globalization.

1 LIVING ON
THE PERIURBAN EDGE

"IF I HAD NOT TAKEN you here, you would not have found this place on your own," Huan insisted as we meandered through lanes half a mile off the Middle Ring Highway in northwestern Shanghai. She steered us clear of uncovered manholes along a path full of puddles; a heavy summer shower had just passed over.

Huan's home turned out to be among two rows of concrete shacks on the roof of a warehouse, part of a dilapidated factory compound tucked behind several real estate developments (see Figure 1.1). The factory used to be a collective enterprise owned by the local village committee. In the late 1990s, the committee leased out the bankrupt factory to migrant bosses, who converted its one-story offices and two-story warehouse into rental units and subleased them to over sixty migrant families. Huan's father found this housing compound through a *laoxiang* (a fellow of the same home origin) when their previous rental place was facing demolition. The family of five, two parents and three children, had lived inside the factory compound since 2006.

The factory compound was shrouded in a sense of enduring temporariness: opposite its entrance sat piles of garbage around a waste-removal cart (see Figure 1.2). Inside the compound, flying dust and metal screeching sounds from a desk-manufacturing workshop filled the air. On the warehouse rooftop where Huan's concrete shack was located, tiny kitchen huts built of used planks lined a passageway less than two meters wide. At the end of the passageway were

FIGURE 1.1. Two rows of rental units on the warehouse rooftop. Photo by the author, July 2011.

two communal squat toilets and two open-air sinks. The inside of Huan's unadorned shack, nine square meters in area, was filled with secondhand furniture and appliances: two full-size metal-framed beds, one shared by two daughters and the other by the parents; a single wooden bed for the youngest son; a dining table; a small color TV set; a standing fan; a refrigerator; a rice cooker; two small desks; and a few cabinets. The family stored most of their bedding, winter clothes, and other belongings in nylon bags, paper boxes, and two pieces of luggage on one of the double beds (see Figure 1.3).

Although the factory did have a street name and number on a plaque at the entrance, the rental units inside were not identifiable. This locational obscurity

FIGURE 1.2. Outside the entrance of the factory compound. Photo by the author, January 2015.

made it impossible for the residents of this small migrant community to have postal or delivery service. Huan had to have all her purchases made on Taobao, China's largest producer-to-customer retail website, sent elsewhere for pick-up. The obscurity also prevented Huan's homeroom teacher (*banzhuren*)[1] from paying her home visits during the three years of middle school.[2]

The difficulty in finding Huan's home and locating it on the map represents the socio-spatial ambiguity and insecurity collectively experienced by migrant youth growing up in Shanghai. When I proposed to visit their homes, most met my requests with reluctance because they were embarrassed by their modest living conditions or they thought I might not be able to find my way there. Often they refer to their residences with imprecise directional terms: for example, "south to the railway," "next to the produce market," "at the airport," "near the bus station," or "in a *xiaoqu*" (neighborhood or housing complex). I usually relied on them to escort me in person on the initial visits.

A street name and a number is an identifier that not only locates a sense of belonging but also enables claims to the city. For individuals, an address allows them to enjoy urban convenience brought by the rapidly growing service economy, such as online shopping and ordering food delivery. For city governments, an address facilitates the documentation and administration of its citizens. Those without a proper address are nonexistent on paper and disqualified

FIGURE 1.3. An interior look at Huan's rental unit on the rooftop. Photo by the author, July 2011.

for rights associated with the place in the eyes of bureaucrats (Mbodj-Pouye 2016). A full residential address is a ticket to proper citizenship and urban life.

The locational obscurity and perpetual makeshift setting of Huan's dwelling attest to the precarious living conditions of migrant families amid China's rapidly urbanizing processes. This chapter examines the migrant households' common practice of renting temporary housing on the city's outskirts, a choice conditioned by the unique political economy of urban development in China. The socialist land tenure system, which designates urban land as state owned and rural land as collectively owned by local villagers (Lin and Ho 2005; Hsing 2006, 2010), makes it impossible for individual migrants to acquire land ownership to build properties in their adopted cities.[3] Meanwhile, state-led infrastructural projects and market-driven real estate developments engender massive, often violent, land grabbing and forced relocation, during which migrants have no bargaining power and have to pack and move without compensation. The consequent high level of spatial fluidity renders migrant livelihood mobile and fragile. This chapter also demonstrates how migrants constantly shape underregulated space on the outskirts of cities while seeking employment and accommodation. Their presence, labor, and living make Shanghai's new urban frontier possible. This symbiotic relationship between the periurban space and migrant livelihood is both empowering and disfranchising amid the late-socialist transformation of China.

"RURAL-URBAN CONVERGENCE ZONE"

Studies of internal migration in postreform China report a high concentration of migrant settlements on the outskirts of cities (Bach 2010; K. W. Chan 2012; J. Fan and Taubmann 2002; Jeong 2011; Siu 2007; Xiang 2005; L. Zhang 2001c). These areas where farms have given way to factories, highways, shopping malls, and real estate projects are called *chengxiang jiehebu* (literally "urban-rural convergence zones") in official terminology. This spatial category draws an interesting parallel to the social category of "peasant workers," which refers to rural-to-urban migrants in official language (see the introduction). In concept, both terms are characterized by temporality and in-betweenness; the transitional temporality in "peasant workers" parallels with the transitional spatiality in "urban-rural converging zones." In reality, while "peasant workers" seek from the periurban space shelter and success, their everyday life practices become essential to the making of such a space.

In Shanghai, more than 80 percent of its nonlocal residents reside outside Puxi, the downtown area on the west side of the Huangpu River (see Table 1.1).[4] Shanghai's Pudong and other exurbia districts offer not only ample work opportunities but also flexible housing arrangements for migrants. These districts used to be rural "counties" (*xian*) until recently. Pudong New District, for instance, used to be Chuansha (literally "river sand") County.[5] As indicated by its name, this area developed from an alluvial plain to the south of the mouth of the Yangtze River where it joins the East China Sea. Over a millennium a large canal and irrigation system for rice and cotton cultivation emerged in this area. And it experienced limited industrial development in its market towns in the late nineteenth and early twentieth centuries. Only after 1990, when the central government picked this area as the experimental showcase to accelerate China's opening up and economic reform, did this area undergo large-scale industrialization and urbanization. The government of what is now Pudong New District, founded in 1992, received preferable tax treatment and other policies to build SEZs for export-oriented production and international trade. Within just a few years, dozens of industrial parks emerged on what used to be farmland to house factories and office buildings and attract foreign direct investment.

Table 1.1. Geographic Distribution of Shanghai's Population, 2014

Administrative Division[a]	District Name	Size (sq. km)	Local Residents (10,000)	Nonlocal Residents (10,000)	% of Nonlocal Resident	Population Density (ppl/sq. km)
Downtown Districts (shiqu or puxi)	Huangpu	20.46	68.20	18.08	26.5	33,333
	Xuhui	54.76	110.97	28.55	25.7	20,265
	Changning	38.30	69.86	17.41	24.9	18,240
	Jing'an	7.62	24.86	5.89	23.7	32,625
	Putuo	54.83	129.61	34.75	26.8	23,639
	Zhabei[b]	29.26	84.85	21.03	24.8	28,999
	Hongkou	23.48	83.82	18.22	21.7	35,698
	Yangpu	60.73	132.37	26.75	20.2	21,796
Pudong New District (Pudong xinqu)		1,210.41	545.12	235.65	43.2	4,504
Inner Exurbia (jinjiao)	Minhang	370.75	253.95	128.60	50.6	6,850
	Baoshan	270.99	202.40	85.56	42.3	7,469
	Jiading	464.20	156.62	91.40	58.4	3,374
Outer Exurbia (yuanjiao)	Jinshan	586.05	79.71	26.96	33.8	1,360
	Songjiang	605.64	175.59	109.08	62.1	2,899
	Qingpu	670.14	120.83	72.49	60.0	1,803
	Fengxian	687.39	116.76	60.81	52.1	1,699
Chongming Island[c]		1,185.49	70.16	15.19	21.7	592
Total		**6,340.50**	**2,425.69**	**996.42**	**41.0**	**3,826**

Source: 2015 Shanghai Statistical Yearbook.

[a] Shanghai has gone through rounds of administrative division and categorization. When the People's Republic of China was founded in 1949, Shanghai had twenty urban districts and ten suburban districts. By 1964, Shanghai's juristic territories expanded extensively, with ten urban districts and ten rural counties. Source: http://www.shanghai.gov.cn/nw2/nw2314/nw24651/nw14926/nw14932/u21aw104103.html (accessed August 10, 2018).

[b] Zhabei District was merged into Jing'an District in November 2015.

[c] Chongming Island was recategorized as a district in July 2016, which signals the state effort to increase urban development for the island.

Pudong's unprecedented economic development has attracted a continuous influx of migrants. From 1990 to 2010, Pudong saw its population grow from 1.4 million to 5.2 million even though the natural population growth rate for native-born residents has actually been in decline.[6] Multistory dormitories in special economic zones have mushroomed to accommodate the influx of migrant workers (Fu 2002). Remaining village houses (*sifang*, literally "private houses") and collectively owned factory compounds offer flexible housing arrangements for those who do not want to be confined by dormitory regulations. Migrants with the means to do so may also rent apartments in newly built housing communities.

In addition to the ample work opportunities and housing options that pull migrants to periurban zones, market mechanisms and institutional restrictions combine to push migrants to these periurban outskirts to look for affordable housing. Living costs in downtown Shanghai, whose long history of industrialization and commercialization since the mid-nineteenth century has left little rental space in the already crowded city core,[7] are higher than those in the exurbia districts. In addition, rural-to-urban migrants are largely discriminated against in the formal labor market in the city core (C. Fan 2002). They tend to concentrate in low-income manufacturing and service work. Nor are they eligible to receive government housing subsidies, which only target local-*hukou* residents of low income.

China's "urban-rural convergence zones," where the majority of "peasant workers" work and live, like periurban areas elsewhere around the world, embody what Erik Harms calls "edge." In his study of the spatial and social reconfigurations on Saigon's urban margin in contemporary Vietnam, he uses the term to describe "the anomalous interface of the rural countryside and the urban fringe" (Harms 2011, 2). Instead of the static term "marginality," "edge"—both a noun and a verb—more forcefully suggests both ambiguity and potentiality. People living on the edge are "neither rural nor urban, neither wholly inside nor outside, but uncomfortably both" (Harms 2011, 3). They experience what Harms calls "social edginess," a state of being that contains both possibilities and risks "associated with moving into, outside, and across the boundaries created by discrete categories" (36).

While most Chinese migration studies use the term "marginality" to define migrant students' peripheral experiences in cities (Han 2012; Kwong 2011; T. Li and Li 2005; Z. Liang and Ma 2004; Ma 2010; Ming 2009; Tang and Yang 2008; Yijie Wang and Gao 2010; Woronov 2004; T. Zhang and Zhao 2006; Zhao 2000), I use "edge" to emphasize the coexistence of risks and opportunities facing migrants, including housing arrangements, on Shanghai's city outskirts. The following sections illustrate how rural-to-urban migrants make use and sense of the periurban space. Their ways of living embody a *social edginess* that entails marginalization and empowerment simultaneously.

MIGRANT ENCLAVE AT LARGE

Huan's family of five has lived in the rooftop shack since 2006. As of 2011, her parents earned approximately 5,000–6,000 RMB (about $760–$910 at the exchange rate of 6.6 RMB to $1) together per month. Huan, the eldest daughter, has been contributing 500 RMB per month to the household income by taking a part-time job in a chain bubble tea shop since she enrolled in a vocational school in 2010. When Huan took a full-time job in a state-owned hotel in 2012, there was no discussion of moving into a better place, despite their growing household income.

As studies of migrant workers' housing choices show, income and life cycle, which are central to housing choices in other contexts, play limited roles in the Chinese case (Bingqin Li, Duda, and An 2009; Bingqin Li and Zhang 2011). Transitional priorities, such as low cost, proximity to work, and flexible arrangement (Bingqin Li, Duda, and An 2009, 142), factor more significantly than safety, comfort, and privacy in their housing choices.

Socioeconomic instability resulting from institutionalized disadvantages against nonlocal *hukou* holders partly explains the persistence of rental housing arrangements among low-income migrant families. Huan's mother, Aidi, works as a janitor in a department store. She has neither employment security nor medical insurance due to her nonlocal *hukou*. She has to renew her contract every year with a labor agency that subcontracts with the real estate management company of the department store. For fear of losing her job, she dares not take any day off, even during Chinese New Year. Huan's father, Dalu, collects recyclables by day and operates a *modi* (motorized pedicab) at night—lines of work dominated by migrants (Swider 2015; K.-M. Wu and Zhang 2016). Motorized-pedicab riding is a risky source of income because, strictly speaking, it is illegal despite its popularity in periurban areas as a cheap and accessible alternative to taxis. The state-employed semi-police force known as *chengguan* (city order enforcers, nicknamed "*heimao*" [black cats], as compared to "*baimao*" [white cats], which refers to policemen) often confiscate motorized pedicabs and detain operators for reasons of public security. There is also a high occurrence of traffic accidents among pedicab drivers as they frequently violate traffic regulations, such as running through red lights and driving against the traffic, under the pressure of severe market competition. Huan's father already had two accidents, the second of which saw him crash into a sedan and break his ribs while riding against traffic. In addition to the sizable hospital and medical bills this entailed, the family was heavily fined for a traffic infraction and was required to pay a hefty sum to the sedan owner in compensation. The lack of access to medical insurance and welfare put an even greater financial constraint on Huan's family. Raising three children in Shanghai also has been a heavy burden on the couple.

In addition to financial pressures, the uncertainties inherent to the factory compound neighborhood contribute to the meager spending of Huan's parents on their housing. Rumors of demolition and relocation have circulated for years. Emerging multistory apartment buildings began to surround the compound. Sounds of hammering from pile drivers nearby reverberated through the shacks, and the tenants had acknowledged the fact that, before long, the factory would be torn down to give way to real estate redevelopment. Yet they lingered for as long as possible. Even though rent had risen from 400 to 700 RMB over the past few years, as Shanghai's real estate market soared, the factory compound remained the cheapest option available to migrant families like Huan's.

In the early spring of 2015, after having lived in the shack atop the old factory for nine years, Huan's parents and other tenants finally received an eviction notice. They were to vacate the premises within weeks. Huan's father frantically searched for an alternative abode and found a similar but smaller migrant community twenty minutes' walk away (see Figures 1.4 and 1.5). To secure a spot, he surrendered two months' rent (800 RMB per month) for the deposit. Over the course of a particularly rainy afternoon, the family borrowed a pedicab to transport their belongings and move their home.

Huan's family took one room in the end of a row of rental units on the second floor of a factory building. The room, with two windows and whitewashed walls, was slightly bigger, brighter, and better furnished than their previous unit. In January 2015, Huan married and moved out to live with her husband in a rental apartment. The family got rid of the single wooden bed and installed a computer desk for the two younger children. They also installed an air conditioner to fend off the summer heat. All tenants shared four squat toilets. Two units shared one of the sinks that lined up in the hallway. Each family set gas stoves in the hallway, as well. Huan's mother even managed to raise a chicken in a small cage wedged between the walls of two adjacent buildings.

In the spring of 2016 Huan's family had to move again. As usual, migrant tenants received neither an explicit explanation nor timely notification of eviction. Rumors had it that the landowner of the housing compound, presumably a local unit of the People's Liberation Army, wanted to take back the land and

FIGURE 1.4. A smaller migrant enclave Huan's family moved into in early 2015. Photo by the author, July 2015.

FIGURE 1.5. Huan's brother on the way out of the smaller migrant enclave. Photo by the author, July 2015.

FIGURE 1.6. A recyclable collection station inside the settlement Huan's family moved into in March 2016. Photo by the author, June 2016.

start a construction project. Thanks to the *laoxiang* network, Huan's parents found another compound hidden behind a produce market about two kilometers away from their former dwelling. A group of migrants converted dozens of portable containers made of steel plates and polyethylene boards into housing units for rent. Each unit, about twelve square meters in size, cost 800 RMB per month. The units in essence were metal boxes with a window and a door and would get very hot in the summer. Huan's family had to keep the air conditioner on whenever they were home. Two portable toilets and a few open-air sinks nearby served the migrant households. Several large garbage bins were provided at the entrance of the compound, as was a recycling station operated by migrants right next door. Nevertheless, the spatial distinction between disposal of garbage and collection of recyclables was often blurred (see Figure 1.6). Meters away were multistory apartment blocks with shiny tiled facades for sale that summer of 2016 (see Figure 1.7).

In late October 2016, the containers were lifted away and the community demolished. Huan's family moved again to another container housing compound,

FIGURE 1.7. The settlement where Huan's family moved into in March 2016. Photo by the author, June 2016.

this time paying RMB 1,200 ($182) for a unit fifteen square meters in size, the inside of which is partitioned into two sections and a tiny bathroom with a squat toilet. It remains to be seen how long this migrant enclave at large will be safe from bulldozers and pile drivers.

INHABITING THE EDGE

Migrant housing choices cannot simply be interpreted as passive responses to socioeconomic instability. Living in a slum-like enclave often enables migrant families to maintain their fringe livelihoods. The lack of management and surveillance in these enclaves accords with the migrants' demand for cheap and much-coveted space for business opportunities. For instance, the factory compounds where Huan's family stayed between 2006 and 2015 offered ample space for the father to park his motorized pedicab and to store any recyclables he collected. In contrast, apartment buildings in established neighborhoods impose excessive restriction on the use of shared space, which would have made it almost impossible for the father to keep his recycling business.

A migrant enclave known as the Night Market on the northern edge of Yangpu District, where many of Huan's friends live, offers a dense web of business opportunities and social relations to its migrant tenants. It is located in a small triangular plot bordered by a university campus, a road, and a railway. Twenty-three local households had lived there in two-story self-built village houses (*sifang*) for decades according to a 2011 local census. Since the late 1980s, migrants began to seize the business opportunities here, selling cheap goods and services on the street, targeting university students. They would sell everything from dumplings, soy milk, and fried rice to stationery, pirated copies of books and CDs, and photocopying services (see Figure 1.8). The local residents leased rooms and built shacks to meet the increasing demands for cheap housing from these migrants, who mainly partake in street vending. Most local residents have gradually moved out to live elsewhere on their rental income. In 2009, according to a rough survey conducted by the local street committee, there were about seven hundred migrants living in this small cluster.[8] This large number was astonishing even to the tenants themselves, who had lived there for over a decade, when all of them were forced to take refuge in a nearby school auditorium at midnight during a severe typhoon in the summer of 2009, and all at once they encountered their own full congregation of tenant residents for the first time. Days of heavy rains reportedly flooded shacks, and water levels rose knee-deep. The local government had to send police cars to transport the migrant tenants as there were concerns that electrocution and contagious diseases could result in serious casualties.

The Night Market resembles an "urban village" (*chengzhongcun*, literally "villages in the city"), as highly concentrated migrant communities on the outskirts of cities are called (Bach 2010; Chung 2018; J. Fan and Taubmann 2002; He 2015; Jeong 2011; Xiang 2005; L. Zhang 2001c). It is much smaller than the "urban villages" in the Pearl River Delta in terms of scale and organization, and the villager-landlords have much less power and interest in profiting from and controlling the community space than those in large "urban villages." It appears as an "uncivil urban space" (Siu 2007) because of its lack of public facilities and proper management. There is only one public restroom in the community, and the dark, muddy alleys are frightening at night (see Figure 1.9). Most households use night soil buckets at home rather than venturing into the alleys to the communal toilets. Challenged by the increasing amount of garbage and refuse that litters the streets, the street committee has had to dispatch daily garbage collection carts to the entrance to the Night Market. When interviewed, even the committee officer did not romanticize the minimal state effort. After all, this community is considered a plot of dead-end land, as the local saying "three [types of] nonintervention" (*san bu guan*) makes clear: little intervention from the state, real estate developers, or local residents due to its awkward location, odd shape, high relocation cost, and low investment return.

Yan grew up in the Night Market with her parents and two younger siblings. Her parents came to Shanghai from rural Anhui Province in 1986 and were among the first to start a food business in the neighborhood, making and selling breakfast, lunch, and late-night snacks. They have been living in the Night Market ever since. Yan's residence was a two-room shack attached to the back of a local resident's two-story *sifang*. The parents live in a windowless room equipped with a big color television and air conditioner, but the low-voltage electricity supply means the air conditioning does not work properly most of the time. Yan's parents use the room only for sleeping and storing their motorcycle. Yan and her younger siblings occupy the other room, where they sleep in two steel bunk beds and have meals and do homework at a long wooden desk between the beds. The family stacks bedding, spare clothes, and random belongings on the empty left upper bunk. The rest of the room serves as dining and storage space. Beside a used refrigerator are big bottles of vegetable oil and soy sauce and bunches of fresh scallions and Chinese parsley. Yan's parents have built an extra tiny brick-and-concrete shack to accommodate two distant relatives, who are employed to help with their food business.

"I hate to live here most when it rains," Yan often complained to me. Water often drips from the ceiling during the rainy season. Yan's parents have plastered the ceiling, but years have passed and it is starting to drip again. In the spring and summer, when it rains frequently, the rooms become extremely damp: the pounded mud floor shines with a film of moisture and grease, and wet laundry hung in the east room produces a whiff of staleness.

Every time I visited Yan at home, I could not help wondering why her family did not move to a better neighborhood for a drier, cleaner, better-lit, and more spacious place. Yan's parents have been successful in running their food cart after two decades of endlessly working hard. Proud of the quality and taste of their food, such as the popular *roujiamo* (a Chinese hamburger that has stewed, shredded pork between a baked bun) and *liangpi* (seasoned cold noodles made from gluten and mixed with cucumber slices), they have gained popularity among discerning college students. Since 2007, they have leased a street-facing booth and transformed it into a stationary business that also takes orders and offers delivery service. The couple makes hundreds of yuan every day thanks to their steady, loyal customer pool. So why don't they move and live more comfortably, given the children's express desire for better living conditions?

"It is not good for the business. It is very hard to find a place like this with such open space to wash scallions and stew pork in large quantities," Yan explained to me. I was puzzled: "Can't you wash them in the restroom, using either a bath tub or a large basin?"

"It's inconvenient. We have to wash dozens of kilograms of Chinese scallions and parsley every morning. Also, the water bill will be sizable." It turns out that Yan's family only needs to pay the landlord a flat rate of 10 RMB ($1.40) per head per month for tap water. To split utility bills, mostly water and electricity, equally among a number of tenants like this is common among migrant communities. In her answer, Yan takes in her parents' capitalist sensitivity to costs, evoking the kind of mind-set that Max Weber (1930) describes as the Protestant ethic that encourages hard work, self-denial of worldly comfort, and accumulating for accumulating's sake.

What Yan did not specify as an advantage of living in the Night Market is the supply chain within the community maintained by chain migration. The small community comprises a complex, supplementary network of business operations: most of the residents are engaged in related retail and services. Cooperation and competition tie them closer together, above and beyond their shared home origins; most of these migrants come from a few places in Anhui Province, and many are related to each other. Yan's parents purchase deep-fried crispy pancakes from a distant cousin who lives down the alley, for instance. The Night Market thus has created an economy of scale and earned a reputation for cheap food, small commodities, and copying services among university students and local residents. Once relocated, the kinship- and place-based networks embedded in such migrant enclaves and the socioeconomic capital that has sustained many migrant families' livelihoods would be disrupted and reduced.

In July 2015, the long-anticipated demolition finally happened. Red banners with slogans promising "democratic decisions, fair procedures, and transparent results" hung outside the entrance to the Night Market (see Figure 1.10). A working committee moved into a street-facing village house to begin the land measurement, property evaluation, and relocation plan. A real estate appraisal company posted on behalf of the district government a meticulous list of the housing survey results, including addresses, property owners' names, and housing types; all the village houses there were categorized as *jiuli* (old alley

FIGURE 1.8. Two food carts ready to serve customers along the main path of the Night Market. Photo by the author, May 2009.

FIGURE 1.9. A muddy lane leading to Yan's home in the Night Market. Photo by the author, May 2009.

FIGURE 1.10. A banner advocating "democratic decisions, fair procedures, and transparent results" at the entrance of the Night Market. Photo by the author, August 2015.

house) and registered by size. One square meter of *jianzhu mianji* (construction area) was set to be worth 28,421 RMB (about $4,000) as of August 2015. The list includes only local-*hukou* villagers, who are entitled to receive monetary compensation and relocation arrangements according to what remains of the collective agricultural land ownership system.

In the high-stake negotiation process, migrant tenants are nonexistent on and off record. While the local villagers frequented the office to check on relocation options or to bargain for higher compensation, the migrant tenants busied themselves looking for rental options while keeping their businesses in operation for as long as possible. Many migrant families kept on living in their shacks amid the rubble since they had paid three months' rent in a lump sum and would not get reimbursed even if they were forced to leave earlier (see Figure 1.11).

Yan's family moved into a furnished two-bedroom apartment with a flush toilet and tiled floor on the ground floor of a five-story *gongfang* (urban public housing projects mostly built by socialist work units between the 1950s and

FIGURE 1.11.   A man collects recyclables in the Night Market, which was to be completely torn down. Photo by the author, August 2015.

1970s to accommodate employees). Nevertheless, Yan's father continued to go to the Night Market every morning to prepare ingredients in the remaining shack. He was not allowed to cook huge pots of braised pork because their *gongfang* neighbors complained about the smell and the grease. He later managed to rent a room in a dilapidated factory compound near the Night Market for the cooking after their shack was finally pulled down. The search among migrants for the edge in both spatial and social senses continues.

RELATIVE LACK OF SLUMS

While migrants search relentlessly for flexible and cheap space to make a living, establish families, and build networks during the rapid urbanizing process, city governments and the urban middle class look at migrant settlements negatively. Words like "dirty" (*zang*), "chaotic" (*luan*), and "inferior" (*cha*) are frequently invoked in daily conversations and official documents to justify campaigns to demolish migrant enclaves. Such denunciation prioritizes a "concept city" over a "pedestrian city" in Michel de Certeau's terms (1984). The "concept city," from an aerial perspective, as found in official campaigns for the 2008 Olympic Games in Beijing or the 2010 World Expo in Shanghai, privileges modern images of high-rises, wide streets, shiny malls, and well-designed parks within a neat scheme of urban planning. In contrast, the mundane "pedestrian city" is often fraught with discordant appearances and experiences. The former tends to dismiss the latter's complex and highly developed form of socioeconomic order beneath its appearance of chaos. Composed of dense, diverse communities, the "pedestrian city" is often perceived as dangerous and backward, an eyesore to be erased in urban planning projects.

The contest between a "concept city" and a "pedestrian city" in Chinese cities, as seen elsewhere, is a process of spatial reorganization "through which social power is expressed" (Harvey 1990, 255). The making of a "concept city," largely dominated and controlled by social elites, creates "spaces of representation," to use Henry Lefebvre's term (Lefebvre 1991), which reflects and strengthens their power. Equally important is that such spaces have become a significant economic resource (Flock and Breitung 2016). They raise the value of real estate and the city in general by projecting the image of modernity and prosperity and attracting investments, businesses, consumers, and tourists.

The "pedestrian city," where migrants appropriate underregulated space for temporary housing, street vending, pedicab driving, and everyday livelihood, recedes amid the hegemonic discourse of urban planning and the "cleansing and beautifying" projects advocated by officials, architects, and developers. The dilapidated appearance of migrants' makeshift dwellings is seen as a blemish, even an embarrassment, to government officials and urban developers in not only aesthetic but also, and more importantly, in economic and political senses. This in turn makes demolition easier and faster, at the expense of migrants, who are left to fend for themselves. In official slogans, demolition and relocation are said to rejuvenate the urban economy and improve people's living conditions. In reality, most often, the opposite is true for migrants, who are deprived of full urban citizenship and hence are "noncitizens" excluded from the urban planning agenda (Harms 2016b).

Jiawen, Huan's classmate, has a hard time remembering clearly how many times his family has moved since coming to Shanghai. Originally from rural Anhui, he accompanied his parents when they came to live in Shanghai the year he entered first grade. Jiawen's father, Gang, takes odd jobs on construction sites and drives a motorized pedicab at night. His pedicab has been confiscated many times, and twice he was detained at police stations for days. Jiawen's mother, Lan, used to work as a janitor, but she has been staying at home since 2006 to take care of a newborn, their second son. Jiawen's family had lived for years in a large migrant community called the Airport, located two kilometers away from the Night Market. The community was built on a long-deserted military airport dating to World War II in northwestern Shanghai. In the 1990s when migrants congregated on the city edge to engage in small businesses, the Airport became a low-rent zone for migrants to survive and flourish. More than three hundred families used to live there, selling groceries, breakfast snacks, lottery tickets, household items, and various services to both local residents and migrant tenants. There were cheap public baths, dimly lit internet bars, open-air pool halls, unkempt hair salons, and smoky mahjong houses. However, Shanghai's rapid urbanization pushed the Airport back onto the real estate market. From 2007, the military authority that owned the land began to drive away the migrant households. By 2009, the once untidy but vibrant migrant community had been dissolved and replaced with untended foliage (see Figure 1.12).

The social space that enabled migrant businesses and livelihoods to prosper evaporated as the physical space of the Airport disappeared (see Figure 1.13). Jiawen's family was forced to leave the Airport in 2007 with many others. This exodus drove up rent in nearby neighborhoods. Jiawen's family had to move farther away to find affordable housing. His father had a harder and harder time finding work because his network thinned out following relocation.

"The impact on my family was huge. The rent went up. Our living conditions have gone downhill since the Airport was destroyed," observed Jiawen. In May 2011, when his family relocated again from a spot his family had moved into for merely two months because of the demolition of the local village, he commented to me bitterly: "I have lost count of how many times we have moved. Perhaps five times? As to why, I do not know. I only know that the places we lived in were always demolished. Because of economic reasons, my family has always been staying in *pinminku* [slums] where migrants gather."

Jiawen did not shy away from using the Chinese phrase for slum, *pinminku*, to describe his family's living conditions. The award-winning movie *Slumdog Millionaire*, translated as *Pinminku de baiwanfuwen*, may help bring back the term and awareness of slums to China. The story of the unexpected success of a young Indian man from the Juhu slums of Mumbai, shown widely in Chinese cinemas in early 2009, has been popular among migrant youth, most of whom watched it on pirated DVDs or online streaming.

FIGURE 1.12. Le, who had grown up in the Airport, took her younger brother to the demolished area to play in summer 2009. Photo by the author, August 2009.

FIGURE 1.13. Luxurious housing projects took shape in 2011 where the Airport used to be. Photo by the author, July 2011.

However, the Chinese media and official documents avoid the term. On paper, China does not have slums. The term has been carefully reserved for use in textbooks when specifically referring to a pre-1949, "old China," an outdated social problem that serves as a testament to the transgression of capitalism brought by the Western powers. In fact, the existence of unofficial migrant communities of different scales in Chinese cities, such as the Night Market and the Airport, is undeniable. These migrant communities have the basic, built-in infrastructure of electricity and water. Yet they commonly lack proper sewage, toilet, and garbage disposal, essentially rendering them slum-like to some extent.

Observers of postreform China frequently express surprise and admiration for "the relative lack of slums" (Wallace 2014, 4) in Chinese cities despite massive internal migration and rapid urbanization, as compared to cities in other developing countries, such as Mumbai in India and Rio de Janeiro in Brazil. Nevertheless, what makes the Chinese case exceptional is not its "relative lack" of such places but the strong determination and capacity of municipal governments to impose "concept cities," to reshape urban space, and to keep slums contained.

Both discursive control and land politics contribute to the state's ability to give the impression of China's having a "lack of slums." The politically neutral term *penghuqu* [shack settlement] has been used to describe dilapidated housing arrangements in Shanghai and other cities. The term, which is sufficiently descriptive, tones down class tensions arising from drastic socioeconomic disparity in the postreform era.[9] Meanwhile, the socialist land-tenure system, where the state and its organs possess most urban land, enables city governments to prevent the development of large-scale slums. Since the foundation of the PRC, the communist government has launched campaigns to improve the living conditions of old shack settlements from the republican era to gain political legitimacy and maintain social order (J. Chen 2012; Honig 1992). The marketization of urban real estate since the 1990s has generated a new wave of *penghuqu gaizao* (shack settlement transformation or regeneration), in which municipal governments work with developers to forcefully relocate local *penghuqu* residents to subsidized apartments in exurbia districts and make space for real estate projects. Meanwhile, the remaining, collectively owned agricultural land and private village houses in the periurban districts help absorb tens of thousands of migrants, preventing large-scale slums from building up in urban centers. Such housing arrangements are often hidden away from the main streets by highways, green zones, and industrial parks. Casual observers are unlikely to know of their existence. The rhetorical avoidance of the term "slum" and the physical destruction and relocation of migrant enclaves conspire to paint a miraculous facade of urbanization without slums in contemporary China.

RECLAIMING GATED COMMUNITIES

When Shanghai's city proper expands, the borderline between the urban and the rural constantly shifts outward, resulting in ambiguous periurban zones prone to continuous cycles of demolition and construction. In the process, small migrant communities on the edge of the city, such as the Night Market and the Airport, are under constant threat of destruction to make way for roads and highways, parks and malls, and residential neighborhoods. Migrants have to move along with the process for employment, business opportunities, and housing alternatives. More and more of them are now moving up, renting in newly built, high-rise housing compounds on the city's edge, a new form of periurban space that is understudied.

Lin's family has lived since 2006 in a multistory apartment complex named Beautiful Harbor with her parents and a younger brother. Completed in 2005, the housing compound is a gated community in design (see Figure 1.14). However, many apartments are vacant and many more are bought by investors, allegedly rich Wenzhou merchants, among others, for speculation and to rent out. In addition to local villagers who were relocated to the apartments to compensate for their loss of land, migrants of various social strata—including wage laborers, college graduates, small businessmen, and young professionals—make up the majority of residents in the compound.

Migrants not only dwell in these new housing compounds but also participate in the very making of them. Migrants lay bricks, guard gates, clean roads, and provide services, including running grocery and convenience stores. Lin's parents have been selling vegetables in a nearby produce market since 1998, and the family has lived in this neighborhood for over a decade. Before moving into the high-rise compound, they had rented a room from a local villager. The village house was demolished in 2006 to make room for another real estate development across from Beautiful Harbor. Lin has witnessed the landscape change dramatically from rice paddies dotted with village houses to open fields filled with rubble and vegetation left to grow wildly and roamed by feral dogs and chickens. A doorframe, filled with bricks, became part of a temporary wall in

FIGURE 1.14.   Beautiful Harbor seen from the outside in northwest Shanghai. Photo by the author, July 2011.

2011 to demarcate the new construction site. Red-ink signs reading "*chai*" (to demolish) were arrayed over the wall. Once when Lin passed the doorframe, she reminisced with me about how they used to live right next door to this place.

These housing projects on the newly developed city edge and their promises of a stable, comfortable living are elusive to migrants who actually shape and inhabit the periurban space. Although the demand for private housing grew in Chinese cities after the socialist public housing system dissolved in the late 1990s, real estate prices have grown much faster than incomes have increased since the mid-2000s, resulting in exorbitant rates that are unaffordable even to middle-income local households, let alone to migrant households. A two-bedroom apartment of one hundred square meters in Beautiful Harbor sold for more than 2 million RMB ($295,400) in 2010 and 4 million RMB ($615,400) in 2016.

In addition to the market's invisible hand, migrants have to overcome institutional barriers associated with their nonlocal *hukou*: no housing subsidies, limited access to housing financing, higher property taxes, and stricter criteria for purchase. Municipal governments have issued multiple rounds of initiatives with the intention to keep prices down and appease the increasingly frustrated local residents. One major way to do so is to raise the criteria threshold for migrants to purchase apartments in their adopted cities. As of 2018, only married nonlocal residents who have not previously purchased an apartment in Shanghai and have paid income tax or social security for five or more consecutive years were qualified for purchasing an apartment. The requirement for consecutive income tax or social security payment technically bars most rural-to-urban migrants engaged in low-income manufacturing and service jobs or self-employment from owning an apartment in the city.

The disequilibrium between supply and demand in China's distorted real estate market results in a high vacancy rate for new housing compounds in the periurban areas. Local residents with means find the Beautiful Harbor undesirable for living because it is on the edge of one of the remotest and least prosperous downtown districts. The high vacancy rate makes it possible for migrants to live in high-rises and improve their living conditions. The new spatial practice of *qunzu* (group rental) has emerged since the late 1990s (Lian 2009; Suda 2016). Lin's family rents only one bedroom and shares the kitchen and the bathroom with two other migrant families in a two-bedroom apartment to reduce living costs. The family paid 700 RMB ($110) per month in 2011, one or two hundred more than those in unofficial migrant housing compounds. Although the living space in shared apartments remains crowded and Spartan, it is considered a better, more hygienic living environment with concrete walls, flush toilets, and steel-framed windows. Twenty-four-hour guarded entrances, tiled walls, ornate fountains, and gardens add a touch of luxury.

In exchange, migrants have to deal with more surveillance and disciplinary rules from property owners who live in the buildings and property management companies aiming to keep property values up. Migrants such as Huan's and Yan's parents have been hesitant about moving into such multistory apartment buildings not only because of the higher prices but also for fear of losing the relative flexibility and freedom to utilize public space in migrant housing compounds. Yet as migrant enclaves have been constantly demolished, they have little choice but, finally, to crowd into such split spaces in these new apartment buildings.

The phenomenon of *qunzu* attracted media attention in the mid-2000s and caused heated discussions in the media over its legality and propriety. In 2007, the Shanghai government introduced a regulation on improving residential rental management to curb group rental practices. It stipulated that a room can only be rented to either an individual or one family, and each tenant must have at least a space of five square meters. The policy cited safety and security concerns as a justification. It received criticism for being out of touch with the social reality. Concerned public intellectuals considered it another measure that discriminates against the poor, especially low-income migrants, to advance the interests of real estate developers and property owners. Even though the implementation of this top-down intervention has been unsuccessful, it nonetheless demonstrates another state attempt to control and reshape the periurban edge that is continually laden with potential and risks for governance.

A ROOM OF ONE'S OWN

Compared to permanent urban residents, migrants with rural *hukou* status are significantly more likely to end up in private rentals (Youqin Huang and Jiang 2007). Studies find that, when other relevant factors are controlled, households without permanent residence are 78 percent less likely to own homes than those with local residency (Y. Huang and Clark 2002). Only five out of fifty migrant families I studied in Shanghai lived in self-purchased apartments as of 2011. They live in either Bridge Town on the eastern edge of Pudong District or in Baoshan District, where real estate prices were still relatively low. All five families made money in lucrative, construction- or logistics-related businesses: one father ran a brick kiln in Jiangsu Province; the other father was a subcontractor; the third father owned two heavy-duty earthwork trucks for rent; the fourth was a trader of construction materials; and the fifth, an owner of a small packaging workshop. The mothers were stay-at-home housewives, supporting the businesses and taking care of the children and housework. These families fell into a more capital-intensive, entrepreneurial category, generating income from capital and employees instead of solely from their own labor.

A few other successful migrants had long been planning to buy apartments in Shanghai, but they missed the opportunity before real estate prices soared in the mid-2000s. They have been renting furnished apartments in established *gongfang* neighborhoods built between the 1950s and 1970s in towns in the exurbia districts with rents ranging from 1,000 to 1,500 RMB ($140–$210) per month in the late 2000s. Like most urban residents, they had not foreseen that housing prices in Shanghai would continue to skyrocket. Xiaming, a watch repairman turned cell-phone vendor from rural Jiangsu, was one of them. As of 2011, he was still waiting for the real estate market to cool down, though real estate agents continued to announce ever higher prices. Xiaming has set his eyes on Bridge Town or nearby towns outside of the Outer Ring Highway, for better prices and network maintenance. After all, his business thrives on the periurban edge, and there is no reason to move into downtown districts where costs are unaffordable. Yan's parents also toyed with the idea of purchasing an apartment in Shanghai for years. However, housing prices where their street food business is located have inflated beyond their wildest imagination. Given the high correlation between location and business, they are unwilling to move away from the current store. In addition, their children are still in school, and they feel economically insecure, which makes any purchase unlikely in the near future.

The extremely low rate of apartment ownership among first-generation migrants also has to do with the migrants' ambiguous sense of belonging. Given the *hukou* barriers, most first-generation migrants expect to retire to their registered home villages. Many have spent significant savings to build big houses back in their home villages or purchase newly developed apartments in towns near those home villages. Huan's parents paid in cash 460,000 RMB ($70,760) for a three-bedroom apartment in 2015 in a county-seat town a thirty-minute bus ride from the husband's home village. These big, two-story houses and three-bedroom apartments often remain empty for years. They, nevertheless, stand as signs of migratory success and social status in the rural community. They also provide a physical and mental safety net for first-generation migrants who do not feel fully settled in Shanghai without access to health insurance or social security. Rural migrants maintain their entitlement to agricultural land in their home villages. In addition, many first-generation migrants have purchased low-cost, state-sponsored, rural health insurance plans in preparation for their old age and entertain the idea of going back to rural hometowns when they retire from *dagong* (working for others). Hence, they treat their rental homes in Shanghai merely as transient places to eat, sleep, and keep their belongings.

The more first-generation rural-to-urban migrants desire to accumulate wealth, the more they are embedded in the urban labor market and the longer they postpone their consumption in their adopted cities. The *hukou* system, which continues to hinder migrants' access to welfare and public goods in their adopted cities, perpetuates this spatial separation between production and consumption among migrant workers (C. Fan 2011; Swider 2015; Zhan 2015; L. Zhang 2002b). This in turn lowers the daily cost of labor reproduction and sustains the supply of cheap, flexible labor for China's urban economy.

In contrast, second-generation migrants are much more inclined to live in cities (Han 2012), not only because there are more working opportunities but also because they grow up there and have taken urban living for granted (see Chapter 6). Farming back in their registered villages is unimaginable for most of them, who do not have the knowledge and still less skills to farm. The desire to own a room of their own and enjoy an urban lifestyle in Shanghai is also stronger among second-generation migrant youth than in their parents. Most of them have grown up in crowded rental settings, sharing beds with their siblings. Neither the parents nor the children have had much privacy in such housing arrangements. Although they seldom express a strong sense of entitlement to privacy or having "one's own room," as found in Vanessa Fong's (2004) study of urban singletons in Dalian, they do occasionally express regret for not being able to live more comfortably in big houses back in their rural hometowns. As they reach adulthood, their need for privacy grows, and their desire for a room of their own grows stronger.

More importantly, these second-generation migrant youths have grown up under an urbanite social convention that one should have an apartment to establish oneself and set up one's own family. Xiaming's only daughter, Limi, who has lived in a rented, furnished apartment since she was born, yearned for the autonomy and freedom to decorate her own room: "Once we buy an apartment, I can start decorating the rooms according to my own taste." Property ownership would give her not only authority over her domestic space but also a new relationship to the city as an owner instead of a tenant and outsider. Studies have focused on the intimate relationship between housing consumption and China's emerging middle class (Davis 2002; Tomba 2004, 2009; L. Zhang 2008, 2010). Yet "propertyness" equally recasts the subjectivity of citizenship among less-privileged migrant workers, as captured by Tiantian Zheng's (2009, 192) account of how a rural migrant prostitute claimed the authenticity of her urban membership based on her ownership of two properties rather than a permanent *hukou* in Dalian, China's northern economic harbor city. Li Zhang's study of real estate development and middle-class formation in Kuming in southwest China also observes that "private home ownership and increasingly stratified residential space serve as a tangible ground on which class-specific subjects and cultural milieus are fostered" (2010, 107). Home ownership in cities becomes the new entrance ticket to urban membership and the marker of insider/outsider distinction in the urbanizing process.

FIGURE 1.15. The living room of Huan's wedding apartment inside a gated community. Photo by the author, January 2015.

FIGURE 1.16. The dining area of Huan's wedding apartment. Photo by the author, January 2015.

However, to have one's own room in Shanghai is particularly hard to realize. Exorbitant real estate prices since the mid-2000s have prevented most migrant youth from seriously considering the idea of purchasing an apartment any time soon. Those who get married in their early twenties rent apartments in either old *gongfang* or new apartment buildings to establish nuclear families and enjoy better living conditions. Huan moved into a two-bedroom apartment (3,000 RMB per month, $425) in a gated community after getting married in early 2015. Unlike their parents, she and her husband spent a whole month transforming the unfurnished apartment into a beautiful "wedding room" (*xinfang*) with the financial support of his parents. They painted the walls, laid a vinyl floor, and hung pinkish curtains and enlarged wedding photos (see Figures 1.15 and 1.16). New furniture and electronic appliances purchased online cost over 10,000 RMB ($1,615). When Yan got married in the fall of 2015, she and her husband also rented a two-bedroom *gongfang* apartment and furnished it with wallpaper before moving in. These apartments have become intimate spaces that provide comfort and, more importantly, anchors for their deeply held aspirations for urban lifestyles and subjectivities.

Immersed in the highly developed mass consumer culture of postreform Shanghai, these second-generation migrant youths no longer postpone consumption for the sake of wealth accumulation as their parents did; nor do they turn their backs on their unfamiliar home villages for delayed consumption. The spatial separation between production, reproduction, and consumption, as observed among many first-generation migrant workers, is no longer desirable or feasible for their offspring.

PERIURBAN LIFE IN LATE-SOCIALIST CHINA

Migrants tend to have less desirable housing than urban natives in general (Costello 1987; Saunders 2010; Skeldon 1977; Tilly 1965, 2006). However, the predominance of minimalist rental housing arrangements among rural-to-urban migrants in urban China has to be explained not only by migrants' transitional needs and market rules but also by late-socialist institutional discrimination. China's *hukou*-based structural inequality and socialist land ownership put rural-to-urban migrants at a disadvantage in the urban housing market. Migrants resort to living in small, often poorly taken care of temporary housing units in periurban areas because rent is cheaper. They suffer from overcrowding, poor hygiene, and lack of tenant protection. Nevertheless, they also benefit from life on the edge by enjoying proximity to work and business opportunities, maintaining a social network based on their native homes, and avoiding state regulation and surveillance. The periurban livelihood entails both marginalization and empowerment for migrants. The shabby rental housing arrangements symbolize and perpetuate the liminal status of rural-to-urban migrants in the cities.

The congregation of migrants on the edge of Chinese cities is no coincidence. It becomes a lived metaphor: in-between people occupying and making in-between space. Living in a society that is at once socialist and capitalist, the Chinese have to confront and reconcile contradictions in everyday life between idealized categories like socialism versus capitalism, the rural versus the urban, and the local versus the outsider. The existence of "peasant workers" and "urban-rural convergence zones" are presumed to be inevitable, transitional, and necessary during China's quest for urbanization and modernity.

Socioeconomic insecurity resulting from institutionalized disadvantages against nonlocal-*hukou* holders contributes to the persistence of shabby rental housing arrangements among first-generation rural migrants. Such spatial arrangements on the urban edge have also been found elsewhere since World War II (Saunders 2010). Doug Saunders calls these congregations, big or small, "arrival cities" for rural-to-urban migrants to make a living and await transition to a full-fledged urban life if possible. The "arrival city" is "both populated with people in transition . . . and is itself a place in transition, for its streets, homes, and established families will either someday become part of the core city itself or will fail and decay into poverty or be destroyed" (Saunders 2010, 11). Saunders's observation resonates with the great urban activist Jane Jacobs's argument for the importance of retaining bad, old buildings in New York City to offer urban mulches for immigrants and low-income households to start small businesses and make a living (Jacobs 1961). Untidy but vibrant, the "arrival cities" are linked to the villages where rural migrants have come from and to the established city at the same time. Although often slum-like in appearance, they are dynamic and crucial entry platforms for migrants to survive, save, socialize, and succeed.

In such "arrival cities," proper state assistance, such as accessible property ownership and social services, education being the most important, are found by Saunders to be crucial in enabling migrants to adapt to an urban lifestyle and achieve upward mobility, especially among the second generation. Given that China's dual-track citizenship still discriminates against migrants in employment, education, and other social services, would migrant families landing in enclaves like the Night Market and the Airport arrive successfully or not? The following chapters answer this question by examining closely the winding path of social (im)mobility undertaken by migrant youth in Shanghai. I turn next to exposing how the normative standards of reproductive choice and child-rearing practices after three decades of top-down one-child policy in urban China disadvantage these youth from their earliest years.

2 THE "REPRODUCTION WITHOUT CULTIVATION" PROBLEM

"WHAT HAVE I DONE? My children are so spoiled! I might not have a lot of education, but I understand the importance of going to school, and I empha-size it. But while I hope to give my children a good education, I've also spoiled them: they don't do any household chores, and they think dirty clothes belong only in the washing machine," complained Simei in a southern Jiangsu accent.

It was an evening early in the summer of 2011, three years after I first met Simei. A petite woman in her early forties, Simei had an older daughter, Lin (born in 1994), and a younger son, Xin (born in 1996). She had migrated to Shanghai in 1998 with her husband, Jianguo, and followed her sister-in-law into the vegetable-vending business. That evening, a thunderstorm was gathering force, and the market where the couple had been selling vegetables for almost a decade was devoid of customers. Simei began to prepare dinner earlier than usual in a six-square-meter storage room across from their booth; both spaces the couple rented from the street committee that managed the market. Lin returned from vocational school to join her mother in preparing dinner, but not before she helped herself to an ice cream. Meters away, Xin, now a ninth grader, slouched in a used armchair. He was enjoying the summer breeze that came through the side entrance while listening to music in his earphones. On a Samsung smartphone his nimble fingers were texting something. He paid no attention to what went on around him, including two chickens that were leaving their crate.

Simei's claim that her children were spoiled surprises me, as it contradicts the popular perception that migrant children do not get enough care and cultivation from their parents. Migrant children are stereotypically portrayed by the media as naive and out of place in the city. Pictures of migrant children helping out their parents in vending booths and playing in debris-strewn places amid sites of demolition stand in stark contrast to the well-dressed city kids being shepherded to extracurricular tutorials.

Some migrant children have rightfully observed the tendency for news reports to pit them against their better-off urban counterparts for the sake of making a comparison. They find the comparison contrived and exaggerated: "Why do they insist on making us look so miserable? I think I have a very comfortable (enough) life, perhaps much better than many urban families." After reading a news feature written based on interviews with her and her friends in 2010, Yang, an outspoken seventeen-year-old girl originally from rural Anhui, protested indignantly: "The moment you put a migrant student against a Shanghai student like that, the migrant immediate looks very pitiful." When contrasted with urban youths who are showered with gifts and attention by both parents and grandparents, migrant children easily appear lacking and inferior.

This chapter zooms in on the topics of reproductive choices and child-rearing practices among migrant households, the majority of which have two or more offspring, and compares them with one-child households—as limited by China's stringent one-child policy targeting urban residents until recently—that predominate in Shanghai. It problematizes the prevalent representation of migrant children as the inferior Other to urban children in Shanghai and argues that the journalistic gaze implies a normative urban-centered view on what childhood should be. The intimate practices of reproduction and child-rearing have become powerful sites for breeding prejudice and exercising exclusionary citizenship in urban China.

FAMILY PLANNING, NATIONAL DEVELOPMENT, AND URBAN CITIZENSHIP

That Simei and Jianguo have two children is not uncommon among rural-to-urban migrant families. More than three-quarters of the fifty migrant families that I studied closely have two or three children, in addition to a few households having four children. Recent reports have also confirmed that most students in migrant schools in Shanghai and Beijing come from families with multiple children (Han 2004; Beibei Li 2004; Meng 2009; Yuan 2010). A survey by Shanghai's Birth Planning Committee in 2011 found that 40 percent of registered migrant households living in Shanghai had two or more children. Considering the large number of unregistered migrants that dodge the census and any related survey studies, the actual percentage of migrant families having two or more children in Shanghai is likely even higher.

Along the Rural-Urban Divide

It should come as no surprise that migrant families have more than one child. The one-child policy is rather a misnomer for China's family-planning campaign between 1980 and 2016, an unprecedented social engineering project in human history (White 2006). This campaign was the major instrument by the Chinese state to curb a surging population[1] at a time of sustained decline in mortality rates due to improved sanitation, nutrition, and health care following the establishment of the PRC (Naughton 2007, 4). The Chinese state first adopted a mild "Later, Longer, and Less" (*wan xi shao*) approach (1973–79), mobilizing Chinese couples to get married later, wait longer, and have fewer children (White 1994).[2] The more drastic one-child-only policy did not start officially until 1980 (Whyte, Feng, and Cai 2015; Whyte and Gu 1987). The tightened policy set a target population of 1.2 billion in the year 2000 (Naughton 2007, 168). However, domestic resistance forced the Chinese government to modify the one-child policy after 1985 (Greenhalgh 2008; White 2006). Since, there have been great variations in implementation by local governments across regions, making generalization difficult. In principle, agricultural households can have a second child if the first one is a girl, resulting in a so-called one-child-and-a-half, or de facto two-child, policy in the countryside. This has created dual-track family-planning policies along the rural-urban divide.

Despite staying long term in cities, most migrant parents still hold agricultural *hukou* and have not been subjected to the one-child policy. Couples with rural *hukou* do have to wait a few years and go through a cumbersome application process to acquire a "birth permit" (*zhunshengzheng*), in order to enjoy the privilege of having a second child without penalty. Children born without a birth permit issued by the local government could not be registered in the *hukou* system and would become "black *hukou*" (*hei hukou*, nonexistent in household registration records). Parents need to rely on *guanxi* and pay fines later to register "black kids" in the *hukou* system so that those children can enroll in school. Administrative hurdles notwithstanding, the relaxing of the one-child policy does allow or even encourage willingness from rural households to act on their preference and have more than one child.

Massive internal migration in the postreform era has allowed rural households to circumvent family-planning policies. Geographic distance and physical mobility make it easier for migrant families to avoid close state surveillance and intervention both at home and in their adopted cities. Jiao's parents, originally from rural Henan, managed to escape the penalties for having four children. After giving birth to two daughters in their home village, the couple migrated to Shanghai in 1996 and made a living selling breakfast food and fruit on the street. There, they gave birth to Jiao, a third daughter, and eventually a son. The couple did not go back to Henan to enter the third and fourth children in the household register. For more than a decade, Jiao and her younger brother remained "black," kept hidden from official records. They managed to circumvent administrative scrutiny by attending private substandard migrant schools, which required few official documents. It was only when these two children graduated from middle school that the family returned to Henan to apply for official IDs so that they could attend academic high school in their hometown. The father sought help from his elder brother, who worked in the public security bureau, to register them and avoid birth-control fines totaling more than 20,000 RMB ($2,860).

In comparison, urban households have been under closer state surveillance via socialist work units (*danwei*) and neighborhood committees (*juweihui*) than their rural counterparts. Urbanites who violated the one-child policy would receive not only fines but also demotion and deprivation of welfare benefits tied to their work position. This is not to deny that the economic and even physical penalties facing rural parents are still significant. Reports of violence against rural families, including coercive sterilization, forced abortion, confiscation of livestock, and demolition of houses, have been abundant. However, the high correlation between urban *hukou*, job placement, and welfare provision, including public housing before the late 1990s real estate marketization, gives city governments more powerful leverage to interfere with urban households' fertility practices.

"The Poor Breeds More"

The Shanghai government has been particularly effective in implementing family-planning policies. In 2001, 97 percent of Shanghai local families had only one child, and only one out of one thousand had more than two children (Liping Wang 2002). The municipal government formed local family-planning committees as early as 1961 in response to the central government's instructions to promote the accessibility and acceptance of birth control. Although birth control efforts were interrupted during the Cultural Revolution (1966–76), Shanghai had already experienced a downward fertility transition before the one-child policy was introduced. Lingering fear of political persecution and physical punishment from the Cultural Revolution also induced compliance to the one-child policy among urban residents. In addition, the city government provided a monetary reward of 5 RMB ($1.70) per month for families that had only one child and had received a one-child certificate by pledging not to give birth to "unplanned children." This subsidy was significant for working-class families when average wages were around 50 RMB ($15) in the mid-1980s under the planned economy. The city's two-decade-long negative rate of natural population growth among local households serves as testament to the success of the one-child policy.[3]

Western media, whose audience generally have a hard time reconciling such state-imposed fertility control, tend to disproportionally report resistance among the Chinese against the one-child policy (Milwertz 1997). However, surveys and interviews with local Shanghainese on the one-child policy suggest a high degree of acceptance and internalization of the policy over time (Nie and Wyman 2005). Although some might consider a two-child family ideal, they would often bring up national concerns about overpopulation when talking about their decisions to have one child only.

From radio and television to newspapers and billboards, "one child one family" has been advertised as the only and the ideal scheme for solving China's population problem (Greenhalgh and Winckler 2005). Although Shanghai was not hit hard during the Great Famine, stories of starvation and even cannibalism in the rural hinterland spread throughout Shanghai as a cautionary tale against overpopulation. The crowdedness in the city center and the traffic during rush hours also convince many Shanghainese that their city is already having an overpopulation problem. It has almost become an implicit duty for Shanghai residents to abide by the one-child policy, or they would not be able to keep up the relatively high standard of living that exists in Shanghai.

The propaganda that personal reproductive desires should align with national development goals has shaped to a large extent the social imagination of family planning. Amid Shanghai's miraculous economic growth, I often heard local Shanghainese compare rural-to-urban migrants who have two or more children with people in populous developing countries, such as India and certain African countries. Such an association with populous Third World countries where economies are sluggish and living standards are low has been encouraged by China's family-planning propaganda. This analogy explicitly correlates high fertility rates with low socioeconomic status at both individual and national levels. According to this reasoning, if one violates the one-child policy, one is an irresponsible citizen and must bear the consequence of hindering national development and causing personal suffering. This analogy helps justify an unapologetic attitude toward migrants' precarious living conditions in the city.

Influence from state propaganda aside, many local Shanghainese interpret their practice and acceptance of one child, one family as proof of their rationality and modernity. Although most of them do acknowledge the factor of state control, they often interpret the result of their having only one child as a rational and responsible choice in answer to modernizing trends. They emphasize that economic rationality and market logic support one child, one family. Even after family policies became relaxed in 2016, when asked whether they would consider having a second child, many Shanghainese would continue to challenge the motivation behind any desire for more: What is the point of having more than one child these days when it is already so expensive to raise just one? It follows that it is irrational to have more than one child given that Shanghai's living costs have risen and competition in school and at work have become more intense since the market-oriented reforms. They want the best for their children. Given that they are not "peasants" and child mortality rate is very low in Shanghai, they prefer pooling family resources to invest in fewer children and increase the quality of their upbringing to succeed amid the more intensely competitive environment. They call the dilution approach among low-income migrant families with multiple children "*yue qiong yue sheng* (the poor breeds more)," labeling it "irrational and irresponsible" as it fails to take into consideration postreform socioeconomic conditions.

Some local Shanghainese also dismiss the traditional notion of *yang er fang lao* (raising children for elderly care in return when old), which is believed to sustain high fertility rates among rural households, including migrant ones. They find this notion no longer applicable to urban China, where the younger generations enjoy high mobility and display strong individuality. Many argue that children today will leave their parents sooner or later for schooling, work, or marriage, and it has become unreasonable to expect children, especially those who migrate to other cities or countries, to live with and take care of their ageing parents. The prospect to having multiple children as old-age security is seen to be diminishing in the urban setting. Of course, many local parents actively use their social networks to help their only child secure jobs within Shanghai and appeal to filial piety and affective bonding to cultivate and maintain close relationship with their adult children (Evans 2010; Sun 2011; Whyte 2005). However, by emphasizing the importance of economic calculation in family planning, local Shanghainese see themselves as more rational and sophisticated than their rural counterparts in embracing the logic of the market economy and contributing to a rapidly modernizing society. The acceptance of the one-child policy hence contributes to Shanghai's urban exclusivity.

Citizenship in Debate

The high degree of acceptance and internalization of the one-child-one-family policy among local Shanghainese exemplifies a Foucauldian mode of governmentality, in which the repressive state exercises its power more and more through strategies of discipline and advocacy of individual self-regulation (Foucault 2010; Rabinow 1984; Rose 2007). Individuals not only regulate but also rationalize their own conduct, including the most intimate reproductive practices (Santos 2016), in line with the Communist Party's agenda and ideology. In consequence, the private domain of reproduction is subject to not only official intervention but also public scrutiny. Those who violate family-planning policies receive heavy criticism from individuals who have internalized the propaganda, in addition to penalties levied by local governments.

In October 2012, Shanghai witnessed a heated debate on whether migrant students deserve the right to take *zhongkao* (high school entrance examination). The debate revealed a collective sensitivity to family-planning practices as a matter of moral responsibility and the governmentality that shapes the politics of urban citizenship. Haite, a migrant eighth grader, initiated the debate. She attracted public attention because of her open call on Sina Weibo (the Chinese version of Twitter) for equal rights to *zhongkao*. Her parents came from Jiangxi Province and migrated to south China in the 1990s. Haite was born in 1997 in Zhuhai, one of the first SEZs, where she got her first name: *hai* from *Zhuhai* and *te* from *Tequ* (Special Zone, referring to Zhuhai SEZ). Since 2002 she has lived with her parents and two younger siblings in Shanghai. However, she remains officially registered in her Jiangxi hometown because of the hereditary *hukou* system. In the spring of 2012, Haite withdrew from middle school because of her ineligibility for Shanghai's *zhongkao*. While being at home and restless, she opened a Sina Weibo account and joined discussions on educational rights.

In October 2012, she invited local Shanghainese to have an online debate on migrant students' right to *zhongkao* in Shanghai. Later in December 2012, Haite, her father, and a few other migrants went to the People's Square across from the Shanghai municipal government building for the third time. They stood next to each other in silence, holding A4-size paper with phrases such as "Give back my right to *zhongkao* [*huan wo zhongkao quanli*]" and "To implement the Constitution, to guarantee human rights [*shishi xianfa, baozhang renquan*]." Soon, the police came to intervene and dispel the group. Haite's father, accused of tearing a policeman's clothes, was detained for a few days.

The debate initiated by Haite turned out to be a very heated one. Tens of thousands of comments from both supporters and opponents led to the closure of her Weibo account three days later. Reports on Haite in major newspapers in Shanghai ignited social commentaries from different walks of life on the internet. Her family's background, her academic performance, and her father's tax history surfaced online, feeding wild speculations about her motives and goals for launching such a public debate. While supporters praised Haite for speaking up and challenging the inequalities in China's education and *hukou* systems, opponents criticized her for being opportunistic and disrespectful of the rules of the game in China's *hukou*-based citizenship regime.

That Haite has two siblings became a key issue in the debate. Her parents' violation of birth control policies was perceived by many commentators as unlawful and irresponsible; hence, they did not deserve any claims of equal citizen rights. Haite and her family were called "locusts" feeding on Shanghai's limited resources. Some netizens pointed out how the Shanghainese had dutifully observed the one-child policy, sometimes despite their personal wishes for more children, to conform with the state goals of population control and economic development. If one asked for equal rights to education as a Chinese citizen, they argued, one should fulfill citizen obligations, such as abiding by birth control policies. Exercising self-discipline regarding family planning has become a way for local urbanites to defend their entitlements in the urban citizenship regime.

The emphasis on responsibility is not uncommon in discussions of citizenship and has its roots in China's education system. The Ministry of Education requires all students to take courses and be tested on the subjects of morality and society (*pinde yu shehui*), ideology and morality (*sixiang pinde*), and ideology and politics (*sixiang zhengzhi*) in primary, middle, and high school respectively. Textbooks that address these subjects are geared toward rote learning and teacher-centered lecturing and are designed to disseminate knowledge, not to stimulate critical examination of the meaning of "citizenship" (Guo and Guo 2015; Zhong and Zhang 2015). The preface of the textbook entitled *Gongmin yu shehui* (Citizen and society), which is used in Shanghai public middle schools for the ideology and morality subject, states that the course is to cultivate "modern, qualified citizens who observe disciplines and laws [*zunji shoufa de xiandai hege gongmin*]." Its lesson 5, "Cherishing Rights, Fulfilling Obligations," first lays out the basic rights, such as physical freedom and the right to vote and labor, granted by the Chinese constitution. It then devotes many more pages to how citizens must carry out certain basic obligations, observing family-planning policies being one. Through these courses, students learn a top-down set of citizenship values that serve the interests of national policies (J. Lu and Gao 2004).

The state-sanctioned discourse on normative citizenship fails to empower migrant youth like Haite to fight for citizen rights. Haite's appeal to the constitution and universal human rights may resemble what the political scientists Kevin O'Brien and Lianjiang Li describe as "rightful resistance," in which disadvantaged groups strategically employ "the rhetoric and commitments of the powerful," such as laws, government policies, and other officially promoted values, to hold the powerful, especially higher-level officials, accountable in China (O'Brien and Li 2006, 2). However, citizen rights such as political rights and physical freedom, as mentioned in the Chinese constitution, cannot be taken for granted in China, where the interpretation and implementation of laws are subject to the political needs of the one-party regime. More importantly, the emphasis on obligations in China's citizenship education weakens and even disqualifies Haite's petition in the first place. Her parents' breach of family planning signals to the public that they have been irresponsible citizens. This in turn makes it hard for them to hold the powerful accountable, disqualifying them in their quest of making "rightful" claims. Rights are closely associated with and often conditioned on the fulfillment of obligations.

Those migrant families in my study who knew Haite neither joined nor supported her protest. They found the notions of constitutional and human rights too distant and abstract if not altogether irrelevant. Most of the migrant parents were less educated and less affluent than Haite's father. Their daily struggles to make ends meet and avoid state regulations that affect their housing and business operations prevented them from knowing and feeling entitled to constitutional rights and human rights in the first place. The absence of labor unions or interest-based associations other than loose networks based on kinship or native-place connection among migrant workers and small businessmen in the city also makes it harder for any collective organization among them.[4]

Haite's open challenge to the status quo has cast her as suspicious to many who have internalized China's passive citizenship regime that suppresses any challenges to state authority. She identified herself on her Weibo account as a "youthful citizen, liberty fighter, and democracy pioneer." Some commentators suggested that she was simply "posing as a dissident" to gain special treatment and perhaps political asylum in the future. Some online posts accused her of being used by anti-China forces from the West. News broke in 2016 via a Sina Weibo announcement that Haite was admitted to Purdue University in the United States. According to an interview of her father, some grumbling netizens even wrote petition letters to urge the university to withdraw the offer.[5] It is unclear whether Haite finally made it to Purdue, and it is impossible for me to verify her father's allegations made during the interview, with some parts of it sounding incoherent and questionable. No matter whose claims are true, the rare open debate over urban citizenship ended in amplified disagreement and distrust.

Since being issued in 2014, two years after the debate, the "Decision on Shanghai Residential Status Management" issued by the municipal government has explicitly mandated that any migrants who violate family-planning policies will lose their eligibility to apply for Shanghai residence cards via the "point accumulation" system. This regulation reflects and reifies the collective sensitivity and discontent, after three decades of social engineering, toward the breach of family-planning policies among migrant families. Any violation of birth planning, which is listed together with "any violation of criminal law" in the decision, discredits migrants from applying for Shanghai's residential status, that is, urban citizenship. Intimate reproductive practices have thus become institutionalized as preconditions for claiming urban citizenship and its accompanied rights to public services in Shanghai. Of course, one must have higher-education qualifications, professional skills, or large amounts of economic capital to meet the minimum requirement. Citizen rights come hand in hand with citizen responsibilities, yet there is no guarantee of such rights even if one fulfills the basic responsibilities.

GENDER, REPRODUCTION, AND URBAN MODERNITY

The higher incidence of violations of family-planning policies among migrant families has been widely attributed to the traditional ideology of "son preference" (*zhongnan qingnü*, preferring men to women, placing more value in a son than a daughter) associated with agricultural economy and rural culture. In the patrilineal family system in China, sons take the family name, continue the lineage, provide money and care to elderly parents, and contribute to ancestral worship rituals. The Chinese patrilineal family system has sustained social, economic, and cultural needs for at least one son in the postreform era, especially in villages where clan organizations and ancestral worship remain important (Y. Lu and Tao 2015; Murphy, Tao, and Lu 2011). The importance of having sons as a form of old-age insurance persists in the countryside, where social security is scanty. The consequent higher valuation of sons often leads to fertility control and child-rearing practices that discriminate against daughters, including sex-selective abortions and late registration of baby girls, especially after the tightening of family-planning policies since 1980 (Feldman et al. 2007; Graham, Larsen, and Xu 1998; Gui 2017; J. Li and Lavely 2003). China's highly skewed sex ratios at birth (SRB), the number of boy infants compared to 100 girl infants who were born within a given period, functions as both an indicator and consequence of the strong social preference for sons. While an SRB between 103 and 107 is considered normal, China's nationwide SRB was 118 according to its 2010 census, and the SRB in Anhui Province, where about half of the migrants in Shanghai come from, was as high as 123 (Yanzhong Huang and Yang 2006; Loh and Remick 2015).[6]

Preference for Sons

Preference for sons indeed remains one factor in shaping migrants' reproductive choices and child-rearing practices. First-generation rural-to-urban migrant parents spent their formative years in the countryside and are understandably more committed to local reproductive ideologies. They married mostly fellow villagers before migration or other rural migrants. Most mothers gave birth, at least to their first child, back in their home villages. The social pressure for having at least a son hence remained strong for them. The highly skewed SRB of rural-to-urban migrants' children based on China's fifth census seems to confirm that son preference persists among rural migrants (H. Wu, Li, and Yang 2005).

In most cases of "over-quota births," the sequence that begins in possibly multiple daughters and terminates in a solitary male testifies to the patrilineal desire of wanting at least one male heir. Such gendered sequences also imply that sons receive more parental care not only for being male but also for being younger. The common gendered offspring sequence—elder daughter(s), then a younger son—means that sons tend to join their parents in the cities earlier, live with them longer, and receive more parental care (Goodburn 2014, 2015; Ling 2017a).

However, it is worth noting that son preference in multisibling migrant families is by no means static. Staying longer in urban areas and assimilating into city lives to a higher degree has reduced son preference among many migrant households (H. Wu et al. 2007; H. Wu, Li, and Yang 2005). This study finds three cases of only-daughter migrant families. The calculation of child-rearing costs in Shanghai and the pursuit of a comfortable lifestyle are more important than filial and patrilineal obligations for those urbanized migrants (Ling 2017a).

Media representations nevertheless have exaggerated such son preference and exacerbated local prejudice against migrant families. The famous comic skit *Chaosheng youjidui* (Over-quota birth guerrilla) makes fun of the strategies and risks undertaken by migrant families to have at least one son. The skit, first played during the 1990 New Year's Eve gala on China's Central Television (CCTV), became a national hit overnight. The skit satirized the efforts of a young rural couple to have a son after giving birth to three girls. They moved across China to escape penalty, left their village house and farming land, engaged in odd jobs in cities, and failed to provide a stable living for their baby girls. This skit, later routinely performed in theaters and on public squares across the countryside, has become a stock propaganda item for birth-planning agencies to condemn the "feudal" ideology of son preference and call for the observance of family-planning policies.

While the comic skit pokes fun at the persistent preference for sons in China after its decade-long family-planning campaign, it perpetuates the denigration of Chinese peasantry as being uncivilized and backward at the end of the twentieth century (Cohen 1993; Kipnis 2001b; Siu 1990). The couple wore baggy blue uniforms from the Maoist era and spoke Chinese with strong accents. They walked stealthily on bowlegs. They could not afford diapers (to prevent their babies from peeing on the street) or fresh fruit (which was believed to be good for the fetus). Nor did they have the sophistication to give proper names to their daughters. The husband was particularly adamant in having at least a son despite the heavy economic and social costs. Although the wife expressed doubt about their wandering for the sake of son preference, she conformed to her gender role in the patriarchal system and conceded the decision to her husband. Such a formulaic portrayal of rural-to-urban migrants reinforces the stereotype that the Chinese peasantry is unfit for the nation's quest for modernization and is to be blamed for China's problems, including overpopulation.

"Unlike Outsiders, We Do Not Prefer Sons!"
The state-sponsored campaign against son preference targets mostly rural households. Urban residents are most receptive to the policy, and it functions as another protective barrier that assures the exclusivity of urban citizenship. Since son preference has become so bound up with the image of the Chinese peasantry in media representations, migrant households that have more than one child are dismissed as *zhongnan qingnü* regardless of individual motives and socioeconomic circumstances. Urban residents who have rationalized and normalized the one-child-one-family policy are quick to dismiss son preference as irrational and backward. "Unlike *waidiren* [outsiders], we do not *zhongnan qingnü*," many local Shanghainese claim while emphasizing the differences between themselves and migrants.

Son preference has indeed shown signs of significant decline in Chinese cities. Modernization theories have long argued that industrialization contributes to the rise of women's status by increasing women's access to education and employment. The rise of women's educational profile and earning power raises first-marriage age and decreases fertility rates. Shanghai, one of China's first treaty ports forced to open to the West after the First Opium War in 1842, has a much longer history of industrialization than most parts of China. The city shows earlier convergence with Western industrialized countries on gender equality issues. The city has been known for its "feminine" qualities, associated with its fashionable and capable female inhabitants (L. O. Lee 1999). The stereotype of "henpecked" Shanghai men buying groceries and cooking meals has been a source of humor for the rest of China, where masculinity is still constructed through men's dominance of women and avoidance of housework (Long 1998). Local Shanghainese ending up with only one child regardless of its sex pride themselves on being not only law-abiding but also open-minded, hence more metropolitan and civilized than their rural counterparts, including the migrants that come to their city.

However, the Shanghai experience owes a lot more to state interventions than to some presumed innate characteristics of the Shanghainese people. The Maoist doctrines, policies, and propaganda that tried to liberate women from patriarchal dominance left strong imprints on urban households' gender dynamics. Women's participation rates in the manufacturing and service industries in the cities rose significantly during the party-led campaigns for women to "hold up half of the sky." Women were mobilized to work hard both in factories and at home to contribute to socialist nation building. The *danwei* system that promised life-long employment also reduced the need for urban residents to have a son for elderly care. Although the *danwei* system has been largely dismantled after market-oriented economic reforms, urban residents continue to have much better access to social security and public provisions than rural *hukou*-holders in the countryside (Gao 2010; Mingjiang Li 2005). The heavy-handed implementation of the one-child policy in Chinese cities has also unintentionally contributed to the rise of women's status. Urban families that end up with only one daughter are compelled to invest in the education and well-being of their only daughters. In turn, daughters who grow up as an only child and conform to the gender norms of being obedient and diligent tend to perform well in China's exam-oriented education system and are empowered by it at home (Evans 2008; Fong 2002).

Studies have shown that daughters turn out to be as accountable as sons, sometimes even more so, in giving financial support to their parents, even after marriage (L. Shi 2009; Xie and Zhu 2009). The adoption of neolocal residence among young married couples in cities makes it less realistic for parents to count on their sons to live with and take care of them. The social norm that expects grooms and their parents to pay for housing and wedding costs, which have been skyrocketing since the commodification of housing and marriage ceremonies in the late 1990s, makes sons even less desirable. Such popular sayings as "daughters are like little warm quilts, while sons are like ill-fitting shirts" testify to the affective bonds between Chinese daughters and their parents (L. Shi 2009, 2017). "What's the point of having a son these days?" The question, often heard in discussions on son preference, shows the decreasing value of sons in both economic and emotional terms in urban families. Those who still show preference for sons are easily dismissed as irrational and backward.

A report with the sensational title "Post-1980s Households Giving away Daughters" offers insights into the discursive practice of differentiation and exclusion built upon a critique of son preference. The report was published on May 29, 2012, the National Birth Planning Campaign Day, in Shanghai's most established local newspaper, *Xinmin* (literally "New Citizen") *Evening News*.[7] It starts with a briefing on the 2010 census findings, highlighting that Shanghai's population growth by birth contributed by migrants is almost equal to what is contributed by local residents. The report continues with the story of a migrant woman from rural Jiangsu Province who gave birth to a daughter less than two years after her first son. The woman was quoted as saying she was prepared to pay the fine of 30,000 RMB for having a second child out of plan because it was easier to make up for the monetary loss with two years of hard work in Shanghai. The careless tone of the quote suggests indifference to and defiance of the family-planning policies among migrant families.

The next section of the report introduced another migrant woman, Ms. Yu, who left behind her six-year-old son in rural Jiangsu. She was reported to have aborted a second pregnancy after four months as she was fearful of the negative effects on her fetus of some medicine she took while sick. An image of a rather careless mother who did not take informed measures to practice the state-promoted *yousheng youyu* (literally "excellent birth, excellent rearing") surfaces between lines. She was quoted saying that the phenomenon of "unplanned birth" persists because of the patrilineal demand of *chuanzong jiedai* (continuing the bloodline through male heirs). In the next quote, Ms. Yu shifted abruptly to the issue of giving away a daughter: "If the child is a daughter, some families would give her away to some other family. These families usually know each other, and the adoptive family would register the girl in their *hukou*." The reporter concludes that concerns about *hukou* registration or a lack of means largely explain why people give away their daughters, and this happens unexpectedly among young couples who were born after the 1980s.

The third part of the report discusses how street-level family-planning committees have been intervening in migrant parents' reproductive practices. It highlights the importance of intragroup influence among migrants themselves. A street committee party secretary was quoted here, saying, "The floating population from outside does not pay enough attention to prenatal examination because of their ideology or preoccupation with doing business, which is not conducive to *yousheng youyu*." The last section, subtitled "Fertility Peak Brings out Social Problems," details how Shanghai's recent population growth—due more to migrants and their two-or-more-children practice than to locals—has imposed great pressure on Shanghai's kindergartens and hospital systems. The news article ends by introducing the new Shanghai Floating Population Family-Planning Policy, which was designed to facilitate the city's economic and social development plans.

The report perpetuates the perception that migrant and local are distinct categories. The deployment of sensational yet misleading titles, such as "giving away daughters," plays to the urban sensitivity toward son preference and its associated rural backwardness. The report selectively chooses stories—paying for "unplanned birth," leaving children behind in the countryside, using abortion to remedy poor prenatal decisions, and giving away daughters—that portray migrants, especially those born in the 1980s, as overly traditional, ill informed, and often irresponsible. It explicitly blames migrants for Shanghai's cramped delivery rooms and intensified competition for kindergarten seats. As China's internal migration tendencies have changed, from seasonal movement to urban settlement, cities have now taken on the responsibility and power of controlling fertility once located in the provincial state apparatus. Shanghai, China's largest receiving city of migrants, has begun to deploy its administrative agencies, mostly street committees, to monitor and facilitate migrants' family planning. Reports like this help contextualize and legitimize the state's power to discipline and punish the migrant population's fertility practices. This report paves the way for legitimizing the continuation of a highly restrictive birth control regime even though Shanghai has a rapidly aging population that cannot sustain the city's economic growth.

In sum, "preference for sons" has been constantly framed in the mass media as a feudal ideology rooted in the countryside and embodied by migrant households. In contrast, city people credit themselves for advancing China's gender equality and developing into a modern society. However, it is not individual qualities, as many city people like to believe, but institutional designs and historical developments that have contributed more to the relative gender equality in big cities. The heavy-handed implementation of China's one-child policy has forcefully compelled urbanites to suppress their desire for sons or more children. Over time, the urbanites interpret the state-engineered, sex-neutral one-child-one-family as proof of their civility and modernity. This is another instance of the "individual self-regulation" mentioned earlier, in which people capitulate to the repressive one-child policy in exchange for urban exclusivity. By claiming that the "outsiders" prefer sons, the local borrows the stereotype to guard the urban-rural, local-nonlocal boundaries and the entitlements attached to local urban citizenship.

"SPOILED" MIGRANT CHILDREN IN PERSPECTIVE

As mentioned in the beginning, media tend to contrast migrant children with urban only children to highlight the formers' lack of material resources and parental care. Migrant parents like Simei nevertheless have a different reference point from the media. When Simei claimed that her children were spoiled, she was referring to her own adolescent experience in the countryside. This corresponds to the common generation gap at a unique moment in Chinese history. Her generation, born in the late 1960s and early 1970s, still experienced the tumultuous effects of Mao's Cultural Revolution and suffered from rural poverty. Simei grew up in a poor farming household in rural Jiangsu with four siblings. She had to quit school at second grade to help with agricultural work and household chores when her mother fell ill.

By comparison, Simei's children, Lin and Xin, are much more privileged in both living and schooling conditions amid China's rapid economic growth. Born in the early 1990s, these migrant children belong to the younger generations who had no experience of Maoist socialism and little knowledge of the Great Famine, the Cultural Revolution, or the Tiananmen Square massacre. Nor did they experience extreme poverty in the countryside before the market reforms set in. They eat meat and greens every day, wear comfortable fashionable clothes, enjoy pop music on affordable MP3 players and smartphones, and have parents who are devoted to backbreaking work to support their study and provide stable living conditions. Despite most migrant children living in crowded rental places and suffering from educational inequality, they are "spoiled" compared with their parents, who endured rural poverty and migratory harshness.

Migrant parents like Simei and her husband, Jianguo, strive to create better living conditions for their children and hope for upward mobility for them through education. The couple has been selling vegetables in the same neighborhood on the north edge of Shanghai's urban periphery since 1998. They are proud that after only one year of selling vegetable they managed to bring both children from rural Jiangsu and school them in Shanghai. This was by no means easy. The couple works long hours, getting up at around 4:00 or 5:00 A.M. and working at the vegetable stand until 6:00 or 7:00 P.M. Jianguo makes purchases before dawn in wholesale markets one hour's ride away on a freight tricycle. Simei takes care of all the housework while helping with the vending stand. They have only one day off throughout the year—the Lunar New Year, the most important Chinese holiday. Their diligence paid off: after paying off the vending stand fee (500 RMB/month as of 2011) and utilities (approximately 200 RMB/month), they make 3,000–3,500 RMB per month.[8] Despite constant worries about the fluctuations of the vending business and the stagnation of real income due to Shanghai's rising living costs,[9] Simei concluded resolutely

from her migrant experience that "it is at least a little better to do small business than a regular factory job." Yet she decided it was even better for her
children to stay away from their vending business and pursue a better living
and higher social status via formal education and stable employment.

Any decontextualized portrait of migrant children as the miserable Other
fails to recognize the efforts of migrant parents in providing necessities and
support to their children. Nor does such a stereotypical representation reflect
on the subjective experience of these children themselves. These children do
not feel as miserable as the media presumes. Without frequent contact with
local peers in daily life, they do not refer to privileged urban only children for
comparison. Instead they look to their previous experience or impression of
rural livelihood and consider themselves much better off than their rural peers.

Of course, this study by design excludes migrant parents who did not bring
any of their children to Shanghai when I conducted field research in 2008–09.
This sample bias may result in an overly favorable portrait of parental care and
living conditions among migrant youth. Recent media attention to millions of
left-behind children (*liushou ertong*) has fueled the social imagination of these
children's plights and improper parenthood. Nevertheless, the practice of leaving children behind in native villages is often temporary, as is shown in the case
of Simei and Jianguo, who brought their children to Shanghai after one year's
separation. The good intentions of migrant parents who leave their children
behind to improve their lives through remittance and its positive effects should
not be denied.

Quality and Quantity in Contention
Despite all the efforts undertaken by migrant parents, their child-rearing practices are still widely perceived to be worse than those of locals. The fact that
most migrant families have more than one child contributes to the perception
that migrant families prioritize quantity over quality. *Waidiren jiushi hui sheng*
(outsiders just know how to breed)—an oft-heard commentary made by some
local Shanghainese—makes an implicit criticism of migrants' deviation from
the rational of "fewer but better" behind the family-planning policy.

Such commentaries and media representations implicitly endorse the eu-
genic notion of *yousheng youyu* at the center of China's population policies
that advocate for less but more qualified children with high intelligence and
strong bodies to realize economic development and national modernization.
The emphasis on quality over quantity in population policies has extended to

child-rearing practices. Raising fewer but better children has become the ideal approach. That most urban households only have one child to invest in has made child-rearing a high-stakes, nerve-racking enterprise. The only child has become "a privileged subject of investment and care" (Kuan 2015, 33) who embodies hope for both individual families and the nation-state. Anxious urban parents consult manuals, seek advice, and consume goods to raise the quality of their only children even before they conceive. Competitive investment in children's health and education has significantly increased since the late 1990s. The popular slogan "winning at the starting line" (*ying zai qipaoxian*) testifies to the internalization of the social Darwinist ideology behind China's family-planning policy.

In the contest of raising "quality" children of high intelligence and strong bodies (Woronov 2007, 2009), Chinese rural households are almost by default at a disadvantage. Although rural households improved their living standards at the early stages of the Maoist revolution and post-Mao economic reforms, rural development has systematically lagged far behind that of urban areas (Davis and Wang 2009; Whyte 2010). The highly uneven distribution of state investment in infrastructure, public education, medical care, and other provisions between the rural and the urban determines that rural families and their children lose "at the starting line."

Despite physical mobility, rural-to-urban migrant families are still caught between the rural-urban divide. Migrant workers have a hard time accessing equal opportunities and benefits in the urban labor market that favors local-*hukou* holders (C. Fan 2002; Solinger 1999). Few employers provide family-friendly dormitories, if there is any housing provision. Educational barriers and lack of child care support in cities compel many migrant parents to leave their young children behind in their home villages. Even when they manage to bring children along and raise them in the city, they often work long hours and live in cramped rental places. The demanding nature of migrant life amid *hukou* discrimination makes it hard for most migrant parents to afford the same time, space, and energy to take care of and engage with their children as their local counterparts do.

The perception that migrants fall short in providing quality parenting is shared by many migrants themselves. Huan's mother, Aidi, used the phrase of *zhi sheng bu yang* (reproduction without cultivation) several times when I paid her home visits over the years. She used the phrase to express her gratitude toward the volunteer teachers, including me, who provided her three children with free tutorials and extracurricular activities via the of NGO J platform, which strives to improve migrant students' learning opportunities in Shanghai. She also evoked the phrase to apologize for her lack of capacity and energy to provide proper guidance for her three children.

Originally from rural Henan Province, Aidi migrated to Shanghai with her husband, Dalu, in 1998 after getting married and having three children. She has been working as a janitor since then. As the eldest daughter in a family of five children, she did not receive much education and describes herself as illiterate. She felt powerless in helping with her children's homework. Her working schedule—two days of twelve-hour shifts followed by one day off—also prevents her from monitoring her children's routine regularly. Her husband, Dalu, is a quiet man with two years of formal education. He used to collect recyclables in the morning and drive a pedicab at night. When he came back home from driving passengers in his motorized pedicab, it would often be after midnight. He could not afford much quality time with his children, still less supervising their homework. Their three children went to school by themselves from first grade and made simple dinners for themselves from time to time.

During a home visit I paid in 2012, Guan, their youngest daughter, merrily joined the conversation to confirm her mother's apology of *zhi sheng bu yang*: "My parents don't *guan* [manage, monitor] us. They don't know much anyway. We decide most things by ourselves." Later at dinner, Guan recalled an incident of her brother Chuan's hurting his head because of a fall from the stairs when he was a boy. She told how their parents just rushed him to a nearby private clinic to get stiches without anesthesia. Aidi apologetically explained that it was at night, and they did not have the knowledge or money to go to a public hospital to do the operation: "It was bloody, and we just wanted to get it tended. He was given some antibiotics afterward." Guan concurred that the somewhat poorly managed situation turned out fine, her brother being a strong young man now with only some scars hidden in his hair. She laughed about it with her mother.

Guan's comments about her parents not "managing" her and her siblings are common among her friends. For Guan, she has enrolled, together with her elder sister and brother, in free tutorials and extracurricular activities offered by NGO J since she was six. It is hence easy and understandable for Guan to make light of the lack of parental supervision since she could seek resources and guidance from the NGO. An extroverted, competitive person by nature, she decided that the absence of her parents' supervision gave her freedom to grow independently, but she did add that her mom constantly reminded her and her siblings to study hard, obey rules, and be friendly and grateful. Their parents may not be able to help them with homework or career development, but their hard work and humble presence have provided a steady moral compass to guide them as they grow up and find their own paths. Guan's willing acknowledgment of the fact that her parents do not manage them shows that emotional ties are not inhibited by the parents' minimal education, long working hours, or lack of resources.

Unlike Guan and her siblings, who have access to educational sources provided by NGOs, most migrant children in Shanghai still rely on family resources to navigate the schooling system. They easily appear inadequate as compared to their local peers. Few migrant families in this study had paid for tutorials or extracurricular activities for their children. Besides the financial constraints that prevent low-income migrant families from investing in such after-school activities, the lack of appreciation of the meaning and significance of such educational investment is an important factor. One of the major difficulties facing the NGOs that aim to improve migrant children's learning experience in Shanghai is that migrant parents were often hesitant, sometimes even resistant, to send their children to the NGOs. The resistance is at least partly based on logistic concerns. Because of their long working hours, few migrant parents could drop off and pick up their children at the NGOs. Most migrant students ride bicycles or take buses by themselves to visit them. Some parents were concerned about their children's safety, especially at night, and hence curtailed their children's visits to the programs. What is more frustrating to the social workers is that many migrant parents discourage their children from participating in extracurricular activities. Several social workers and volunteer tutors complained to me that most migrant parents only welcome straightforward tutorials on main school subjects, such as mathematics and English. They consider music lessons and other nonacademic activities "useless." Those parents worry that such extracurricular activities will distract their children from formal schoolwork and potentially lower their exam scores.

The fixation on exam scores among first-generation migrant parents testifies to their desire for upward mobility via formal education for their children. When asked what they expected of their school-age children, many express their preference for *haohao dushu* (studying hard). Yet their understanding of studying well remains largely confined within the exam-centered formal education system that emphasizes textbook-based rote learning and equates academic achievement with exam scores. However, China's quality education reforms since the 1990s have called for a departure from the tradition of exam-centered learning by rote. An all-round approach is now encouraged to boost creativity among Chinese students and increase China's human capital and its competitive advantage in the global order. In the ongoing debate on China's educational reforms, quality trumps quantity. The social workers' frustration over migrant parents' emphasis on numeric scores rather than extracurricular development mirrors the local's moral judgments about migrant families' violation of the one-child policy.

In addition, the popularity of Western child-rearing and educational advice has contributed to growing investments in English camps, musical instrument lessons, and other after-school activities among urban middle-class families. In Shanghai, as in other developed societies, the accumulation of cultural capital via learning a musical instrument or speaking foreign languages has become instrumental to middle-class formation (Bourdieu 1984; S. Wang, Davis, and Bian 2006). It is mostly educated Chinese urbanites who have access to the overseas media and education that actively promote ideas from developed countries. Studies on the relationship between child-rearing, globalization, and nation building in Chinese cities show that the appropriation of global sources of value helps urbanites to distance themselves from their rural counterparts (Anagnost 1997; Naftali 2009, 2014; Leslie Wang 2010; Xu 2017). Their eagerness serves two purposes: to appropriate global sources of value and to differentiate and distance themselves from domestic Others, noticeably their countrymen from the rural hinterland. Migrant parents, the majority of whom did not receive more than a basic education in the countryside, indeed have a hard time grappling with and acting on the changing scripts of child-rearing.

Concerted Cultivation Versus Natural Growth in Shanghai

The perceived local-outsider differences in parenting in urban China resemble the contrast between what the sociologist Annette Lareau (2011) calls "concerted cultivation" and "natural growth," two approaches toward child-rearing among middle- and working-class families in the United States. Lareau argues through her careful ethnographic records of twelve white and African American families that social class has powerful effects in shaping daily arrangements of family life and interaction between families and schools. American middle-class parents, either white or black, "deliberately try to stimulate their children's development and foster their cognitive and social skills" (Lareau 2011, 5) through organized activities. In contrast, working-class and poor families are often too busy with making ends meet to organize their children's after-school activities. Nor are the adults comfortable or adept at interacting with teachers and administrators. In consequence, middle-class children harbor a sense of entitlement, while working-class children show a sense of constraint in institutional settings. It is through such seemingly insignificant routines and patterns that inequality is reproduced across generations.

Lareau's observation is applicable to Shanghai today. Normative parenthood in Shanghai is based on the dominant discourse of child-rearing circulated through maternal magazines, parenting counseling, product advertisements, and educational programs targeting China's rising middle class after the market reforms (Kuan 2015; Naftali 2009; Zelizer 1985). Educated urban parents are eager to adopt modern child-rearing concepts and practices believed to exist in the developed West, especially in the United States. Best sellers entitled *Harvard Girl Liu Yiting* and *Quality Education in the US* have been ubiquitously available in bookstores in big cities since 2001. Thousands of domestic WeChat accounts devoted to child-rearing advice (*weixin yuer gongzhonghao*) have also emerged since 2013. These accounts post daily articles on various child-rearing topics, from healthy ways of conception and breastfeeding techniques to reading lists for different age groups and school interview preps. Successful accounts attract millions of registered followers, who avidly read and repost how-to articles on their mobile phones. The large readership enables many privately run accounts to become profitable businesses through taking ads and direct sales of toys and children books, among other goods.

Most of this child-rearing advice, often told through individual stories, resembles the cultural repertoires of "concerted cultivation" observed in Lareau's study. The role of parents, especially mothers, is regarded as essential in shaping children's cognitive capacities, social skills, and moral characters. Most writing circulating on WeChat presumes parents' social and ethical obligations to provide for their children a comfortable, loving environment and stimulating learning opportunities. Of course, "a dominant set of cultural repertoires about how children should be raised" (Lareau 2011, 4) is still yet to permeate the whole of Chinese society. Nevertheless, it is fair to say that in China's major cities, like Shanghai, where the most educated and affluent tend to cluster, there is indeed an emerging sociocultural logic that favors concerted efforts in breeding children out of both indigenous emphasis on cultivation and modern child-rearing principles borrowed from the West.

Aidi's self-deprecating manner reflects less actual lack of confidence than a way of self-presentation to the public. Her self-criticism reveals the power of middle-class-specific child-rearing discourse that devalues those who cannot afford concerted cultivation. Migrant parents of lower socioeconomic status are not unaware of the normative child-rearing practices: stories of child-rearing anxieties in urban China in dramas, advertisements, and talk shows are frequently present on television, the dominant media where they get information and entertainment. This hegemonic discourse hence allows little alternative space for Aidi and others like her to represent themselves in ways other than being apologetic.

This self-deprecating manner also perpetuates migrant parents' feeling of disempowerment against the context of drastic reconfiguration of parent-child relations in postreform China. It breeds insecurity in exercising parental authority over their children or communicating with their children's teachers. Like the working-class and poor U.S. families in Lareau's study, migrant parents often lack knowledge of "the rules of the game" that "govern interactions with intuitional representatives" (Lareau 2011, 6) when dealing with teachers and school administrators. They might not be as aware of their children's school situation, or they might dismiss the school rules or teachers as unfair. In either case, they are less equipped and confident in negotiating with institutions like schools and hospitals to their advantage.

Public school teachers in Shanghai often comment regretfully how migrant parents lack the consciousness or capacity to communicate and collaborate with the teachers and school authorities in supervising their children's homework. Although local students attending the Bridge School, a nonelite public school, are mostly from working- and lower-middle-class families in vicinity, and most of their parents are not as invested in education as the teachers wished, the local teachers tend to grow more sensitive toward migrant parents' lack of skill and disposition to interact with them. "You know, some *waidi* parents don't show up to the teacher-parent meetings. If they do, they often show up late." Teacher Gao, a veteran English teacher in the Bridge School, where I conducted year-long participant observation, once lamented the influx of migrant students and its effect on her teaching experience: "Some [migrant parents] even have their dirty pants rolled up; they might have just got off work from some construction site or vending booth. What could you expect from them to help supervise the students' homework at home?" While Teacher Gao excused migrant parents by showing sympathy toward their poor working conditions, her compassion implicitly justifies the school's lowered expectation of migrant students, as well as local prejudice against the outsider represented as the stereotypical "peasant worker."

Differentiated teaching and caring practices contribute to migrant parents' disengagement with school authorities. As the next chapter will show, migrant students' ineligibility to take the entrance examination for high school in Shanghai have significantly shaped the attitudes and practices of the faculty. The teachers are discouraged to spend equal amounts of time and energy on migrant students, many of whom leave Shanghai by eighth grade. A few migrant parents complained to me how they felt unfairly treated by the schools. In consequence, they felt discouraged to participate in school events, including teacher-parent meetings. A mother whose son attended the Bridge School was very upset at the school arrangement that put her son in a class composed of mostly migrant students and a few bad-behaving local students at the beginning of eighth grade (see Chapter 3). She went to the first teacher-parent meeting to raise her concern but did not get a satisfying response. She said, "Some Shanghainese teachers simply look down upon *waidiren*. If that's the case, why should I bother to see those teachers again? I just told my son to stay put in school till he graduates with a middle school certificate." Such miscommunication resulting from institutional barriers mixed with local prejudice contributes to migrant parents' disengagement with the schools, which in turn perpetuates the impression that migrant parents fall short in not only capacity but also in conscientiousness when it comes to delivering good parenting.

Unlike their U.S. counterparts, low-income migrant parents are less inclined to defend their "natural growth" approach as an accomplishment. Aidi's comment about "reproduction without cultivation" reveals a deeply felt sense of guilt among low-income migrant parents for not living up to the rising standard of child-rearing in Shanghai. Although socioeconomic disparity in the postreform era has reached an alarming level, class (re)formation in post-Mao China is still in process (D. Goodman 2014; Woronov 2015; Zavoretti 2017; L. Zhang 2008). The public still see upward mobility via educational achievement as possible amid China's rapid economic growth. This may explain why migrant parents emphasize formal school education and buy into the promise of studying well for upward mobility. Even when they cannot practice concerted cultivation, they still aspire to, or at least respect, such efforts. This puts them in a rather precarious position in the increasingly commercialized child-rearing and education systems.

GLOBAL BIOPOLITICS WITH CHINESE CHARACTERISTICS

China's three-decade-long family-planning campaign is one of the most intensive cases of a "global biopolitical enterprise" (Santos 2016, 1324) concerned with nation-state building through population policies. The Chinese state has made it a national duty for individual citizens to align their reproductive choices with the state agenda of population control and national modernization. Those who violate birth-control policies are subject to penalties, including fines, confiscation of property, forced abortion, demotion, or deprivation of social benefits. Recent years have seen more moderate measures and relaxed policies in response to China's aging problem and labor shortage. The campaign has nevertheless managed to propagate the notion of *yousheng youyu*, whose aim is to improve both individual and national fitness. It has created a mode of governance in which individual self-regulation aligns with official agenda so that the state power is not only repressive but also creative, at least for some social groups. The urbanites who are subject to the stringent one-child policy, for instance, internalize the one child, one family mind-set and feel empowered to make moralistic judgments about migrant families that have more than one child and demonstrate preference for sons.

The politics of citizenship unfolds in the intimate realms of reproductive choice and child-rearing practices. In the same way that migrants' rentals on the city outskirts are seen as a signal of trespass, in the birth-control policies and "quality child" discourse, migrant families are often represented as irresponsible and inferior, hence deemed ineligible for equal citizenship. The negotiations over urban inclusion and exclusion often boil down to quality versus quantity and citizen right versus citizen obligation. The state-promoted emphases on quality and citizen obligation help legitimize urban exclusion and naturalize structural inequality in the name of personal failure in embodying modernity in postreform China. The attendant value judgments and social discrimination extend from child-rearing to child education, which will be elaborated on as our focus shifts to their schooling experiences.

3 OUTSIDERS IN PUBLIC MIDDLE SCHOOL

ON THE FIRST DAY of the 2008–09 academic year, Principal Chen of the Bridge School in Bridge Town invited me into his spacious office and gave a talk to prepare me for my year-long research there. He emphasized how important my research topic was, as there had been a steady increase of migrant students at the Bridge School and other public schools since the 2000s. In fact, migrant students made up almost half of the sixth graders enrolled at the Bridge School. Principal Chen agreed to let me sit in on one of the ninth-grade classes and to have access to the teachers' office to conduct participant observation throughout the academic year. Curiously though, he repeatedly reminded me that Class Five, which I was to sit in on, was "not representative of the school's situation or quality of education." He urged me not to make any generalizations based on that group alone.

As I approached the Class Five classroom with Teacher Zeng, the *banzhuren* (homeroom teacher), I understood why Principal Chen had warned that this class was not representative of the school. To begin with, the classroom was half empty. While other classrooms had over fifty students each, Class Five had merely twenty students, enough to fill only the front three rows. Nonetheless, the classroom was bursting with noise: the students chattered away boisterously. One boy was asking his deskmate to let him copy his homework; two students were chasing after each other in the back; a group of girls were animatedly discussing a newly purchased popular teen magazine. Teacher Zeng and

I paused in surprise at the entrance for a few seconds as he prepared to enter the classroom to take control.

At that moment, a female class monitor was trying to collect a 50 RMB ($7.40) fee for insurance from the Red Cross and for subscribing to a newspaper, both required of each student by the school. A male student immediately protested vociferously, challenging the necessity of both the insurance and subscription. Teacher Zeng had to step in by reiterating the school's policy in a flat, soft voice, only to meet cries of "No money!" One male student shouted, "What a waste of money! I've always been fine. The school is just trying to rip us off." The class monitor tried to tamp down all the grumbling by saying, "Aiya! It costs just 50 RMB!" But two boys responded mockingly, "We know your family has money. We get it! Ooh . . ."

Newly assigned to Class Five, Teacher Zeng needed a moment to adjust. "Who's missing today?" he asked, once he finally had control of the half-empty classroom. Some students pointed to an unoccupied desk with a pile of textbooks sitting quietly inside its slot, and one of them reported matter-of-factly, "Nan is no longer with this class. She went back to her hometown last weekend."

Having studied myself in a nonelite public middle school similar to the Bridge School, I was taken aback by both Class Five's small size and its disorderly scene. China's public middle schools emphasize discipline and obedience in classes, including morning study sessions. I expected to see Class Five students reading English and Chinese texts aloud in a regimental manner, just as other ninth-grade classes at the Bridge School did. I also found it hard to imagine students' openly disregarding and even defying rules in front of a homeroom teacher. In this regard, Class Five seemed, indeed, an anomaly. More importantly, I wondered: How did Class Five end up with only twenty students? What happened to those students during ninth-grade, the last year of their compulsory basic education?

The story of how Class Five came into being stems from the very design of the Chinese education system. The "exam closure"—that is, the deprivation of migrant students' right to participate in local high school entrance examinations (HSEE) and to attend high school in their adopted cities—has been instrumental to the *segmented inclusion* of migrant youth in Shanghai. Although the Shanghai government has invested millions of dollars since 2008 to accommodate migrant students in its public school system, segregation between local and migrant students today persists, and migrant students have not been included on equal terms. Despite their increasing presence, migrant students are treated as almost invisible by the current evaluation system in public schools. In consequence, they often face negligence, both pedagogically and socially. Existing scholarship has detailed the labor market segmentation that has developed in Shanghai and other cities in which rural-to-urban migrant workers are discriminated against and underpaid due to *hukou* barriers. The case of Class Five suggests that segmentation starts much earlier for second-generation migrant youth, before they join the labor market.

THE MAKING OF CLASS FIVE

Class Five may be an exception unrepresentative of the situation at the Bridge School, but the rationale behind its formation and operation is common and deeply embedded in China's territorialized public school system. Even though every Chinese citizen has since 1985 been entitled to free basic education (first to ninth grades) under the mandate of China's Nine-Year Compulsory Education Law, individual eligibility has been closely tied to one's registered place of *hukou*. Public primary and middle schools take in only local students who are registered within their county or district without charging them tuition fees. Meanwhile, public schools receive most of their funding from local governments at the county (in rural areas) or district (in urban areas) level. These are the principles of *jiujin ruxue* (schooling in the vicinity) and *difang fuze* (local funding responsibility). They fail entirely to take into consideration the massive internal migration phenomenon, especially family migration, since the onset of the economic reforms.

Because of the highly territorialized school funding and admission structure, migrant students who do not have local *hukou* status are not covered by local state funding and have to pay tuition. They are, in this way, designated subaltern schooling subjects. Since local students enjoy priority in admission, migrant families also need *guanxi* (connections, social network) and must pay extra fees (*jiedufei*, literally "borrow study fees"), a few thousand renminbi or more per semester to secure their children seats in public schools.[1] Given that most first-generation rural-to-urban migrants take on low-end jobs in these cities and do not have much economic and social capital, a large percentage of their children end up staying put in private, substandard migrant schools operated by migrant entrepreneurs (Han 2004; Kwong 2004; Z. Liang and Chen 2007).

It was only in the late 2000s that free, basic public education became significantly more accessible to migrant students in Shanghai and other major cities. China's central government has been pressing local governments to increase spending on migrant children, whose number rose to over 35.8 million according to the 2010 national census. This official pressure arose partly in response to the public demand that every citizen, including migrant children, should have the right to education (Han 2012; Kwong 2011). More importantly, practical concerns—social stability and economic development—compelled local governments to invest more in migrant children, as having a better education, it was thought, would keep them off the street and improve their contribution to the country's human capital. The Shanghai government, for instance, committed itself to closing down all substandard migrant schools by 2010 and absorbing their migrant students into public schools for free.[2] Public schools started to receive *shengjun shiyefei* (a subsidy for operational expenses per student) for each migrant student they took in. The city also upgraded and converted 152 qualified private migrant schools into *gongzhu minban xuexiao* (publicly sponsored, privately run schools).[3] Such fiscal and administrative measures combined to increase free education opportunities for migrant students who were able to produce the necessary documents, including their parents' proof of employment and residential status in Shanghai.

However, migrant students have still been denied the eligibility to take local HSEEs and attend academic senior high school in their cities of residence. Upon reaching ninth-grade, migrant students are forced to choose: they can return to their hometown to attend senior high school and try their luck with the national university entrance examination or attend a vocational school in Shanghai or enter the labor market.[4] This results in an outflow of migrant students who are nearing the end of their secondary schooling. About one-fifth to one-third of migrant students studying in public middle schools in Shanghai "go back" around eighth grade to their registered home places.

The shrinkage of the student body imposes significant administrative and operational challenges on school administrators. It is common for public middle schools, especially those in Shanghai's periurban areas, where migrant families congregate, to dissolve a class if too many migrant students depart and it becomes too small. The remaining students and teachers are reassigned to other classes. The making of Class Five is a case in point. In the fall of 2005, the Bridge School enrolled 350 incoming sixth graders, about half of whom were local students and the other half, migrants. These students were divided into six classes.[5] By fall of 2007, more than 50 migrant students from that cohort had left Shanghai to attend school in their native places. In response, the Bridge School closed one class to reduce costs. The eighth-grade students were redistributed

Table 3.1. Eighth-Grade Student Composition in the Bridge School, 2007–2008

	Total Number	Shanghai hukou	Non-Shanghai hukou
Class 1	62	38	24
Class 2	51	41	10
Class 3	52	31	21
Class 4	68	30	38
Class 5	37	5	32

Source: Bridge School internal archive of student records.

in September 2007 into five classes, four of which were intentionally kept larger (more than 50) than the standard size (around 45) because the school foresaw that more migrant students would leave Shanghai on reaching ninth-grade. Class Five accommodated the remaining 37 students (see Table 3.1).

THE PERCEIVED LOCAL-NONLOCAL DIVIDE

What made Class Five distinct from the other four classes, in addition to its much smaller size, was that most of its students did not have a Shanghai *hukou*. Indeed, Class Five was often called the *waidi ban* (nonlocal/outsider class) in Bridge School everyday lingo. Such had not always been the case though: it had five local (Shanghai) students when it was first formed at the beginning of eighth grade. Yet as of the beginning of ninth grade, it was a class of twenty composed entirely of students with nonlocal *hukou*.[6] The five local students assigned to Class Five, all of whom were male, were widely considered *wenti xuesheng* (literally "problematic students," troublemakers). During eighth grade, the five local students had either dropped out or were dismissed for serious misconduct. Their departures to some extent testify to the effectiveness of using class redistribution as a strategy to force out the most troublesome local students by containing them in a marginalized group and leaving them to their own devices until they hit bottom.

Of course, public schools like the Bridge School are obliged by local governments to ensure that most local students within its vicinity complete nine years of basic education. The school administration and faculty hence have more incentive to spend time and effort on local students of poor academic standing so long as they follow school rules. The moral economy in the public school system values students' obedience to authority and holds teachers accountable for providing basic remedial tutoring to poor students. This explains why a few underperforming and mentally challenged local students who complied with school rules were retained in Class Four. The teachers often arranged for those students to come to the teachers' office after class for extra drilling and tutoring. The teachers also encouraged the cooperation of parents and used other means to ensure the students could graduate with the basic certificate. Only the most rebellious and least promising local students, like the five "problematic students" in Class Five, were left in this group to eventually fade out of the school system.

When asked how they felt about being grouped together with the "problematic students" in Class Five, the migrant students would often reference their nonlocal, outsider status: "[We are targeted] just because we are *waidiren* [outsiders]!" More than half of them dismissed the claim that their academic performance was particularly poor at the end of seventh grade when the redistribution took place. On several occasions, to express their indignation, they singled out one slightly mentally challenged local student in Class Four who barely passed the exams: "Look, even that *baichi* [idiot] sits in Class Four every day!"

However, the presumed local-nonlocal divide was not as clear-cut as the migrant students thought. Ninety-three migrant students were assigned to the other four "normal" classes to study with local students at the beginning of eighth grade when all the students were redistributed (see Table 3.1). Many teachers admitted that a fair share of those migrant students was on a par with some of the better local students, demonstrating similar levels of intelligence and diligence. I also observed cases of friendly relations between local teachers and well-behaved or academically talented migrant students at the Bridge School and other public schools. Since academic performance and graduation rates remain the key criteria for school evaluation by education bureaus and parents, it is impractical for the Bridge School to distribute and discipline its students solely along the local-nonlocal divide.

THE CEILING EFFECT

While the students of Class Five and their parents emphasized the local-nonlocal distinction, the school administration used the poor academic performance of these students to justify the redistribution. The Bridge School's administration explained the rationale behind reshuffling the students, which consisted of not only financial but also pedagogical concerns:

There weren't enough students to fill six classes. To run an extra class would incur a lot of costs, including wages for the teachers. Subsidies from the district government were preset by the number of students,[7] so we reshuffled the classes and grouped those underperforming migrant children into one class—previous experience indicated that since they couldn't take Shanghai's *gaokao*, they would often slack off leading up to ninth grade and have a negative influence on other students.

In addition to reducing operational costs, the school administration anticipated the negative effects of the exam closure on migrant students. It emphasized a tangible "ceiling" effect to justify the reassigning of underperforming migrant students to Class Five. Some migrant students did complain that being barred from taking the HSEE affected their ability to focus in school. Local students were spared such uncertainty and underwent the common drilling to prepare for the HSEE. This "ceiling" for migrant students resembles to some extent the "glass ceiling" experienced by women who, after reaching a certain position, face insurmountable obstacles to further promotion in a corporate structure and are discouraged from committing themselves to career advancement. However, unlike the implicit gender-based ceiling that women face in the corporate world, the explicit ceiling that migrant students encounter is the direct result of top-down, *hukou*-based policies. As the next section will show, the causal relation between the "ceiling" and migrant students' "slacking off" is far from being as clear as the school administration claimed. The school's systematic negligence in dealing with migrant students often prevents these young people from performing well in school in the first place.

Public school administrators and teachers have also emphasized the problem of self-selection among migrant students, arguing that those who are academically less promising are more likely to choose to stay in Shanghai because they are less likely to succeed in the HSEE back in their hometowns anyway. Teacher Gao, a well-respected English teacher who had taught at the Bridge School for almost three decades, tried to make sense of Class Five, observing:

Unless formal vocational schools can take them after graduation, few migrant students will complete ninth grade here because the policy has prohibited them from taking *zhongkao* in Shanghai. The academic performance of many remaining *waidi* students has been poor, so they have been put together to form a separate class [Class Five]. This class is very noisy. Their homeroom teacher struggles to keep them in order. They don't want to study. The school thinks that since

> these students will gradually leave during ninth grade, why not put them together in one class so that it would be easier to keep them from disrupting other classes?

It is true that migrant students who study well are more likely to go back to their native places as early as seventh grade to increase their chances of passing the HSEE there and obtaining a university education. However, the presumed correlation between academic performance and remigration back to the hometown is problematic. As Chapter 5 will show, whether to leave Shanghai or not is a far more complicated decision than is often presumed, and it is made not only in regard to educational opportunities but also family relations and lifestyle choices. Migrant children who have grown up under the same roof as their parents in Shanghai often find it hard to imagine, and still less actually to adapt to, attending boarding school and life in general without their parents in the rural parts of China. Furthermore, the opacity of education policies complicates the decision: rumors in 2008 about the possibility that Shanghai's high schools would become open to migrant students, for example, induced a lot of speculation that left many migrant parents and their children in limbo.

The narrative that migrant students would disengage academically and become a negative influence on their local peers because they had no hope of sitting in the HSEE fails to recognize the structural constraints that conditioned the students' choices and behaviors in the first place. The underlying logic resonates with those of similar institutional discriminatory practices targeting second- or third-generation immigrants in France, the United States, and other Western societies (Alberio 2012; Ogbu and Simons 1998; Windle 2015; Zanten 1997, 2003, 2005). A closer look at the daily operation of and students' experience in Class Five and other public middle schools in the following section suggests that this narrative was at best overstated, if not unfounded. The differences between local and migrant students were more a matter of perception than a reality. In fact, it was the school's presumption of difference and adoption of a differentiating approach that aggravated the kinds of problematic behavior the migrant students were accused of exhibiting, all of which consequently gave rise to the noted ceiling effect.

SEGMENTED INCLUSION IN PUBLIC SCHOOL

As mentioned, denying migrant students eligibility to take the HSEE in Shanghai is part of the governing mechanism of segmented inclusion, intended by the Shanghai municipal government to selectively incorporate and manage its growing second-generation migrant population. Without physical border controls, the local state, aiming to achieve a preferred hierarchical composition of its urban population, relies on daily operations to differentiate residents on the basis of what they are and are not entitled to. Within the microsphere of public middle schools, minute but persistent differentiating practices against migrant students, based on the premise of their exam ineligibility, are common.

Spatial Stratification

The well-advertised state effort to incorporate migrant students into the urban public school system for basic education seldom describes the kinds of actual public schools into which migrant children are allowed to enroll. Recent research, along with this study, has found that most public schools open to migrant children—the Bridge School being a prime example—are the "nonelite public schools" (*putong gongban xuexiao*) located outside Shanghai's urban core (Miao Li 2015; Xiong 2010a). This corresponds in part to the geographic distribution pattern of the migrant population that concentrates in the periurban zones of Shanghai (see Chapter 1).

The center-peripheral spatial differentiation is also embedded in the hierarchy of public schools in Shanghai. Elite public schools[8] (*zhongdian xuexiao*, literally "key schools") with better facilities, more qualified faculties, and richer extracurricular activities are mostly located in central urban districts. The Shanghai Education Bureau has stopped using the word "key" since 2005 in the hope of cooling down the "school selection fever [*zexiaore*]," in which families compete intensely to send their children to the few elite public schools, often engaging in intensive *guanxi* building, investments in tutorials, and even bribery to this end. However, the distinction between the elite and common schools remains as pronounced as ever. Elite public schools continue to enjoy wider recognition, enroll students with higher test scores, receive more state funding, and produce higher university admission rates than other schools. It is telling that Shanghai residents still refer to elite public schools as "key schools" in daily conversation. Given the limited spaces available in elite high schools, municipal governments tend to take a protectionist approach and exclude migrant students from the competition. Migrant students are more likely to attend public schools on the lower end of school quality and reputation. This significantly reduces their chances of succeeding in China's increasingly competitive tertiary educational market, which clearly favors elite high schools and their graduates.

Spatial stratification exists within the schools as well. Although class reshuffling only took place in the beginning of eighth grade in the Bridge School when there was a significant drop in the number of students because of the outflow of migrant students, many other schools make clear divisions between local and nonlocal students from as early as first grade in anticipation of the sizing problem. Some schools set up *waidi* classes separately as soon as they start enrolling migrant children for free under the direction of the Shanghai Education Commission. In daily conversations, the teachers and the students themselves often refer to the classes as "Shanghai classes" or "*waidi* classes."

In some public schools that have taken in migrant students from defunct migrant schools, those migrant students are put into special *waidi* classes that are separate from other existing classes. These public schools argue that the poor teaching quality in private migrant schools has made it hard for migrant students to catch up with the Shanghai curriculum. A 2010 survey conducted in twenty elementary schools (eleven public schools and nine migrant schools) in Shanghai confirmed that migrant students in general scored three points lower than Shanghai students on standardized Chinese and mathematics tests. The sociologists who ran the survey concluded that "school type is the most important determinant of Chinese and Mathematics test scores" and suggested that "the overall test score gap between migrant students and Shanghai students would shrink from 9.7 to 6 for Chinese and from 13.6 to 8.3 for Mathematics" if there were no school type difference (Yuanyuan Chen and Feng 2013, 86). The study presumed that migrant students in public schools would, in time, catch up with their local peers. However, it neglected the fact that many public schools accepting migrant students had no intention to level the playing field for them. From the outset, the setting up of *waidi* classes denied migrant students equal access to public school resources and the chance to catch up with local peers.

Spatial stratification is most evident when migrant students are allocated to specific, designated areas on school campus and so kept separate from local students. The City Middle School, for example, designates its own Class Five as the "Migrant Class" from sixth to ninth grades and always assigns it a ground-floor classroom (Xiong 2010b). Students in Class Five there refer to the Shanghai classes as "the classes above [*shangmian de ban*]," a vivid metaphor that captures both the spatial and social hierarchy embedded in the binary labels of local and migrant. In another public middle school in northwest Shanghai, all migrant students transferred from a defunct migrant school nearby after its forced closure in the winter of 2009 were put in a separate building. Such spatial segmentation allows little time for them to meet and socialize with local peers during breaks between classes. Some teachers have even warned migrant students against hanging out with local students, lest they become a hindrance or negative influence.

Some schools use spatial relocation as a reward for migrant students of good standing. Jixue, an intelligent girl from rural Anhui but brought up in Shanghai since the age of three, was transferred to a "Shanghai Class" in fifth grade because of her outstanding academic performance. The school issued a certificate of honor to encourage her to study harder: "Jixue, student of the *waishengshi xuexiban* [literally 'Outer-Province Class,' class composed of students from other provinces], has studied hard and maintained excellent scores. As an encouragement, the school transferred her to Class Three of fifth grade to study together with the Shanghai students. We hope she will keep on studying hard and achieve yet higher goals."

When I asked Jixue about the certificate hanging on the wall of the bedroom that she shared with her parents and two elder siblings, she explained with indignity:

> How ironic! I did not feel even a faint moment of glory or happiness. My mom hung it up there. She just wanted me to study hard and hoped that I could go to university someday. I feel the harder I study, the deeper I fall into a whirlpool of cynicism. I feel like I am no more than a commodity, being tossed around from place to place and used as a tool to draw attention.

The transfer from an "outsider class" to a "Shanghai class," bestowed as a special honor to high-achieving migrant students like Jixue, is indeed ironic. It signifies the collective subordination of migrant students rather than individual achievement. Jixue was only recognized as equal to local Shanghai students after achieving high exam scores and dissociating herself from her migrant fellows, which reifies the unworthiness of those remaining behind in the "outsider classes." Her feeling of being objectified as a showpiece to glorify the public school reveals a deep sense of alienation from an education system that treats migrant students as second-class subjects. The removal of spatial segregation in Jixue's case hence highlights the marginalization, rather than empowerment, of migrant students as a collective in the public school system.

Temporal Differentiation

In addition to spatial stratification, migrant students may also experience different schedules in school. The weekly timetable for Class Five at the Bridge School exemplifies this. To my surprise, Class Five had one physical education (PE) class at 8:00 A.M. on Wednesday and two PE classes on Friday morning, with mathematics in between. No other classes but Class Five had such an odd schedule for students to run and jump before and after working on numbers and formulas. Morning is widely believed in China to be crucial for learning, as the Chinese saying "morning hours are the best time of the day [*yiri zhiji zaiyu chen*]," confirms. In almost every public school, students are required to arrive at school around 7:00–7:30 A.M. to have a good start with morning study sessions. Mild morning exercises are believed to strengthen both the mind and the body, but strenuous physical activities are considered exhausting and hence disruptive

Table 3.2. Class Five's Weekly Schedule in Fall 2008, Bridge School

	Mon.	Tues.	Wed.	Thurs.	Fri.
7:30–7:50			Morning Self-Study		
8:00–8:45	Chemistry	Math	Physical Education	Chinese	Physical Education
8:45–9:00			Morning Meeting/Exercise		
9:05–9:50	Chinese	Physics	Physics	Math	Math
10:00–10:05			Eye Exercise[a]		
10:05–10:50	Chinese Extra Session	Morality & Ethics	English	Physics	Physical Education
11:00–11:45	Music	Sports	Chemistry	Society	Chinese Tutorial
11:45–13:00			Lunch Break		
13:00–13:45	Math Extra Session	English	Chinese	English	English
13:55–14:40	Society	Drawing	Morality & Ethics	English Tutorial	Chemistry
14:50–15:35	English Extra Session	Chinese	Math	Chemistry Tutorial	Physics Tutorial
15:50–16:35	Class Activity	Self-Study	Math Extra Session	Self-Study	
16:45–17:30	Extra Tutorial	Extra Tutorial	Extra Tutorial	Extra Tutorial	

Source: Bridge School internal document.
[a] China's Ministry of Education requires primary and middle school students to practice together during break a set of massages aimed to relax ocular muscles and raise awareness of eye protection.

to academic study. The students of Class Five complained about being tired after those PE classes, sometimes using it as an excuse to fall asleep at their desks.

Class scheduling should be interpreted with great sensitivity to the power relations and negotiations between various stakeholders in the Chinese schooling system. It is a delicate, complex exercise of allocating and coordinating limited resources that often requires days for school administrators to finalize a timetable. The fact that Class Five was assigned two PE classes early in the morning shows the school administration's deliberate minimization of their expectations of Class Five. Neither eligible to take the HSEE nor possessing a promising educational outlook more generally, these migrant students were presumed to be able to afford the consequences of this curricular manipulation.

The spring 2010 schedule of another public middle school, which had been asked by the district government to take in most of the migrant students from a nearby, recently closed migrant school, is even more telling with respect to differential treatment. Not only were these transferred students (in seventh to ninth grades) put into separate migrant classes; they were also asked to come to school ten minutes later, end morning classes forty-five minutes earlier, eat lunch thirty minutes earlier, and finish their school day almost two hours earlier than the other students. In contrast, local students in the "Shanghai classes" stay in school till 5:10, drilling with mock exams in preparation for the HSEE (see Table 3.3).

The early dismissal from school seems rational and justifiable to school administrators because migrant students cannot take the HSEE in Shanghai. In principle, public schools should emphasize "comprehensive basic education." However, in practice teachers and administrators devote most of their energy

Table 3.3. Class Schedule of the City Middle School

Item	Shanghai Class	Outsider Class
Morning Self-Study	7:30–8:00	7:40–8:00
Morning Exercise	8:00–8:15	8:00–8:15
Classes	8:20–11:30	8:20–10:45
Lunch	11:30–12:10	11:00–11:30
Noon Self-Study	12:10–13:00	12:00–12:30
Classes	13:00–17:10	13:00–15:25
Class End	17:10	15:25

Source: City Middle School internal document.

to HSEE preparation. Ninth grade is a crucial stage for preparing for the HSEE through endless review sessions and mock examinations. Few new topics are introduced in ninth grade. Student performance on the HSEE is measured in numeric scores and admission rates, from which school evaluations and reputations are derived. Barred from this central project of the schools, migrant students are effectually discounted as redundant. Their differentiating experiences of time and rhythm at school contribute to their segmented inclusion in the public school system.

Workload Variation

The differences in schedule between migrant and local students at the City Middle School directly translate into differences in the academic workload between the two groups. Migrant students in separate migrant classes were given less homework in several public schools I visited. Their assignments also tend to place emphasis on mechanical learning by rote—copying texts instead of writing essays and reviewing fundamental mathematics concepts instead of solving problem sets. Few supplementary exercise books are used, especially for math and science subjects. The problem sets assigned for migrant classes are sometimes less difficult or complex, as some students find out after comparing their homework with those of the students in the Shanghai classes.

The discrepancy is most distinct in ninth grade when the local students are drilled with mock exams after class and the migrant students are asked to leave school. Although the Shanghai government prohibits public schools from charging students for extra tutorials at school, exam pressure and school competition have led to the integration of freely provided tutorials into the official curriculum. Many public schools pay teachers extra to conduct these tutorials. For the most part, these tutorials are not available to migrant children. Some schools have even used this as an excuse to let migrant students finish school earlier than their local counterparts.

Class Five at the Bridge School was offered extra tutorials by the school in the first semester of ninth grade (see Table 3.2). This was a consequence of protests by dissatisfied migrant parents during a highly emotionally charged teacher-parent meeting in the second semester of eighth grade. At the time, many migrant parents still wanted their children to study hard and get high exam scores. They argued that, although their children could not compete in Shanghai's HSEE, they might still do so in their native places. In addition, because there were calls in state-controlled newspapers to open Shanghai's

HSEE to migrant students, some parents were anticipating a possible change in policy. Several migrant parents were small-business owners in Shanghai, among them a kiln factory owner from Jiangsu Province, a restaurant proprietor from Jiangxi, and a logistics company boss from Anhui. Their comparatively high economic status, even in comparison with many local Shanghai parents, gave them the confidence to voice their discontent, unlike most working-class migrants, who often felt uncomfortable confronting teachers or bargaining with school administrators.

However, by the second semester of ninth grade, most tutorials of Class Five had turned into self-study sessions, during which the students would be left to themselves to do whatever they liked. Occasionally the class head teacher or a teacher in charge of a specific subject would show up to keep order. To explain this, the school blamed the migrant students' mounting disinterest in the sessions and disorderly behavior; still, the tutorials were not canceled. They carried on in the schedule, for security reasons rather than academic concerns. Legally, public schools are held responsible for students' personal safety during school hours. The school gate, watched over by two security guards, was supposed to remain locked until 5:30 P.M. when, officially, all classes were to have concluded. The fear of students getting injured through accidents or involved in fights off campus during school time prompted the Bridge School's administrators to adopt the cautious approach of keeping Class Five together in these self-study sessions. The school acted more as a warden than an educator to these migrant students.

Faculty Allocation

In line with the warden attitude, the faculty assigned to separate *waidi* classes tended to be the least experienced and respected teachers. Every public school strategically allocates teachers to classes in an effort to balance teaching loads and attain the best possible student examination results. Typically, there is little controversy when it comes to the assignments of teachers of such minor subjects as PE, visual arts, and music, which are largely considered superfluous and inconsequential in China's exam-oriented system. However, when it comes to the main subjects (*zhuke*) that will be tested on the HSEE—including Chinese, mathematics, English, physics, and chemistry—the stakes involved with faculty allocation are high. Each *zhuke* teacher is usually responsible for two to three classes per semester. Each class would often end up with different sets of teachers, and they would be locked into teaching a particular class for the entire three years between seventh and ninth grades. Thus, the matter of which teacher of what perceived quality is assigned to teach which class is seen as of paramount importance and reflects and reifies the implicit rankings of classes and their students. The most experienced or capable teachers are usually assigned to *haoban* (literally "good classes," classes reserved for students of good academic standing), to further improve the best students' academic performance and ensure the school's success rate on the HSEE. Studies find that when schools are evaluated on a biased, achievement-based scale, teachers instructing disadvantaged students may respond with frustration and reduced effort (Downey, von Hippel, and Hughes 2008). This is often the case with teachers in charge of migrant-only classes in Shanghai's public schools. Recent studies also show that students with higher expectations experience more positive learning outcomes, and teachers play important roles in forming students' expectations.[9] Teachers' lower expectations of marginalized students contribute to the perpetuation of educational attainment gaps.

Not surprisingly, Class Five in the Bridge School was assigned a relatively weak faculty team when it was reshuffled at the beginning of eighth grade. Its Chinese and English teachers did not teach the other four classes at all. What struck me as peculiar was that these two teachers did not have desks in the ninth-grade teachers' office. Since all other *zhuke* teachers responsible for ninth grade were based in the teachers' office, their absence signified a marginality of both their positions and the standing of Class Five on campus.

The Chinese teacher Wu was a man in his forties from Chongming Island, Shanghai's last rural county. He spoke Mandarin Chinese and Shanghainese with a slight but distinct Chongming accent, which marked him as a "nonlocal" among the faculty, most of whom were natives of Bridge Town and other townships in Pudong. Teacher Wu liked to make jokes whenever the students in Class Five looked disengaged or even fell asleep. If his jokes did not work, he rolled his eyes and kept on lecturing without making any effort to engage the students further. His forced casual manner interspersed with cold jokes was not well received by the Class Five students. Quite a few complained about his negligence and blamed him for their slipping results on Chinese tests: "This Chinese teacher doesn't go through the texts with proper care. In seventh grade, we used to copy down a lot of notes from each lecture. Now Teacher Wu simply goes on and on, without paying much attention to much else."

Teacher He, the English teacher of Class Five, was in her late forties. She had transferred to the Bridge School as a spousal hire a decade before. Trained in Anhui Province, she did not have the qualifications to meet the Shanghai Education Commission standards required for employment as a permanent English teacher at the Bridge School, so she was not on the school's official faculty payroll. Essentially, she was a part-time staff member employed specifically to teach Class Five. Being a migrant herself, Teacher He often related to me her sympathy for the students of Class Five, commenting on how bright and yet how unfortunate these students were because of *hukou* restrictions. Yet, despite her compassion, Teacher He had a hard time connecting with the students. Her commands were not authoritative, and her teaching style was mostly ineffective. Her provincial accent when speaking English and weak voice further cost her the respect of her students. Toward the end of the 2008 fall semester, she started to resort to using a cassette player to play recordings of the English texts in class, as she stood by. The students paid little attention to her lectures.

A homeroom teacher, *banzhuren*, plays an important role in a Chinese student's school life, much like main-subject teachers. As in most public schools, at the Bridge School, a main-subject teacher usually assumes that role and stays with the same class for consecutive years to maintain control and consistency. Class Five, however, was assigned three homeroom teachers within two years. The first *banzhuren* was a PE teacher whose office was located on the opposite side of campus next to the dining hall—a ten-minute walk from the Class Five classroom. In contrast, the ninth-grade teachers' office was on the same floor as the ninth-grade classes in an adjacent building block. Furthermore, the low status of PE teachers in the exam-centered school system immediately placed the Class Five *banzhuren* at a considerable disadvantage in his attempts to earn the respect and cooperation of his homeroom students. In the second semester of eighth grade, he was replaced by a recent female graduate from a teacher training college who worked as a mental health counsellor at the Bridge School; however, her gentle manner, in addition to her lack of experience and teaching credentials, did not endear her to the students either.

The third homeroom teacher was Teacher Zeng, a chemistry teacher in his late twenties. He had recently transferred over from a less prestigious public school in another town, which was a step up for his teaching career. Taking on the homeroom teacher duties of Class Five was a chance for him to prove himself a capable faculty member in the school. Teacher Zeng fared better than the previous two and stayed with Class Five throughout ninth grade. He also taught the class a *zhuke* (i.e., chemistry). Since he was a legitimate member of the ninth-grade teachers' office, the Class Five students looked on him as a genuine *banzhuren*, like those for the local classes. Shy but amiable, Teacher Zeng also demonstrated a supportive, caring attitude for the students, though he still had trouble keeping order in classroom. "He was nice, very patient, and never lost his temper," said the students. One year after graduation, half of Class Five went back to the Bridge School on National Teachers' Day, officially designated as September 10, to visit Teacher Zeng as part of their class reunion. They thought he had not only been kind and patient but also had given them what they had missed in eighth grade: a sense of being cared for by a proper homeroom teacher.

Evaluation Discount

The above-mentioned differentiating practices in the Bridge School and other public middle schools have largely been the consequences of China's school evaluation system that puts the greatest value on student performance in standardized examinations, especially the HSEE. Public middle schools receive higher rankings, more generous operation subsidies, and better student quota numbers from the education bureaus if their students produce higher exam scores. As much as China has been pushing for *suzhi jiaoyu* (quality education) reform since 1999 to reduce student academic workloads, alleviate exam pressure, and promote well-rounded development to cultivate a creative and entrepreneurial population for national development and modernization, it is generally agreed that *yingshi jiaoyu* (examination-oriented education) persists, especially in nonelite public schools.

Although Shanghai pioneered in advancing *suzhi* education reform that has been recognized as the most successful of the kind in China, the teachers of the Bridge School and other nonelite public schools frequently expressed dissatisfaction with this project. They argued that the reform brought deleterious consequences for their teaching load and student competition precisely because there were no effective alternatives introduced for the evaluation of students. In short, numeric scores have remained the key criteria for high school and university admissions and the most important index for officials, administrators, and parents to evaluate a nonelite school. When textbooks are revised to be more interactive or less demanding, they often become harder to teach. In addition to adopting new pedagogical approaches and preparing different teaching notes, teachers often need to make up for what has been omitted from the textbooks. A recently revised mathematics textbook, for instance, leaves out several important concepts and equations that, nonetheless, are important for solving certain problem sets that are still tested on the HSEE. To produce high exam scores, the teachers have to cram those concepts in class and hold extra tutorials to make up for what is missing from the new curriculum.

The *suzhi* education reform, thus, has unintentionally widened the gap between elite and nonelite public schools. Many nonelite public schools face the outflow of local students of higher socioeconomic status. The emerging middle-class families in big cities like Shanghai are willing and able to pay extra for better *suzhi* education either in elite public schools or private schools outside of their registered districts (Mok, Wong, and Zhang 2009). Making matters worse still, the influx of migrant students to nonelite public schools has been contributing to a phenomenon similar to "white flight" in U.S. cities, in which people of European descent migrate out of racially mixed urban centers to ethnically homogeneous suburbs. Some local parents have explicitly expressed concerns about the mixing of locals and migrant students in a single class. Some teachers have complained about the low *suzhi* of rural-to-urban migrant parents, many of whom received little formal education and engage in manual work or small-scale business. They consider it impossible to implement for migrant students the *suzhi* education that is oriented to middle-class dispositions and child-rearing practices (Woronov 2008; Kuan 2015) when the students' parents have neither the means nor awareness to supervise homework, pay for tutorials, or arrange extracurricular activities (see Chapter 2). The teachers in these schools feel victimized, instead of empowered, by the *suzhi* education reform and, as a result, cling firmly to the exam-oriented evaluation system.

Because migrant students are not allowed to take Shanghai's HSEE in late June, their student status, in effect, ends in April once they finish the graduation exam (*huikao*), which is much less challenging than the HSEE. When local students stay in school to make a final effort to memorize texts and improve exam skills under the close supervision of their teachers and parents until late June, migrant students have little to do in school. Many schools simply have asked migrant students not to come in to school at all. They would only need to appear in school again to receive their diplomas in early July.

In anticipation of the absence of migrant students in Shanghai's HSEE, schools and education bureaus tend to disregard migrant students' performance in the evaluation system as early as seventh grade. The education bureaus do not take into account migrant students' performance on the frequent interschool or interdistrict examinations (*tongkao*). At the Bridge School, migrant students' scores are often recorded on separate spreadsheets on the teachers' computers, as they are not counted toward the school's average performance score. This adds a further insidious disincentive for school administrators and teachers to provide quality education to migrant students. The liminal status of migrant students renders them invisible in the evaluation system and inferior within the broader education system.

MUDDLING ALONG IN LIMBO

Even as they experience the differentiating treatment, most migrant students still remain in middle school. Sixteen is the mandated legal minimum age for work in China. It is very difficult for middle-school dropouts to find formal employment. The expansion and marketization of tertiary education since 1999 has also raised the bar for entry-level jobs. Dropouts can find odd jobs in unofficial sectors, but those are often temporary and offer meager compensation. Besides, as living standards continue to rise in urban China, more and more parents consider their teenage children too young to work. As a result, most migrant students who chose to stay in Shanghai completed middle school.

The question nevertheless remains as to what migrant students should do with so much time in school during which so little is expected of them. The consequence, as is evident in Class Five, was the practice of *hun* (muddling along), in which they learned to do the minimum schoolwork required and find ways to get through all that classroom time, which, in the end, would have very little to do with their future life chances. Examinations gradually lost their disciplinary function, especially when the migrant students realized that the graduation test would not be nearly as difficult as the HSEE that local students would face. They learned that as long as they passed the 60-percent mark, they would receive the middle school certificate; even if they failed, there were still chances to retake the test. "I will graduate anyway" was the general feeling shared among the students of Class Five.

In the last semester of ninth grade, the students of Class Five came to realize that most vocational schools they could apply for did not require high scores. The whole class, thus, devolved into utter listlessness in the last months (see Figure 3.1). They chatted, napped, and checked out their hairstyles in pocket mirrors. Some hid headphone cords underneath their shirts to listen to music during class. A few even carved words on the wall out of boredom. The strategy of *hun* has proven sufficient for the students to graduate with a middle school certificate with minimal effort. In June 2009, except for two students who returned to their hometowns to repeat grade nine in order to take the

FIGURE 3.1. A ninth-grade student napping during class in Class Five at the Bridge
School. Photo by the author, October 2008.

HSEE there, the students in Class Five otherwise all entered public vocational
schools in Shanghai despite having underperformed on the final examination.

The migrant students' energy was directed not to study but toward social
and leisure activities off campus.[10] Without the burden of homework and mock
exams, they spent their after-school hours and weekends wandering the streets,
visiting clothes stores, stopping for cheap snacks, and playing online games in
illegal internet cafes.[11] Since they still relied on monthly allowances from their
parents, their spending power was limited. Yet they had already become more
active and savvy consumers than their local peers, who were generally confined
to either the classroom or their home to do schoolwork.

Migrant students who are lucky enough to take class with local students have to deal with the limbo as well. Because it is usually migrant students of good academic standing that are put into mixed classes, they often suffer from an acute sense of failure due to high expectations from their parents, their teachers, and themselves. Migrant students of high academic standing like Jixue have to face the reality that they can lose their spots in high school in Shanghai to even those local students who do not perform as well academically. These high-achieving students are often continually subjected to their teachers' well-intentioned advice that they return to their registered hometowns to compete with students there. They are also advised not to go to school after the graduation test in April. Staying at home for three months until the July graduation ceremony can be very trying for these teenagers. Boredom exacerbated by hours of watching television day and night often turns into deep frustration. Some try part-time jobs, working in supermarkets, wedding photo studios, or fast-food chains, to kill time and make money. However, the realization that only menial jobs of the most menial sort are available to middle-school graduates intensifies their frustration with the void they feel in their lives in the months before starting at vocational school in the fall.

The teachers experience a similar path of escalating disengagement. In the first semester of ninth grade, the main-subject teachers still tried to deliver prepared lectures to Class Five. From time to time they gave motivational speeches on the importance of studying hard, reminding them of filial obligations to their parents, who worked hard to support them, and encouraging them to continue their education with inspirational success stories. However, the fact that these migrant students could not compete in the HSEE and their learning outcome bears little consequence on their teaching evaluation or school performance made it hard for them to exert more effort than what minimum professionalism required. The Class Five students' disengagement also wore away the teachers' willingness to meet the educational and emotional needs of individual students. Many frustrated teachers gradually adopted an approach of "keeping one eye open and the other shut," requiring only a minimum standard from the students and abandoning any hope of inspiring or motivating them. In turn, the students felt less cared for, and hence further disengaged with school learning.

In recent studies, discrimination against migrant students in public school is often presumed to be primarily rooted in teacher prejudice. However, as Lisa Yiu observed in two public middle schools in Shanghai, teachers often feel "disempowered from caring for migrant students" (2016, 261). They are caught between conflicting policies of citizenship and education—those that claim to give migrant students citizenship rights to basic education and include them in the public schooling system and yet exclude them from the competition for higher education and so full citizenship in Shanghai. This incongruence renders well-meaning teachers as frustrated as their migrant students.

"ONCE THE HEART GOT WILD, IT BECAME DIFFICULT TO REIN IN"

Being pooled together with the "problematic students" in Class Five created a strong collective sense among the migrant students of being mistreated. It highlights the otherwise unmarked distinction and hierarchy between locals and migrants. As all are Han Chinese, migrant and local students usually cannot tell each other apart in school. The requirement of school uniforms, the predominant usage of Mandarin Chinese in class, the shared popular cultural references, and the limited consuming power among teenagers make everyday interactions between migrant and local students quite equal and unmarked. Many students at the Bridge School told me how surprised they were to learn about their classmates' *hukou* status at the beginning of ninth grade. It is the school's top-down intervention through classroom redistribution, spatial separation, and workload differentiation that eroded the sense of equality between local and migrant students.

A strong feeling of unfairness in many migrant students led to disruptive behavior by those Class Five students seeking an outlet for their discontent. They grew sensitized to the discrimination against them on campus and became increasingly disruptive in class. They were quick to feel agitated whenever they encountered any instance of local students with Shanghai *hukou* not being held to the same standards. When accused of vandalism or other misconduct, such as kicking and flinging open the door or chasing each other in the hallway during the breaks between classes, they would talk back and argue that local students in other classes were behaving equally badly, if not worse. Limi, the only daughter of a self-made couple originally from Jiangsu Province who ran their own eyewear retail store, felt indignant even two years after her graduation: "Because of class reshuffling, the *waidi* students were put together with bad [local] students. That was unfair, and I was very upset. Everything had been going rather well in my former class. Why should *I* [emphasis Limi's] be relocated?" If the unfairness sowed the seeds of defiance, the everyday practice of such petty resistance could take on a life of its own and grow into something larger, bringing to life the saying "Once the heart got wild [*xin ye le*], it became difficult to rein in," as the students admitted to slacking off and letting their disruptive behavior become habitual.

In the very beginning of ninth grade, when I first observed Class Five, I noticed efforts among the students, especially those who chose to sit in the first row,[12] to make up for time lost in eighth grade after classes were reshuffled and the time when the two homeroom teachers had come and gone. They explicitly stated that they hoped the stabilization of the class after the departure of the five "problematic students" and the arrival of a new homeroom teacher would put them back on track.

I offered free English group tutorials on Friday afternoons and Saturday mornings from the beginning of the fall semester in order to get to know the students better and to help them improve their language skills. Almost everyone attended the first three sessions out of curiosity and an apparent willingness to improve. However, the number of attendees gradually declined, and I had a difficult time getting them to keep coming. Junjie was the one who stayed with my tutorial the longest. Though he was the tallest student in class, he chose to sit in the first row when ninth grade started so that he could stay away from the disruptions coming from the third-row group. He is the younger son of a successful subcontractor originally from rural Anhui. He was still contemplating going back to his registered hometown for his senior high school. His elder sister had studied high school there and had later been admitted into a *dazhuan* (three-year college). Good at mathematics, Junjie was making efforts to improve his overall grade point average. He tried hard to keep up with school assignments and took notes during class. However, the prolonged uncertainty produced by the *zhongkao* policies and the downward spiral of order and motivation in the class diminished his incentive to work hard. Toward the end of the fall semester, Junjie started to join the other students in muddling along both in and outside of school and enjoying social solidarity with his classmates—a sense of shared defiance.

INCLUSION ON UNEQUAL TERMS

More and more migrant students have gained free access to public schools for nine years of basic education since the late 2000s in Shanghai and other major cities. However, the closure of the local HSEE to migrant students in their cities of residence makes it impossible for them to be included in school on equal terms. Regardless of their academic performance, those who choose to stay in Shanghai are ineligible to sit in the local HSEE and become "invisible" in the school evaluation system, which discourages school administrators and teachers from investing in migrant students' academic learning. Differentiating and even discriminative practices against migrant students regarding spatial arrangement, faculty allocation, course scheduling, and work assignment are common in public middle schools in Shanghai.

Migrant students must cope with the void they come to feel in the last year of middle schooling when their learning efforts will have little consequence for their life chances or their schools' ranking. Many have adopted the practice of *hun*, exerting minimal effort on schoolwork and disengaging from the school's disciplinary regime geared to produce higher exam scores, which in turn justifies and invites the school's discriminating practices against migrant students. The vicious circle reproduces and reinforces the migrant students' precarious position in the education system.

Migrant students' disengagement, nevertheless, cannot be equated to a rejection of formal education, as found in studies of minority education in industrialized societies (Ogbu 1978, 1990; Ogbu and Simons 1998; Okano and Tsuchiya 1999). The students of Class Five and most migrant students in other public schools have not rejected education and school authority entirely. In fact, they often expressed the wish that their teachers would *guan* (manage, care) more, and they often showed their discontent more with the local prejudice directed at them rather than the institutional discrimination against migrants as a whole. The graduates of Class Five showed little resentment toward the school during their periodic class reunions. More than a dozen voluntarily visited their teachers at the Bridge School on Teacher's Day in 2010 and 2011 and interacted with their teachers rather fondly. They described their "chaotic" years as "pretty happy" and dismissed their own behavior as "being young and immature." Those middle school days seemed distant already as they were navigating their way in Shanghai's rapid socioeconomic transformation, pursuing the only available routes to their future through vocational school, internships, and entering the job market.

4 "BAD STUDENTS GO TO VOCATIONAL SCHOOLS!"

IN LATE FEBRUARY 2009 at the Bridge School, Teacher Yao, a recruiting officer from Newtown Vocational School (NVS), was having a hard time promoting her school to Class Five. A girl suddenly raised her concern over the school's reputation: "I heard your school has a lot of hooligans [*liumang*]!"[1] Teacher Yao responded in defense: "I've also heard such things, but I would say no school is free from *liumang*, including elite middle schools and universities." As the students kept silent, she continued: "Our school was not born with *liumang*. They are sent from other [middle] schools. So you might feel that once you enroll in our school, you would be considered *liumang* too. But it is not true."

NVS's association with *liumang* epitomizes the social stigma of vocational schooling in urban China today. Despite the state's promotion of vocational education over the past decade to assist economic restructuring and national development, the inferiority of vocational schooling along the educational ladder persists in both social perception and objective reality. Teacher Yao's defense emphasizes the passivity of the school as a recipient of failed competitors in the Chinese education system without denying the notion of *liumang* itself, which often conflates poor academic performance and misbehavior with lack of morality in the school setting.

The fear among migrant students of being lumped into the *liumang* category is particularly real. As we know, they are still barred from taking the HSEE, which results in systematically depriving higher-education opportunities to migrant students regardless of individual performances and preferences. Since there are few postsecondary education alternatives in cities, they are more vulnerable to being labeled *liumang* than their urban peers. What follows examines how migrant students have adjusted to and experienced the limited opening up of public vocational schools in Shanghai since 2008. Ethnographic details reveal the process of segmented inclusion and highlight the local state's direct involvement in reproducing migrant youth as cheap semiskilled labor for the lower rungs of the labor market through the *hukou* institution and restrictions on educational eligibility. However, tension persists between state intention, market demand, and individual aspirations over the limited choice of specializations and career trajectories after enrollment.

SCHOOL, REPRODUCTION, AND MIGRANT YOUTH

When migrant students of good academic standing are channeled to the lower-status vocational education that is filled with local students who failed in the HSEE, to what extent are social hierarchies reproduced or transcended? Sociological studies of youth cultures have long argued that schools are primary sites for producing and reproducing social inequalities and class differences (Collins 2009). This insight may seem a given for understanding education and the social position of migrant youth in urban China today. The negative effects of *hukou*-based barriers on their nine-year basic education, by way of diminished learning motivation and academic performance, has been established here in Chapter 3 and in other studies (Yuanyuan Chen and Feng 2017; Goodburn 2009; Han 2004; Kwong 2004; Z. Liang and Chen 2007; Ming 2014; Yuan 2010; Zhao 2000). The consequent marginalization of migrant students in China's educational system has led some scholars to evoke the notion of class reproduction, as exemplified in the works of Paul Willis (1981) and Pierre Bourdieu and Jean Claude Passeron (1977), when predicting the educational and work outcomes for migrant youth (Lan 2014; Xiong 2015). However, whether the *hukou*-based ceiling effect that channels migrant students to vocational schools conforms to the class reproduction analyses of education based on studies in the developed West deserves more careful and contextualized analysis.

Bourdieu and Passeron were among the first to offer structuralist accounts of educational reproduction by examining the conduct and organization of classrooms and curricula and showing how cultural and economic inequalities were perpetuated in French schools. Willis's classic study of the school-to-work transition among white male working-class "lads" in a late-industrial English town, on the other hand, emphasized individual agency. It did so by demonstrating how the students' "counter-school subculture"—which entailed outright disrespect of teacher authority, defiance of school regulations, and rejection of mainstream academic success—eventually condemned them to a shop-floor existence and hence class reproduction. All of these "lads" would, like their parents, remain in the working class. Despite differences in theoretical explanations, both approaches see class reproduction—as part of a long-term process in capitalist societies with long-established class structures—being a fully embodied practice. For Bourdieu and Passeron, it would be the lack of cultural capital, whereas for Willis it would be the subculture of resistance to school authority.

However, second-generation Chinese migrant youth are situated in different socioeconomic structures and cultural environments. As the following sections show, while they may be produced as a type of underclass if the *hukou* policy has its intended effects, the manner of class reproduction differs from the above-mentioned paradigms. Willis emphasizes the importance of an extant masculine shop-floor culture outside of school and its intersection with the counter-school culture in driving class reproduction. In late-socialist China, although first-generation rural-to-urban migrants are often grouped under the single label of "peasant worker" on government documents and in newspapers, the high degree of heterogeneity among those population in terms of age, education, occupation, home of origin, and economic status runs counter to such a simplistic explanation. In particular, a large percentage of parents of migrant students remaining in Shanghai for vocational education are self-employed in the informal sectors of the urban economy, working as construction contractors, pedicab drivers, garbage collectors, street peddlers, and small businessmen. The lack of an articulated class culture or solidarity among migrant families makes it impractical to presume a causal relation between cultural production and class reproduction as suggested by Willis. Meanwhile, working-class machismo in general has lost its appeal among Chinese youth after the collapse of the socialist work unit system (Moore 2005; Rosen 2004; Song 2010). The highly segmented production process that exists under global capitalism has further pushed manual labor to the bottom of the production chain, which is increasingly mechanic, repetitive, and hence demeaning (Anagnost, Arai, and Ren 2013; C. K. Lee 2007; Tsing 2000). Recent studies find among migrant youth equally strong preferences for indoor office work or entrepreneurial undertakings as their urban peers

(Han 2012; Lan 2014). Tensions have arisen between individual aspirations for mobility and prestige and the state agenda of reproducing a new generation of workers for low-skilled manufacturing and service industries.

China's entrenched rural-urban divide and academic-vocational distinction further complicate the process of class reproduction. The channeling of migrant students to secondary vocational education, an inferior alternative reserved for academic "failures" in China's examination-oriented education system, reflects and reifies the social hierarchies that discriminate against the rural and the nonlocal. Nevertheless, school is not deterministic in reproducing dominant power structures without room for reinterpretation and repositioning. The inferiority of vocational education puts migrant students and their local classmates on relatively equal terms, resulting in the type of closer interaction and stronger bonding that is rare in academic middle schools. The inferiority of vocational schooling also induces a classroom culture of *hun* (muddling along), during which migrant students' disengagement with schoolwork and active pursuit of urban consumption and entertainment better prepares them for the urban service-oriented economy. Their practice of *hun* can be seen as "student resistance without counterculture" (Kipnis 2001a, 485), which does not articulate counter-school subcultures as represented by the explicit expressions among the "lads" while rejecting school norms and criticizing school's role in reproducing social inequality. In contrast, migrant students' noncompliance results from their sense of deprivation due to *hukou* barriers and the fact that vocational schooling does not live up to the individual and social ideal of a proper secondary education. Such cultural practices reveal internalization rather than rejection of school values. Nor do they directly contribute to the reproduction of the cultural identities of an existing class as in the case of the "lads." The time and space provided by vocational schooling instead enable migrant students to gain urban habitus and form networks across boundaries, both things that were unavailable to first-generation migrants. Vocational schools thus have become a unique site where migrant youths can reposition themselves in the urban environment during China's rapid socioeconomic changes.

SEGMENTED INCLUSION VIA VOCATIONAL EDUCATION

Chinese cities, Shanghai included, have gradually shifted their focus from the exclusion to the passive control, and then on to the proactive inclusion, of the migrant population to facilitate local economic development while maintaining sociopolitical stability. In 2008, the Shanghai municipal education commission tentatively opened thirty-two public vocational schools on a trial basis to admit over two thousand "peasant workers' children." The number of schools and students allowed to participate in this initiative has steadily increased since then. Migrant students had to meet three criteria for enrollment: be under the age of eighteen, have been studying in Shanghai for at least two years, and have Shanghai residence cards or temporary residence cards. Admitted migrant students paid the same tuition—2,400 to 4,000 RMB ($330–$552) per year on average—as local students.

Like "ethnic minorities" in the United States who benefit from affirmative action policies, migrant students could receive substantial subsidies and fellowships from the government if they meet certain criteria. In 2008, migrant students from low-income families were eligible to receive a national fellowship of 1,000 RMB ($140) per year. Those whose parents held rural agricultural *hukou* status enjoyed an annual subsidy of 3,000 to 4,600 RMB ($415–$635). The Shanghai municipal government also granted performance-based scholarships (500 to 1,500 RMB) for migrant students. By combining these various forms of financial support, qualified migrant children with rural *hukou* could enjoy three years of formal vocational schooling for free in Shanghai.

The opening up of public vocational schools, such as NVS, to second-generation migrant youth can be seen as an important measure taken by the municipal government to include this ever-growing social group in its formal labor market. In particular, the labor shortage across China, especially in skilled manufacturing and low-end service jobs, demands a solution (K. W. Chan 2010; Park, Cai, and Du 2010). Meanwhile, policy makers and social observers see unemployment among migrant youth as a potential threat to social order.[2] To accommodate migrant youth in vocational schools for three years is one way to delay the pressure of unemployment and maintain sociopolitical stability.

The policy change also reflects and responds to the rapid growth and marketization of vocational schools in the past decade, which has increased competition among schools for student enrollment. Shanghai's decade-long negative local population growth and China's drastic expansion of university admission since 1999 have exacerbated the competition. Even state-funded vocational schools, such as NVS, have to aggressively promote themselves for survival and success. The director of NVS's student enrollment and placement office repeatedly described the recruitment process as a "battlefield." Migrant students living in Shanghai hence become a lucrative pool for enrollment and the attendant government subsidies available for vocational schools.

The urban inclusion of migrant youth via public vocational schools has nevertheless been segmented. Only a small percentage of vocational schools were allowed to enroll migrant students and receive government subsidies. Only certain *zhuanye* (specializations) are available to migrant students, many of which are manufacturing and service oriented, such as mechanics, cooking, hairstyling, logistics, hotel services, and automobile repairs. The official admission announcement clearly states the rationale for such a restrictive opening up: "The specializations that are open to migrant workers' children should be the specializations most needed for the front operation in advanced manufacturing and modern service industries. These industries are the most needed for our social development, but they are also greatly insufficient and demand stabilization" (Shanghai Municipal Education Commission 2008).

The available specializations reinforce the practice of labeling migrants as cheap manufacturing and service workers at the low rungs of China's urban labor market. The municipal government offers extra fellowships of 1,600 to 3,000 RMB ($220–$415) each year to migrant students who enroll in specializations that are considered harsh and dirty and are thus unpopular with local residents—such as cooking, hotel services, and lathe operation. Such financial incentives contribute to the state-sponsored scheme of producing second-generation migrant youth as *xinshengdai nongmingong* (new generation of peasant workers), as official documents and news reports label them.

However, the state-sponsored reproduction scheme does not receive consensus approval from migrant youth. Unlike their parents, most of whom are manufacturing workers or self-employed in the low-skilled service sectors, second-generation migrant youth share with their local peers the aspiration for white-collar professional jobs that are indoors and socially prestigious. Noticeably, most migrant students in this study chose less labor-intensive specializations, such as computing, accounting, and business English, which promise, at least nominally, office work. Those few male migrant students who majored in lathe operation came from worse-off families. The main incentives for them are the high placement rate on graduation and the potential of a significant increase in salary after several years of experience, due to the scarcity of such skilled manual laborers.

Specializations associated with low-skilled service work are often shunned even though the salary rates for such specializations upon graduation are of the same range as the specializations associated with high-skilled ones. As Robin Leidner's (1993) notion of the "service triangle" suggests, migrant students tend to view having to interact with customers in low-skilled service work as reaffirming of their lower status and thus make it even less appealing than manual work. This is particularly true for gender-specific service work.

Many vocational schools offer hotel service management (*jiudian fuwu guanli*) to female migrant students, a major considered to be an "urgently needed profession in short supply" (*shehui jixu jinque hangye*). The growing commerce, tourism, and finance industries in Shanghai demand a large number of semiskilled young females. Nevertheless, most migrant girls and their parents dislike this major because of its negative association with prostitution. Yan's mother, a food cart vendor from Anhui Province, resolutely rejected hotel management despite the government subsidy offered for this specialization: "Hotel management is basically hotel services. It is not good. Not good for girls. It does not have a good reputation for girls. We all have been *dagong* for years. We know what is happening behind the scenes in those places. Too many bad things."

The suspicion and moralistic critique of specializations like hotel service map onto the much larger collective labor experiences of rural-to-urban migrant women over the past two decades. Harsh labor conditions and low incomes did push a large number of migrant women to work as masseuses and hostesses in the gray zone of "erotic service" (*seqing fuwu*) under the guise of hotels, saunas, karaoke bars, and hair salons (Zheng 2007, 2009). Although many do not sell sex, the reputation of migrant women in these service sectors has been stigmatized. Eileen Otis (2011) has described how the formally employed, local urban female workers in a luxurious hotel in southwest China adopted "virtuous professionalism" to distinguish themselves from informally employed migrant workers who provided sexual services at the rear of the hotel. The contrived efforts of "virtuous professionalism" testify to the marginalization of female migrants in China's discriminative labor regime and social imagination. Although Yan's mother and her peers did not express explicit prejudice against those migrant women because they are also subject to such labeling, their careful avoidance of such specializations as hotel service reveals a certain degree of internalization of the stigma.

Yan's mother instead hoped her daughter would specialize in nursing, which she considered to have better reputation. However, she realized that without Shanghai *hukou*, it was unlikely that her daughter would become a nurse, still less be able to work in a state-owned hospital on a formal long-term contract.

Very few nursing schools were open to migrant students, and the specialization offered was *huli* (clinical care) instead of *hushi* (nursing), the former being lower ranked, lower paying, and usually only for a short-term contract. Yan ended up choosing finance as her specialization though her family was unsure what exactly is taught in that subject.

The official directive also specifically mentions that "migrant students' *hukou* should not be relocated into the schools' collective *hukou*" in order to prevent migrant students from being localized. In comparison, university students from other provinces are not labeled as migrants in the first place. They also change their *hukou* to the university's collective *hukou* upon enrollment so that they become "local" and enjoy the social benefits associated with the local "collective *hukou*" during their four years of higher education. The educational hierarchy clearly plays into the *hukou*-based segmentation of opportunity structured into the lives of migrant youth.

THE ANTITHESIS OF A CHOOSING INDIVIDUAL

Although migrant students seem to have several options upon the end of nine years of basic education, institutional barriers combined with market forces have made most options only marginally viable. While it is too expensive to purchase admission into private urban prep schools that focus on university admissions, it is too early and disadvantageous to immediately enter the job market given the increasing qualification requirements in China's rapidly modernizing economy. Meanwhile, the option of returning to their registered hometowns for senior high school, which is often taken for granted by urbanites and policy makers as the proper and unproblematic solution, is perceived among both migrant parents and their children as risky and difficult due to lack of parental supervision, curricular disparity, social alienation, and cultural differences between the city and the countryside (see Chapter 5). Vocational education thus becomes the most practical option for the majority of migrant students in cities like Shanghai. Financial incentives provided by the Shanghai government have also drawn more qualified migrant students to vocational schools. In May 2009, all the students in Class Five at the Bridge School enrolled in vocational schools, except two girls who decided to attend academic senior high school in their hometowns. The majority of migrant students who participated in NGO J's activities also ended up with vocational schools in Shanghai between 2008 and 2011.

The decision-making process was full of confusion and arbitrariness. The absence of "feel for the game" (Bourdieu 1990, 9) in choosing schools and specializations, which is often associated with the educated middle and upper classes, is common among migrant students. As ninth graders, they are not mentally prepared for the transition from academic student to professional apprentice. Chinese public middle schools concentrate on preparation for the high school entrance examination and offer students little advice about career development and vocational training, since the latter is considered the last resort for those who fail to pass the examinations. Meiyun, an articulate student originally from rural Chongqing, commented:

> Perhaps in my mind I still think of myself as a student. But all of a sudden, I was given a chart and asked to choose what I want to specialize in for the future. I did not know what to choose at all. I felt ninth grade was the time when I had the least understanding of myself. I didn't know what else I could do besides studying books.

Limited access to information, local networks, and institutional support make the selection process even more difficult for migrant students and their parents. None of the six public middle schools I visited had a career development office. Their main sources of information were posters and promotional sessions by vocational schools in the spring semester of ninth grade, weeks before enrollment. Most migrant students in the Bridge School enrolled in NVS and another vocational school three bus stops away from where they live. Both schools had good *guanxi* with the Bridge School, so they were able to hold on-campus promotional sessions and won over the students because of geographic proximity and information accessibility. The students also clustered in a few specializations to maintain friendships and keep solidarity.

The complex classification of industries and specializations makes it harder for both students and parents to make deliberate choices. The specializations are named using a kind of shorthand, usually two or four Chinese characters, such as "digital control" (*shukong*, lathe operation), which conveys only vague meanings. Most students speculated on the pros and cons of specializations by guessing from the names. Meiyun, for instance, was attracted by the major named "exhibition" (*huizhan*), but any high expectations she had based on the interesting-sounding name were soon subverted when she confronted the harsh reality: "The enrollment officer told me the specialization of exhibition wanted students with a nice figure and pretty face. I was quite upset after hearing this and asked, 'Are you really training people to design exhibitions or just to be "ceremony girls" [*liyi xiaojie*]?'[3] I felt very disappointed."

Only a few migrant students whose parents had extended social networks made calculated choices. One girl went to a medical vocational school to study pharmaceuticals at her father's insistence after rounds of consultations with his former colleagues in the army. Another girl chose a commerce vocational school in another district because her father, who ran a small logistics company, wanted her to learn commerce. The migrant students who participated in NGO J's activities relied exclusively on the staff's help in searching for and choosing between vocational schools. The online research and campus tours offered by NGO J did lead those students into vocational schools with bigger campuses, better facilities, and more specialization choices. Their parents, busy with work and hampered by a lack of local connections, were happy to entrust their children to the NGO's guidance.

A certain degree of indifference toward vocational education among both migrant students and their parents also contributes to uninformed decisions. Most migrant students and their parents still aspire to the widely held cultural prestige of a university education, even though they might adjust their educational expectation when encountering the structural barriers that prevent them from taking the *zhongkao*. The deprivation of the right to prepare for the *zhongkao*, which has become a normative rite of passage "assumed to be the central experience of the Chinese adolescent" (Woronov 2011, 83), makes them upset and angry toward the end of ninth grade. Similarly, migrant students are unable to participate in the prevalent narrative of "speaking bitterness of the *gaokao*." By complaining about exam preparation, Chinese youth demonstrate their endurance of pressures and pains and construct positive self-identities in the face of their elders' constant criticisms of their generation's privilege and material comfort (Cockain 2011, 114). Migrant students are forced out of the bonding process, which is important for local students, and feel disappointed.

The concentration of specializations available to migrant students in manufacturing and service industries further reduces their motivation to invest in the selection process. Few migrant students in the Bridge School consulted with their parents about school choices; nor did they inquire about schools other than NVS and the other local vocational school that had connections with the Bridge School and made promotions on campus, even though there were dozens across Shanghai from which to choose. In March 2009, I obtained from an educational bureau officer the whole list of Shanghai vocational schools taking in migrant students and their admission quotas and made copies for the entire class. To my disappointment, most students just took a look of the sheet and tucked it into their desk slots. Few of the students bothered to take their copies home to discuss with their parents.

Nevertheless, since the planned economy ended in China, the importance of developing choice-making skills has been growing: one needs to choose not only commodities and fashion styles but also jobs and social relations. Lisa Hoffman argues that the act of choosing is "not a natural pre-existing state of the self but rather a cultivated form of personhood" (2010, 82). Her study of young professionals in the northeast city of Dalian demonstrates how Chinese university graduates are trained as self-enterprising "talents" to adopt the idea of self-development and make careful choices to advance both individual careers and national development in the postreform era. In comparison, middle school students are still drilled to study for standardized examinations and follow a determined path to a university education. Only then will they be qualified as "talents" (rencai). Yet, as scholars of Chinese education have shown (Hansen 2015; Kipnis 2011; Woronov 2015), the idea that one has to study hard and assume full responsibility for his or her own success in the examination system has already taken root in basic education. Individuated subjects who exercise self-discipline for self-interest are shaped through the discursive practices of schools and mass media, including popular child-rearing advice (Kuan 2015).

Migrant students, including highly qualified ones like Meiyun, are nevertheless denied the chance of becoming "talents" by taking the normative path at grade nine due to institutional barriers. They are instead forcibly channeled to vocational schools by the municipal government to become manufacturing and service workers. In light of Foucault's notion of governmentality (Foucault 1988), choice is more a technique of governance than evidence of a lack of any governance, because disciplinary power exists in the very formation of desires. The absence of career development offices in middle schools enhances the educational desire for gaokao and a university degree and discredits other forms of desire and aspiration. This consequently prevents migrant students, as well as local students in poor academic standing, from acquiring the same self-enterprising skills as those required for educated "talents." Migrant students are not only denied the eligibility to sit in zhongkao but also the chance to become a choosing subject for nonacademic opportunities, which helps produce them as new-generation workers at the lower rungs of the labor market.

VOCATIONAL EDUCATION AS
THE STIGMATIZED ALTERNATIVE

"Bad students [*chasheng*] go to vocational schools!" This was among the first responses from the migrant students in the Bridge School to Teacher Yao's. Perceived as an inferior alternative to academic senior high school in urban China today, vocational school involves a social stigma that has to be understood historically. Although China has a long history of an apprentice system of guilds and private workshops, state-sponsored, institutionalized vocational training is a modern invention originally established during the Mao era to train skilled laborers for the urban *danwei* (work unit) system (Thøgersen 1990). In the planned economy, vocational education provided a practical means for obtaining stable employment and was popular among working-class youths (Unger 1982). When tertiary education was still rare and educational achievement low, vocational school graduates were considered well educated, respected for their skills, and envied for their secure job placement. However, the social prestige of vocational education has rapidly diminished in the postreform era after the dismantling of the work unit system, which broke down the "iron rice bowl" of lifelong employment and social benefits. Furthermore, the resumption of tertiary education after the Cultural Revolution and the expansion of university enrollment since the late 1990s made vocational education secondary and inferior.

In practice, low entry scores add to the stigma of vocational education. Because of student shortage, financial constraints, and intense competition, many vocational schools are willing to lower requirements for academic performance valued elsewhere in China's formal schooling system (see Table 4.1). Nevertheless, as T. E. Woronov observes about China's examination-oriented education system, "test scores are more than just the quantitative expression of educational mobility. They condense and represent all social value for youth" (2011, 83). The social prestige of a university education comes not only from the degree itself but also from the enormous labor and discipline required during the long preparation process. Vocational students are hence rendered as a "status group of negative honor" in the Weberian term (Weber 1978), lacking intelligence, discipline, and even morality—the so-called bad students.

Of course, one has to achieve high scores to get into a reputable vocational school that promises better jobs. For instance, the entry scores for Gongsha and Shanye as shown in Table 4.1 are comparable to one for an academic senior

Table 4.1. Sampling of Admission Scores for Vocational Schools in Shanghai, 2008

School Name	Specialization	Admission Score[a]	Breakdown of Scores of Lowest-Ranked Admitted Students	
			Oral English	Total Score of Math, Chinese, and English Exams
Shanye	Accounting	467.0	B	328.0
Zheda	Multimedia	469.5	D	321.5
Gongsha	English	510.5	A	367.0
Donghu	Hotel service and management	336.5	D	224.5
Qunxi	Culinary arts	89.0	D	39.5
Hada	Digital lathe operation	109.5	D	59.5
Xinzhe	Automobile repair	79.5	D	37.0

Source: Internal document of the Pudong Education Bureau.
[a] "Admission score" (*luqu fenshuxian*) is the lowest score for students enrolled in a particular school/specialization in a particular year. Shanghai's high school entrance examination has a maximum possible score of 630, composed of Chinese (150), Mathematics (150), English (150), Physics (90), Chemistry (60) and Physical Education (30). Unlike academic senior high schools that have requirements for minimum scores set by district education bureaus, most vocational schools do not set minimum scores for admission, which explains some of the extremely low entry scores.

high school in Shanghai. However, migrant students enjoy a much smaller quota for such top vocational schools, and most available specializations for migrant students are for those with lower entry scores. Because of *hukou* barriers, migrant students who fare well in middle school are forced to reconcile with undesirable vocational schools and specializations.[4] The low entry barrier in general exacerbates the fear among migrant students of being lumped into the category of *liumang*.

In addition, the perceived lower socioeconomic background of enrolled students contributes to the bad reputation of a vocational education. The changing definition of childhood in laws and social conventions has prolonged the length of adolescence in modern societies, where the legal working age has been repeatedly pushed up to protect "children's rights."[5] In Shanghai, where the GDP per capita has topped other Chinese cities, working at sixteen often indicates poverty or catastrophic academic failure. Lin, daughter of a vegetable vendor couple originally from rural Jiangsu, did not hesitate to point out the class composition of her classmates after finishing her first year in vocational school:

After all, this school is not a very motivating setting that would make you feel like working hard. From what I observed around me and what the teachers told me since I work in the Student League, the students of vocational schools are either from single-parent families [*danqin*] or from lowest-income families [*dibaohu*]![6] There is nothing good about their family backgrounds! I helped the teacher sort out *dibao* students' archives: a thick pile of documents. Every class has some.

In big cities like Shanghai, more and more local urbanites are able to heavily invest their accumulated wealth in their only children for better schools and higher education. Nevertheless, there are also inevitably "losers" from the economic reform: laid-off workers from state-owned enterprises and villagers remaining on farms in the suburban districts. Short in economic, social, and cultural capital, children from those low-income households are disadvantaged in the intense competition for elite schools and higher degrees. Many resort to vocational schools to gain minimum credentials and basic training for future employment. In turn, the perceived low socioeconomic status of such vocational students adds another source of social stigma to vocational training.[7]

Lin subconsciously excluded herself from the "troubled" local student pool. She spoke as an onlooker instead of a member. Her anxiety over her local classmates' bad family backgrounds reflects an anxiety over the conflation between "bad students" and "migrant students" because of imposed *hukou* restrictions. Lin had not failed in her examinations or behaved badly in class; nor was she from a single-parent or *dibao* family. Her status as a vocational school student was solely the result of her nonlocal *hukou* status. However, once lumped together under the label of *sanxiaosheng* (students of three types of secondary vocational schools),[8] she would constantly risk being considered as *liumang* or *chasheng* by outsiders, sometimes even by herself when she used such phrases to refer to her classmates.

Vocational students are also considered to be of low *suzhi*. As mentioned in the introduction, the malleable term *suzhi*, widely used in the Chinese discourse since the late 1990s, has often been used by urbanites and officials to devalue the labor and social existence of rural and migrant populations and cast them as lacking education, culture, and civility (Anagnost 2004; Jacka 2009; Kipnis 2007; Sigley 2009; Tomba 2009). Now the term has taken on a new meaning when it refers to vocational students, who used to be mostly urban kids. Meiyun, the articulate top student originally from rural Chongqing, evoked the notion of *suzhi* while expressing her disappointment with the students during campus tours organized by NGO J before deciding on a vocational school:

> As to the students' *suzhi*, I saw what vocational school students would be. Well . . . I just felt there were things different from what *gaozhong* [academic high schools] would have—for instance, smoking. I smelled the odor of someone smoking the moment I entered the campus . . . Right out of the school gate, girls and boys would walk hand in hand or cuddle into each other, all kinds of behavior. That's what I mean by "what vocational school students would be." The scene was completely different from what I imagined about *gaozhong* before: students are busy every day, holding books in their hands while walking around.

Meiyun associates good *suzhi* with proper behavior for teenage students, such as no smoking and no public displays of affection on campus, which belongs to the moral economy of the formal academically oriented educational system. Yet she herself had to confront the conflict between the moral discipline she had been socialized to throughout basic education and her semi-forced entry into the negative social group of vocational students, labeled as "bad students," because of her nonlocal *hukou*.

PASSING TIME IN INFERIOR VOCATIONAL SCHOOLING

While vocational schools are considered inferior to academic senior high schools in the score-based educational ranking system, the course offerings of vocational schools seem to be equally inferior in the eyes of migrant graduates. Substandard teaching and aging faculty are common. The marketization of vocational schools gives administrators the incentive to employ retired teachers and teachers from other provinces to reduce costs. Unlike the examination-oriented education system that pushes high school administrators, teachers, and students to work hard to produce scores and pass the constant external inspections from above by education bureaus (Kipnis 2011), there are few *tong-kao* (district- or citywide unified examinations) to rank vocational schools and students. The supervision and evaluation of teachers' performance is hence much more relaxed, which reinforces the perception that there is no good teaching in these schools.

The courses offered in vocational schools turned out to be disappointing as well. The emphasis on practical skills was rather illusory. Keen on playing computer games and surfing the internet, six male students from Class Five at the Bridge School applied for the specialization of "computer." Nevertheless, the teacher taught little math or computer theory because they anticipated the enrolled students' poor academic performance. Ming recalled his two years' learning experience as such:

> What we've learned basically is typing [the other three students concurred si-multaneously] throughout the four semesters . . . The teachers just assigned us articles to type, and you practiced on your own in class. We used to say, "Nine years of Chinese classes is not as good as half a year's online chatting on QQ [China's most popular free instant messaging system]. You improve both your typing speed and your Chinese."

Middle school graduates often feel maladjusted and neglected in such learning environments, as is evident in the following conversation among four migrant students who enrolled in the Informational Technology School in the fall of 2010. They received free vocational schooling from government subsidies because of their "peasant workers' children" status, but they were not used to the accompanying freedom and purposelessness, which made the middle school days they once disliked seem somewhat sweet and memorable:

> LIN: How come I feel time passes so slowly? Before when I was in No. 3 Middle School, right after lunch the teachers would assign you something to do. So time flew before the afternoon class began.
>
> QI: Yep, you blinked your eyes and the class resumed.
>
> LIN: Right! It was not long before the class resumed. After lunch, I just sat there doing schoolwork, nothing else—a feeling of urgency and superfast being. But once I got into the vocational school, I became disoriented, just feeling things slow down and time is prolonged.
>
> MEIXIA: As compared to middle school, I find there is a huge gap.
>
> JIAWEN: I prefer middle school. The intense feeling of competition made me feel fulfilled, but now I feel I get quite *tuifei* [listless]. Under pressure, I felt very uplifted when I felt I made progress. In middle school, there was a lot of homework. Here, the teachers, TMD,[9] leave no homework. I just watch cartoons back home [*laughter*].

The ample time available to vocational students marks an acute departure from the highly structured disciplinary regime required by the examination-oriented education system. The goal of vocational education is instead geared to the production of manual labor power rather than mental power (Willis 1981, 145–46), or "talents" in Chinese. Such labor is supposed to be flexible and adjustable to idle time. It accommodates "new organizations of production, such as subcontracting, outsourcing, and employment of large numbers of temporary and part-time workers," which results in "increasingly segmented, deskilled and globalized" processes of "flexible accumulation" fraught with volatility and insecurity (Ong and Nonini 1997, 12). Vocational students are not expected to form the same productive use of time as university graduates in high-income professions, the latter of whom are motivated and pressured to work hard in a "white-collar sweatshop" (K. Z. Ho 2009, 83) to demonstrate and internalize their rightful superiority and entitlement in the job market.

Discouraged by inferior curricula, faculties, and teaching methods, migrant students join their local peers in the classroom culture of *hun*, passing the time and getting by with minimum effort in class and schoolwork. As Meiyun observed of her class, "there were all types of students in class. Some love reading romance, some love reading comics, some love sleeping in class, and some love putting on makeup. Of course, the species who love studying is very rare." Some migrant students, especially those of good academic standing, also intentionally adopt the practice of *hun* to protest against the inferior curricula and poor teaching in vocational schools. The imposed enrollment in vocational school imbues a sense of unfairness and makes them more sensitive than their local peers to the perceived inadequacy of vocational schooling.

The teachers are often complicit in producing a passing-time culture in vocational schools by delivering badly prepared lectures, assigning little homework, showing nepotism in student evaluations, and turning a blind eye to students' negligence in class. The job placement rate matters most to vocational schools in terms of advertisement and recruitment, but the rate is easy to manipulate (see Chapter 7). As Qi rightly observed, "our school has a 99.99 percent job placement rate [*laughs*]. Every [vocational] school says that though." Therefore, instead of round-the-clock supervision, vocational school administrators and teachers tend to take a much more laissez-faire approach focusing on preventive mechanisms to maintain school order and ensure students' transition to become half-skilled laborers so that they can meet the market demand for low-end industrial or service workers.

Migrant parents take a similar laissez-faire approach to their children's vocational education. Some teachers complained that the parents expected the teachers to act as mere babysitters while the parents could be exempt from educational responsibility. The "daycare" perception is indeed common among parents of both local and migrant students, and many simply want to keep their teenagers off the streets and out of trouble and for them to gain the minimum qualifications necessary until they are ready to join the labor market. Xiaming, a self-made watch repairman and later eyewear retailer from rural Jiangsu, started working as an apprentice at the age of sixteen and came to Shanghai alone two years later, setting up a tiny watch repair booth out of planks in an open market seven days a week. Nevertheless, his plan for his only daughter, Limi, who studied in Class Five at the Bridge School, was rather protective:

> She is too young! At the age of only sixteen, she is still like a child knowing nothing. I promise to put her in [vocational] school for two or three more years so that she can have some fun before work. If the vocational school turns out to be too bad, I would send her to a training program so that she can get a certificate for eye examination. With that, she can open up her own store.

Migrant parents like Xiaming are less willing to have their children experience the same hardships they endured during migration. Hence they treated vocational schooling as an expedient cushion for their children to grow into full adulthood.

Bing, from Class Five in the Bridge School, quit vocational school after one year of study and started working in a restaurant. His family's precarious financial condition and the lack of parental support largely explained his early entry to the job market. When the students of Class Five from the Bridge School commented on their classmate Bing's decision to quit, they shared their parents' reasoning and constantly evoked the term *hun* (muddling) to rationalize their choice of going to vocational school:

> JIANXIN: To put it directly, going to vocational school is to *hun suishu, hun shijian* [muddle through this age, muddle through this time], that's all it is about.
>
> JUNJIE: *Hun suishu*, as you grow older, you can start working.
>
> MING: People of our age think like this: actually it's pretty good to study in school, because studying is just like playing. It is really harsh to go to work, you know? Our parents have the same idea. No matter how bad your scores are, they still want you to have a certificate. If both sides agree, we go to school.
>
> JUNJIE: To put it straight, we just try to *hun wenpin* [to get a certificate with minimum efforts]. The teachers in the school are just like labor agents; they would recommend you to get a job. The so-called one hundred percent recommendation rate. If you really mess it up, it is not the school's fault.

The culture of passing time may seem to resemble the counterschool sub-culture that Willis found among the British working-class "lads." However, its underlying mentality differs significantly from the lads' articulated subculture. Similar to what Chapter 3 discussed about migrant students' passing time in ninth grade, the practices of slacking-off and disrespecting teachers in class result more from those students' critique of the inferior quality of vocational teaching. Their complaints about insufficient training and frustrations over the lack of supervision actually reveal their internalization, rather than rejection, of the examination-oriented school values. Furthermore, the practice of mud-dling along does not articulate a critique of the role of school in reproducing inequality as the "lads'" counterculture does. Although they are doubtful about the relationship between their studies in vocational schools and their future jobs, they still recognize the importance of educational credentials for social mobility in postreform China. Many of them attended *gaofuban* (prep classes for people without an academic senior high school diploma to prepare for tests to get into junior colleges) in the hope of getting into three-year colleges either full- or part-time after vocational school (see Chapter 7). Well aware of the increasing demand for certificates, they have become reconciled with the infe-rior option of vocational schooling, treating it as a provisional moment, during which they can have fun and acquire some minimum employment qualifica-tions before embarking on work and adult life.

NEGOTIATING BOUNDARIES IN VOCATIONAL SCHOOL

Enrolling in urban public vocational schools not only temporarily suspends en-try into the labor market but also provides social space for second-generation migrant youth to negotiate their social positions in Shanghai before doing so. Unlike socially prestigious academic senior high school students of the same age, vocational students have more independence from parents and a more active so-cial life and can afford more fashionable consumption because they have more time and less pressure. Most vocational schools end classes at two or three in the afternoon, leaving enough time for migrant students to join their local peers to explore urban ways of living. They take off school uniforms to put on their own clothes and engage in shopping, playing basketball, singing karaoke, practicing hip-hop dancing, eating street food with friends, and taking part-time jobs. By participating in these activities, migrant youth are able to accumulate urban habi-tus and form local networks, which was much harder for their parents' generation.

Huan, the eldest daughter of a pedicab driver and a recycle collector originally from rural Henan, has been working four to six hours almost every day in a bubble tea chain store. In addition to contributing to family savings, in which she takes great pride, she is able to buy low-cost but fashionable clothes in large retail markets because she has the time and knowledge. She also makes friends with work colleagues, who are all local Shanghainese of a slightly older age. Later she started dating a local worker there. In her third year at vocational school, she secured through school recommendation an internship in a state-owned hotel's bakery.

Migrant students' interactions with local peers and their acquisition of urban habitus navigate the increasingly porous boundaries between the rural and the urban, the local and nonlocal, in rapidly urbanizing Shanghai. As mentioned in the introduction, all of the migrant students in this research are ethnically Han Chinese and speak standardized Mandarin Chinese together with their local peers at school. Having grown up in Shanghai, most migrant students reported that they understood the Shanghai dialect to varying degrees and often used popular Shanghainese expressions. Although the fact that they were unable to speak the Shanghai dialect well does produce local prejudice from time to time, emphasis on personal characteristics, such as being fun and friendly among youth at vocational school, helps reduce regional-based distinctions.

Socioeconomically, migrant youth are largely on par with their local classmates, a majority of whom come from working-class or rural households. Migrant students who attended vocational schools in Shanghai are often either students of good standing who do not want to leave Shanghai or students of relatively stable family conditions under no pressure to join the labor market immediately after ninth grade. In addition, their "peasant worker" status ironically gives migrant students certain benefits that are not accessible to local students: government subsidies and scholarships, as well as the support of NGOs that target migrants only. Therefore, although migrant students are still the minority in Shanghai's vocational schools, taking up about one-fifth or one-sixth of the student body, because of the relatively low quota for migrants in each school, their numerical minority does not necessarily translate into a minority status in school.

Chapter 1 shows that migrants tend to concentrate in Shanghai's suburban districts because of lower housing costs and more employment opportunities in factories inside nearby industrial zones, as well as informal economic sectors. Correspondingly, most of the vocational schools available to migrant students are located in suburban districts. In these periurban spaces, migrant youth have more interactions and relations, not with the dominant group at the urban center but with less dominant groups, such as local farmers who have become recently urbanized during land appropriation for public infrastructure or real estate development. The widely assumed binaries of the rural and the urban have been losing relevance as neither migrant students nor local students fit neatly into these binary categories.

The lack of marked ethnic and socioeconomic distinctions allows local and migrant students to build different social connections beyond home origin and *hukou* status, connections that are rarely found among first-generation migrants. A recent study of two vocational schools in Nanjing, the provincial capital of Jiangsu Province, also finds that the social stigma of a vocational education places both local and migrant students on a similar footing regarding life chances and social status at an early stage in the larger culture of "failure" (Woronov 2011, 91). Unlike in middle school, where migrant students are barred from the normative path of *zhongkao* and often singled out for being "outsiders," in vocational schools both local and migrant students belong to the "negatively honored status group," in Weberian terms. By shopping together, exchanging video games, copying each other's homework, and sharing stories of sleeping in class and arguing with teachers, migrant students established bonds and friendship with local classmates.

Dating across the subgroups is also common at this stage, during which the boundaries of rural and urban, local and migrant, have become more permeable and less relevant in the eyes of youth. Of course, it remains unclear whether *hukou* status would remain a barrier as the students negotiate marriages and start families. Given the importance of *hukou* in determining one's eligibility to purchase an apartment, registering newborns, and schooling children in Shanghai, the stake of having a local *hukou* may become higher and the local-nonlocal boundary might be hardened again.

CHANNELED INTO INFERIORITY

Restricted in eligibility for testing for a university degree, an increasing number of migrant youths have been channeled to socially inferior vocational education since the late 2000s. The limited opening up of schools and granting of government subsidies for migrant students enrolled in specializations leading to "dirty, dangerous, and demeaning" jobs represent the efforts of city governments like Shanghai, by combining their administrative powers with market mechanisms and cultural criteria, to foster a new generation of migrant laborers much needed for its manufacturing and service industries.

Given the resilience of the *hukou* system and the intensified competition in the labor market during China's further integration with the global economy, these migrant students may be produced as the underclass of China's rural-urban dividing citizenship regime. However, simplistic evocations of inevitable class reproduction gloss over the complexity of class-formation processes in China today. Unlike reproduction theories of education based on accounts of Western industrialized societies, little evidence exists among Chinese migrant youth of a class reproducing itself through any lack of cultural capital or rebellious culture at school. Instead, the role of the state cannot be overstated in class reproduction through restrictive policies in the education sector in a late-socialist setting.

Nevertheless, these migrant students are by no means passive victims of such a state-led reproduction scheme. They consciously take advantage of their rural nonlocal status to gain government subsidies specifically for migrant students and a few more years to play and grow up before entering the job market. By engaging in the culture of passing the time, they minimize efforts directed toward examinations and obtain credentials to compete in the labor market. Newly available vocational schooling has also enabled migrant youth to form friendships and social networks with local peers and blur the rural-urban and local-migrant boundaries, a situation that is rarely reported in studies of first-generation migrant workers. The channeling of migrant youth to subsidized public vocational education thus contributes to both disfranchisement and empowerment of migrant youth at the intersection of the rural and urban, local and migrant, worlds in rapidly changing Shanghai. The only other schooling option for migrant students, as discussed in the next chapter, requires them to enter a school system in rural hometowns, where, in most cases, they arrive as strangers.

5   TO GO HOME OR NOT

When I entered eighth grade, my teachers started to pressure me to leave Shanghai. Every other week they would say to me: "Why are you still here? You should go home. We don't want to keep you here." . . . They have confidence that I can pass the entrance exam and get into a high school there. So they pressed me to go home, as if they were driving a guest out of their sitting room.

Meiyun, a top student in a public middle school in northeast Shanghai, grew frustrated for being continually reminded by her teachers that she should return to the rural exurb of Chongqing in southwest China from which she originally came. She was brought to Shanghai in 2000 at the age of six by her parents, who moved to Pudong on the eastern edge of Shanghai in 1998. The couple has worked ever since in a privately owned rubber-parts manufacturing plant, laboring long hours for overtime wages and living frugally to save money. Due to their long working hours and financial strains, they decided against having a second child, even though China's family planning policy allowed rural households with a female first child like theirs to do so.[1] Meiyun hence shoulders all her parents' aspirations for a better life. This only intensified her anxiety when she had to decide whether to return to her hometown to pursue a university education, the desirable path for upward mobility in China.

The "guest in the sitting room" metaphor Meiyun associated with her school vividly captures the spatial and temporal liminality of migrant students in the exam-oriented education system. They can receive nine years of basic education in Shanghai but are still barred from sitting in the city's *zhong-kao* and *gaokao*, standardized enrollment tests for academic high school and universities, respectively. Since the content of textbooks, curricula, and examinations vary regionally, migrant students who want to pursue university education need to go back to their registered places of birth before ninth grade to familiarize themselves with local textbooks and prepare properly for the local examinations.

However, institutional barriers, regional disparities, and sociocultural bias make it hard for returnees to realize their university dreams. This chapter first problematizes the notion of "returning home" and its assumption that going to their registered home places enables migrant students to obtain higher education. It then situates migrant families' educational desire within a larger political-economic structure and contextualizes the motivations behind educational remigration. The third section presents the agonizing process of deciding whether to go back or not in the face of policy uncertainty and regional disparity. What follows delineates the physical, emotional, and sociocultural aspects of the difficulties experienced by returnees while adapting to the rural schooling system.

THE PROBLEMATIC ASSUMPTIONS OF "RETURNING HOME"

The exact number of Chinese migrant students moving to their registered hometowns for schooling is unknown. According to my field research in middle schools in Shanghai and Beijing, between a fifth to a third of migrant students in each school left for their registered hometown around seventh or eighth grade. Given that over 35 million migrant children were estimated to have been growing up in Chinese cities at the time of the 2010 national census (National Bureau of Statistics 2012), the number of migrant students returning to their places of origin may reach half a million each year.

In addition to the practical obstacles to identifying and counting these returning migrant students in survey studies, the binary rural-urban analytical framework "in which geographical movements were viewed as occurring in one direction only—rural to urban" (Gmelch 1980, 135) still persists in migration studies in China, as well as elsewhere (Ghanem 2003; Hatfield 2010; Klimt 1989). Although there are a growing number of studies on the education of migrant children in their adopted cities (Miao Li 2015; Y. Lu and Zhou 2013; Ming 2014; Lu Wang 2008; Woronov 2004; Xiong 2010a) and those "left behind" to grow up in the countryside without parental care because of the emigration of adult laborers (Y. Lu 2012; Murphy 2014; Murphy, Zhou, and Tao 2016; Xiang 2007; Ye and Pan 2008), few researchers have focused on those returnees who sojourn between the rural and the urban (Koo, Ming, and Tsang 2014).

The assumption that these students are going back "home" within a unitary ethnically Han Chinese cultural system has also undermined the significance and urgency of studying such returnees. In official documents and media reports, this remigration is considered a "return" (*hui*) because these migrant youth belong, at least administratively, to the countryside from which their parents came. In everyday conversations, migrant students and their parents also use the phrase *hui laojia* (going back to the old home or native place) to refer to their remigration.

To go to one's place of origin was often viewed in the past as a natural process of reclaiming one's material and metaphorical place in the world. However, this notion has proven to be highly contested in the era of globalization (Escobar 2001; Horst 2011; Knörr 2005; Louie 2000; Potter, Conway, and Phillips 2005). More and more people live in "homeless" conditions, in which the sense of certainty associated with one's home place has become quite unattainable. Instead, linkages with multiple places provide plural centers of human existence to which people have different physical, psychological, and emotional attachments and hence form differently territorialized, if not wholly deterritorialized, identities (Deleuze and Guattari 1987; Gupta and Ferguson 1997).

China's second-generation rural-to-urban migrant youth are one of these deterritorialized groups within nation-state boundaries due to the rural-urban, local-nonlocal dividing *hukou* system. Although they are registered as rural residents, they are city dwellers with little experience of or attachment to rural life. They grow up among local Shanghai residents, but they are still cast as outsiders. Most of them seldom visit their home villages except for rare occasions like Chinese New Year, the death of a close relative, or when applying for an identification card during their formative years. A "structure of feeling" (Williams 1973) that supports a sense of bias against the countryside also prevails in China's paramount urban-oriented modernization project. The rural has become, both materially and ideologically, the antithesis of progress and modernity in public discourse and individual sensibility since the early twentieth century (Cohen 1993; Guang 2003; Siu 1990). "Poor," "dilapidated," "backward," and "drab" are common adjectives used by migrant youth to describe their home villages after brief visits.

Such "old homes" can hardly serve as "symbolic anchors of community for dispersed people" (Gupta and Ferguson 1992, 11) as observed in many transnational migration and diaspora studies (Leonard 1992; Malkki 1992, 1995). This makes remigration to native places among migrant youth particularly intriguing and raises many questions: How do migrant students and their parents decide whether to leave their adopted cities for schooling? How do returnees negotiate the rural-urban relationship while adapting to school life back in the hometown? How do such negotiations affect their sense of identity? How do we understand the process of emplacement and displacement in an increasingly deterritorialized world driven by massive migration and rapid urbanization (Appadurai 1990)? The remigration of millions of Chinese teenagers to their registered rural hometowns for schooling presents an odd yet significant case for anthropological studies of displacement, inequality, and identity formation. The generally poor schooling conditions in rural China make it all the more essential for us to examine critically the motivations, experiences, and consequences of this phenomenon of "returning" for higher education.

EDUCATIONAL DESIRE TRAPPED IN THE RURAL-URBAN DIVIDE

In global terms, among the wide variety of motivations behind return migration, education is not a common one. The adopted cities where migrants live are generally considered to have better schooling systems and more educational resources, especially for those migrants coming from poor regions that suffer from economic stagnation or political uncertainty. For migrant youth and their parents, educational desire often plays a strong factor for emigration out of, rather than back to, their home villages and towns. The Chinese case is different not because return migrant students do not want better education. Indeed, they return out of their strong desire for success in the state-sanctioned examination system.

First-generation migrant workers may have failed to achieve educational success because of rural poverty and family constraints, but their desire for their children to achieve upward mobility through formal education is strong. Almost every migrant parent I interviewed expressed a preference for his or her child to *kaodaxue* (sit a qualification test for university) if possible.[2] The desire for a university degree derives from both individual experiences and collective beliefs. Most migrant parents were born in the 1960s or early 1970s in the countryside and received at most a primary school education. They were often quick to relate their difficult life in the city to their lack of education. Aidi, Huan's mother and the vegetable vendor who quit school in fourth grade to help with farming and household chores in rural Jiangsu, reasoned that she could not get better jobs in Shanghai because of her lack of *xueli* (educational qualification). Thus she spared her two children from household chores in the hope that they could study well.

The strong belief in a positive correlation between education and upward mobility dates back to the imperial era in China. "Studying well and proceeding to officialdom and prestige" was a deeply embedded social value generated by the civil service examination system (Elman 2000; P.-T. Ho 1962). Although the civil service examination was abolished in 1905,[3] China's modern education system and the NUEE have deep resonances with the imperial civil service examination (Kipnis 2011). They serve the same functions of selecting talent from around the nation, promoting standardized curricula, structuring social mobility, and legitimizing political order by instilling the ideology of meritocracy into commoners. Although the postreform era has witnessed the rise of entrepreneurs and the nouveaux riches of once humble backgrounds and often minimal education, university graduates are still most likely to hold professional jobs and prominent positions in government bureaus, state-owned enterprises, and large corporations. University graduates also make up the core of the rising middle class and have been shaping the landscape of China's "consumer revolution" (Davis 2000).

Since the *gaokao* resumed in 1977 after the end of the Cultural Revolution, the process of *kaodaxue* has become the normative path for Chinese youth aspiring to upward mobility.[4] Stories of students breaking down after day-and-night drilling for exams or parents investing their life savings on a small apartment in a desirable school district circulate widely in newspapers and everyday conversations (Kuan 2015). An exam economy centered on *gaokao* preparation has generated both consumer demand and employment opportunities for private tutorials. In fact, Benjamin Elman has commented on the civil service examination system in late imperial China, and it applies surprisingly well to the NUEE today: "the examinations represent the focal point through which state interests, family strategies, and individual hopes and aspirations are directed" (1991, 10).

For rural Chinese, the annual *gaokao* has carried a particular promise of success because it has been one of the few means for them to break out of the confinement of their rural *hukou* and change their destinies:[5] to graduate from university and obtain a city job may gain them a nonagricultural *hukou* in an adopted city. Although only a small number of rural students make it to universities, in part, because failure rates are extremely high,[6] success stories propagated by state media, local governments, school administrators, and individuals continue to spread the desire for education across the country (Kipnis 2011).

Nevertheless, *hukou* barriers have circumscribed migrant families' educational pursuits. In the cities, migrant students have the ambiguous status of "being outside, and yet belonging" (Agamben 2005, 35), which prevents them from accessing local resources on an equal footing with urban youth (see Chapters 3 and 4). China's entrenched rural-urban disparity and educational stratification makes it even harder for migrant students to fulfill their educational aspirations. Stark economic disparity across regions after three decades of uneven development, especially between the eastern coastal urban centers, such as Shanghai, and the rural hinterland, has exacerbated the long-existing stratification of educational resources and opportunities (Ding and Liang 2012; Guo 2007; Hannum 1999; Hannum and Park 2007; Kipnis and Li 2010; Rong and Shi 2001). The decentralization of educational spending since the mid-1980s (Wong 2004) means that rich regions can afford to spend more on local schools than poor areas. A reverse pyramid scheme of school investment has intensified educational stratification: rural schools making up the larger bottom level receive the least, while urban schools in big cities comprising the smaller top level are endowed with the most. China's city-oriented development has resulted in a high concentration of educational and other resources in big cities. This has created an "advantage of proximity": the closer one stays to big cities, the more opportunities one has.

To make things worse, most Chinese universities are assigned annually specific student quotas for each province by the Ministry of Education. Students have to compete not only in terms of absolute scores but also relative ranks within his/her registered province. The university enrollment quota system is highly unbalanced, privileging economically advanced, eastern coastal provinces, which are home to a large number of prestigious universities and enjoy much higher quotas for local urban residents.

Although the annual NUEE is held simultaneously across China, different regions use slightly different tests based on different textbooks. In particular, municipalities like Shanghai and Beijing have the privilege of designing for their residents their own textbooks and NUEE, which are generally regarded as slightly easier. Consequently, the average Shanghai student enjoys a higher chance of getting into a first-tier university than a top Anhui student because of the educational, economic, and political resources that Shanghai's urban citizens enjoy. By pushing migrant students back to their hometowns, the place-specific educational system helps maintain China's socioeconomic hierarchy and its dual-track citizenship regime.

"TO GO BACK HOME, I'D HAVE TO CLIMB THE MOUNTAINS."

To go home or not to go is something most migrant students have to decide at some point in their early teens. Since this decision will determine to a large extent one's educational trajectory and coming-of-age experience, the decision-making process generates tremendous anxiety and agony especially for high-achieving students. Meiyun and her parents have long debated, since she entered sixth grade, whether the merits of their educational desire outweigh their preference for Shanghai. Their indecisiveness and frustration have partly arisen from an internalization of *kaodaxue* as the normative path for Chinese youth: "I used to take my parents' words to heart: going to primary school, testing in to middle school, then high school, and then, alas, university. This was the only path I knew of in the past—the only 'right' path for me. But when I learned at sixth grade that I wasn't allowed to take the *zhongkao*, I realized this path had always been wrong for me."

China's regional disparities and Shanghai's superior command of educational resources make this decision even more difficult. Test scores in Shanghai indicate little about how return students will perform in their much less resource-endowed but more competitive native places. Migrant families of lower socioeconomic status also suffer from asymmetric information and are unable to navigate the complicated examination and university admissions systems. In response to the precarious situation, many wait, betting on policy changes and delaying the decision until the last minute. Meiyun and her parents, for instance, kept on waiting in hopes of a policy change:

> I had classmates who went back at the beginning of sixth grade. But I was still secretly hoping that the regulations would change. My parents were thinking along the same line: what if [the HSEE] opens up right after you go back? They were afraid of losing what was really a betting game: what if you go back while those who stay get the right to take the *gaokao* in Shanghai? This has been on my mind throughout middle school.

Given that the decision to remigrate has to be made in a student's early teens, migrant parents play a significant role in the process. If they decide to send their children back to their rural home, they need to locate in advance a proper middle school in the home region and transfer their children's *xueji* (registered place of study) back there. Because of *hukou*-based nativism, they often must rely on *guanxi* and gifts to ensure admission. They also need to find a means of accommodation for their returning children.[7] It is impossible for returnees to stay alone in a village unless their grandparents or relatives can take care of them. Since middle schools and high schools are located in county towns or cities, it often takes hours for rural students to commute between home and school, so most parents pay for boarding schools to save some trouble and ensure their kids' safety. They have to save for boarding fees on top of tuition and daily allowances.[8] Given that a large proportion of migrant households have two or more children (see Chapter 2), the parents need to calculate carefully the cost of remigration and allocate family savings strategically among different children.

Besides logistical and financial concerns, academic performance and personal qualities matter in the decision-making process. Those who experience academic success are more likely to be sent back since they are more likely to succeed in the competitive NUEE. In the exam-oriented education system, test scores have weakened the preference for sons among migrant households (Ling 2017a). Girls are equally considered for remigration if they are academically promising. Ironically, boys are often kept in Shanghai, forgoing the chance of attending high school because of the gender stereotype that boys tend to be unruly and susceptible to bad influences.

Migrant students actively negotiate with their parents in the decision-making process. The authority of parents that can wield over their children in a traditional sense has declined and is rare today. Three decades of family planning policies have contributed significantly to the rise of the status of children in relation to parents (see Chapter 2). The closer affective ties between parents and children also make it more likely for the children to engage in negotiations rather than just follow instructions without discussion. The younger generation born in the 1980s and 1990s has experienced much more autonomy in choosing consumer goods and lifestyles than their parents (Y. Yan 2009, 2010). It is almost impossible for parents to force their children to choose one way or another without the children's agreement.

Meiyun's parents had been cautious about making such a big decision for her. Right before the spring semester of ninth grade, they took their first home-visit trip to rural Chongqing during the Chinese New Year of 2010, ten years after taking Meiyun to Shanghai. This trip was triggered by the death of Meiyun's great-grandmother, but they also had a burning agenda: to have Meiyun familiarize herself with her native place and to push her to decide whether to go back there for schooling. The parents had packed her belongings in case she decided to stay in Chongqing. "If you decide not to go back to Shanghai, I will call to notify your teachers. They were pushing you away anyway," Meiyun's mother said, divulging her plans.

After ten days of firsthand experience, Meiyun returned with her parents to Shanghai. "To go back home, I would have to climb mountains," she concluded. "After ten years, I found my old home was no longer suitable for me." When five months later I asked her about her decision, she recalled of the visit:

> What I remember most about that home trip is a lot of climbing—Chongqing being a mountainous city. You need to climb two hills just to get a pair of chopsticks in the market. One trip takes two hours easily, and you can't even ride a bicycle. You have to walk all the way. My first impression was that mountains are high and roads are difficult. My second impression was that my old home is really backward. Our county, situated in the southwest, was very remote and not part of the city district. I can only describe the margins of Chongqing City as *hen nongcun, hen xiangxia* (very countryside, very rural). I feel it was different from Shanghai in almost every aspect. There were no high-rise buildings. The village I stayed in was even more backward. The houses, built by villagers themselves, were OK; but there were hog pens right next to the houses, and next to us were mountains and fields.

Meiyun's view of her old home, common among migrant students, confirms the hegemonic discourse in China that regards the countryside as the backward Other to the city.

The mountains Meiyun considered cumbersome to climb also seem to be metaphorical. When she met her cousin of the same age who grew up in Chongqing, they talked about their experiences at school and their plans for after graduation. Meiyun observed shrewdly the growing gap between them, which she recognized as another mountain to climb if she were to go back:

> When I asked what she planned to do after high school, she said, "Testing into university." When I asked her where she wanted to attend university, she said she would go to Shanghai, just like what I thought: testing into a city. The more

prosperous the city is, the better. I asked her why she didn't consider Chongqing since her family was in Chongqing. She said Chongqing was not as good as Shanghai. I had always been curious about what kind of learning environment I would face if I were to choose to go back there, so I asked my cousin whether her school had newspapers. The answer was no. I asked her whether she liked reading newspapers; she said she didn't read newspapers and only listened occasionally to the news on the radio. She had no idea what *tougao* [submitting articles to newspapers or journals] was. Even a third grader in Shanghai would know this, but she, a ninth grader, didn't. This was rather trivial, but it did shape my choice. After chatting with her, I recalled what my teacher in Shanghai once said to me. At that time I was complaining in the teacher's office that I would not have followed my parents to Shanghai had I known one day I would face such a tough decision. My teacher responded, "You shouldn't think like that. You have seen a lot after coming here, at least much more than your peers back in your hometown." I responded with a simple nod then; but after talking to my cousin, I finally realized what an enormous difference ten years could make.

Meiyun's keen observation of the disparities between her native place and Shanghai informs her decision not to go back to her native place for higher education. It seems a formidable challenge to "climb the mountains," in both the physical and metaphorical senses, to reach her desired destination: a university. She also doubted whether the gains of testing into a university would outweigh the loss of leaving Shanghai. For Meiyun, the social and cultural capitals she gained at school in Shanghai, as exemplified in the knowledge and practice of *tougao*, were too dear to give up. And for those who do choose to go back home for high school, their journeys, as discussed in the following sections, prove to be as trying as Meiyun foresaw.

Placement in Rural Schools, Displacement in Suzhi Education

The earnest persuasion of Meiyun's teachers assumes that the physical movement of leaving Shanghai and returning to rural Chongqing would enable Meiyun to reclaim her legitimate place in the examination system. However, the right to take the NUEE does not guarantee a smooth transition at school and less success still in the NUEE. China's entrenched rural-urban disparity makes it questionable whether migrant students can successfully place themselves after relocation to their registered native place for high school. City schools and rural schools represent two "fields," in Bourdieu's terms (1990), which set different rules and values for resources available to students. Migrant students are forced to operate in two different "fields" before and after remigration (Koo, Ming, and Tsang 2014). They have difficulty in transferring their economic, social, and cultural capital acquired in adopted cities to their registered places of origin because the rules of the game change once they have crossed from one "field" to another.

Since textbooks, teaching practices, and evaluation criteria vary by region, migrant students have to return to their registered hometowns at least one year before taking the HSEE at the end of ninth grade. This explains why Meiyun's teachers became anxious about her staying too long in Shanghai. They believed such a delay would jeopardize her chances of scoring high and advancing to a competitive local high school, which is the key to success in the NUEE. It is impossible to assess whether Meiyun's teachers made the right prediction given that Meiyun chose not to go back to rural Chongqing and forgo the path to the *gaokao*. Nevertheless, the following experience of Zhihui, who did return in eighth grade, demonstrates that a few years' adjustment remains insufficient to overcome the vast differences between the rural and urban schooling systems in postreform China.

Born in 1992, Zhihui grew up in rural Anhui before joining her parents in Shanghai in 1999. Her parents began by helping fellow migrants sell fruit in 1997 but later switched to the more stable and profitable bicycle- and motorcycle-repair business. The rapid increase in scooter and motorcycle purchases among both residents and migrants in the late 1990s brought them a profitable business and enabled them to bring their elder son, Zhijun, and younger daughter, Zhihui, to Shanghai two years later. Since 2008, Zhihui's parents have been leasing a street-facing, twenty-square-meter store for 10,000 RMB ($1,460) per year. Zhihui's father employs two young distant relatives from rural Anhui to help repair bicycles and motorcycles. He also regularly drives to wholesale markets at dawn to purchase parts in bundles and then sells them to small repair booths and individual users. Zhihui's mother works as a cashier and helps deliver parts to customers. Once the store opens around six in the morning, customers stream in and out almost continuously until eight or nine at night. Every time I visited Zhihui, her parents were busy, and it was hard for me to start a conversation without feeling guilty about distracting them from their work.

The repair shop run by Zhihui's parents is like a battlefield, where every inch is in use and everyone is fighting for more time and more transactions.[9] However, Zhihui had been excused from the family business and housework.

An intelligent student with good academic standing, Zhihui went back to her native place in Anhui in 2007, after eight years of schooling in Shanghai. She attended a private boarding school for eighth and ninth grades, did well in the HSEE, and got accepted by a top academic senior high school there. Everyone, including her parents, teachers, friends, frequent customers, and herself, expected her to become a university student.

The competition in high school was nevertheless far more intense in Anhui than Zhihui had expected. She was forced to study harder than ever to just catch up:

> I decided to be a diligent student. So it was inevitable for me to get up earlier and sleep later. I adjusted my alarm clock from 6:00 A.M. to 5:50 A.M., then to 5:40 A.M. Although it was only twenty minutes' difference, how precious it was to me at that time! I would even carefully calculate how to eat breakfast faster.

Zhihui was by no means alone in exercising such extreme self-discipline. In her own words, she worked hard "just like a chameleon changing colors to blend in with its surroundings." Studies of schooling experiences in rural China have testified to the comparatively intense workload and competition there (Hansen 2015; J. Wu 2012, 2016) due to lower university enrollment quotas allotted to hinterland provinces. Most middle schools in rural regions have to devote their curricula and faculties to preparing students for the NUEE.[10] Both students and teachers become complicit in the exacting discipline regime under the huge pressure of *gaokao*.

Those who cannot get used to the exam-focused schooling system often quit before taking the HSEE. Huan, who went back to rural Henan in sixth grade, returned to Shanghai one year later after failing to adjust to the intense school life: "I could not put up with it. We had fourteen classes every day and tons of homework. It was very tiring to have all the classes, and the teachers were also very strict." Her rural schooling experience contrasted sharply with what she had in Shanghai, even though she had to study in substandard migrant schools for primary education. Abundant in both economic and educational resources, public primary and middle schools in Shanghai have better facilities, smaller classes, shorter school hours, higher teacher-to-student ratios, and greater varieties of extracurricular activities. The higher standard also puts pressure on migrant schools to keep up to some extent. This was especially so after 2008 when the municipal government closed down the most underqualified schools and invested millions in upgrading and monitoring the remaining migrant schools.

Differences between rural and urban areas have become even more pronounced amid the state-promoted *suzhi*-oriented educational reforms since the late 1990s. As discussed in the introduction and Chapter 2, *suzhi* discourse as a form of governance weaves seamlessly into the modernization project embraced by the Chinese state to justify socioeconomic inequality for the sake of national development and political legitimacy. In the educational realm, *suzhi jiaoyu* aims to foster well-rounded youth with creative-thinking and practical skills to enhance economic development and national competitiveness (Murphy 2004; Woronov 2008). It has generated repeated calls to reshape curricula, textbooks, and the evaluation system, but results have been highly uneven.

The growing emphasis on *suzhi* education over *yingshi* education puts rural and migrant students at an even greater disadvantage. Although there is no clear definition of "*suzhi* education," it has come to be associated with urban schools and middle-class youth who can afford English and computer classes, sports, and extracurricular activities (Yi 2008). In contrast, most middle and high schools in rural China still devote their academic programs to preparing for the NUEE. Limited investment in libraries and computer labs, among other resources, also constrains rural students' potential to learn anything beyond the material presented in standardized textbooks (Y. Lu 2012; Murphy 2014). When Zhihui visited Shanghai during the winter break of 2008, one of her former teachers there commented half-jokingly that she had become a bit *tu* (literally "earthy, unfashionable, lacking sophistication") after studying for a year and a half in Anhui. Speaking sympathetically to her, the teacher said her eyes looked dulled and her manner timid, not as lively as before. He went on to recommend that Zhihui read novels, beyond what was assigned in school, to minimize the mind-numbing impact of *yingshi* education. Her personal embodiment of a different schooling style, though trivial, suggests the failings of the *yingshi* education in the countryside.

Zhihui's two attempts to seek alternatives to the NUEE for university education show the enlarged rural-urban disparity under the *suzhi* education reform. First, she was sponsored by NGO J to go to Beijing and take free TOEFL preparation classes in the summer of 2010. This opportunity led Zhihui to consider the idea of studying abroad, which has become increasingly viable and desirable to urban youth in big Chinese cities (Fong 2011).[11] Yet, lacking preparation and access to information, she had great difficulty in catching up with the cram classes. In the end, her low score on the TOEFL examination and the formidable financial costs of studying in the United States dashed her hope of studying abroad and bypassing the NUEE.

In the spring of 2011, Zhihui was thrilled to learn about the *zizhu zhaosheng* policy (pre-NUEE admission administered by individual universities). Since 2003, top Chinese universities have been granted the freedom to recruit a small number of students through their own "quality-oriented" examinations and interviews before the annual NUEE to compete with Hong Kong and overseas universities for top students in an effort to retain them in China. This policy has also been advertised as part of the *suzhi*-oriented education reform intended to create more opportunities for students and help universities to discover talented students that would otherwise be potentially overlooked by the rigid, one-dimensional NUEE system.

Zhihui was optimistic at first: "I hoped to prove myself through means other than the *gaokao* to get into university. Sometimes I still believed I was unique and had an advantage." However, later she recalled the whole process with much anger and disappointment. All the top Chinese universities gave "recommendation quotas" only to elite high schools located in big cities. Zhihui's school, among the best in her county, was beneath consideration. There was a supplementary online self-recommendation form for applicants, but it only asked for officially recognized honors and allowed no space for individual experiences, hobbies, or extracurricular activities. Besides, only one university would give humanities students like Zhihui a face-to-face interview.

Despite the odds, Zhihui summoned all her courage to travel six hours by bus to Hefei, the provincial capital of Anhui Province, to take the preadmission test in February 2011. She would soon find out that this required her to be tested in physics and chemistry on top of the major subjects of Chinese, math, and English. As a humanities student, Zhihui was exempted from all science subjects in eleventh and twelfth grades in order to focus on preparing for the humanities subjects on the *gaokao*. She left the testing site feeling defeated, and her bid for preadmission went nowhere. Back in her home county, Zhihui moved out of the crowded dormitory and rented a small apartment near school to have better conditions in which she could prepare for the *gaokao*. Her mother joined her in the last three months to cook for her and do her laundry. Zhihui did not score as high as expected in the NUEE in June 2011 and enrolled in a university in Anhui instead of a top university in Shanghai as she and her family would have preferred. She felt she had not succeeded.

Zhihui's sense of defeat resonates with many other students from the rural hinterland. Many left the preadmission examination disappointed because they "could not even understand most of the questions" (Pan et al. 2011). One student recalled that she was asked in the preadmission test which university the prominent Chinese anthropologist Fei Xiaotong had attended.[12] "I did not even know who Fei Xiaotong was!" she said. "But students from Tsinghua Affiliated Middle School [one of China's most prestigious middle schools located in Beijing where Fei attended high school] would surely know the answer" (Pan et al. 2011). The emphasis on comprehensive knowledge and creative thinking contributes to the drastically shrinking percentage of rural *hukou* holders among admitted students in China's top universities after the *suzhi*-oriented reforms (C. Li 2012). In 2010, 62 percent of NUEE candidates had a rural *hukou*, but only 17 percent of Tsinghua University's class of 2010 was rural *hukou* holders (Pan et al. 2011). The decrease in the number of rural students in top universities (Ding and Liang 2012; C. Liang et al. 2012; Tam and Jiang 2015) both testifies to and contributes to the increasing closing off of upward mobility in China today (Bian 2002; Davis and Wang 2009; Selden and Wu 2011).

ALIENATION AT "HOME"

Educational remigration subjects migrant students to physical, emotional, and sociocultural alienation in their registered hometowns. The journeys back "home" are often lonely and isolating. Since a majority of migrant families have more than one child (see Chapter 2), parents are unlikely to move back just because of the educational remigration of one child. Lots of migrant students undertake the journey by themselves. Parents may accompany them on the way on the train or long-distance bus to ensure their safe arrival, but most parents have to return to their adopted cities for work to be able to afford their children's tuitions and living costs.

Cut off from former social ties in the adopted cities where they grew up, return students are forced to live independently from as early an age as thirteen (around sixth or seventh grade), much earlier than most of their urban counterparts. As mentioned earlier, return students are most likely to live in boarding schools throughout the academic year and only visit relatives over weekends or public holidays. They are also separated from their childhood friends in Shanghai, and they have to make new friends in a new environment. Occasional phone calls with their parents, siblings, or friends are the only means of maintaining social ties. They may visit their families in the big cities during winter and summer vacations, but the pressure of examination preparation is enormous, and they often have to go back weeks earlier to attend extra tutorials before school starts.

The early separation from their parents is emotionally trying for migrant teenagers. Huan, the eldest daughter of a janitor and collector of recyclables originally from rural Henan (see Chapter 1), went back to rural Henan in sixth grade. She returned to Shanghai after one year due to the hardship and loneliness she experienced. The failed "homecoming" sojourn was surprising because Huan was considered quite independent and had begun doing housework and caring for her younger siblings from as early as the age of five while her parents were busy with agricultural work: "Every day when it grew dark, I would miss my family, because I'd never been away from them before. Every time I heard my parents' voices on the phone, I could not help myself and I would cry. My mom's heart ached for me. Although they scolded me for not being strong enough, I know their hearts ached for me. So they let me come back."

Huan, like many return students, spent most of her time in crowded, barely decorated classrooms and school dormitories.

> It was too *ku* [bitter, hard] back in my old home. . . . We lived with over a hundred students in one big dorm and had classes with 105 classmates in one room. It was very crowded. We bought our meals from a canteen. Usually fifty cents for a steamed bun with a spoonful of meat and vegetables to insert in between, just like a hamburger. The best meal was the 1.5 RMB [around $0.20] lunch box— rice with potato—that's the best. [M. L.: What did you eat?] I usually ate the best option, or I would still feel hungry if I only ate a bun [*laughter*].

In addition to emotional and physical difficulties, sociocultural differences also mark "home" journeys undertaken by second-generation migrant youth. Le's failed attempt at educational remigration is revealing here. A tall, outspoken girl originally from rural Anhui, Le grew up with her parents in a crowded migrant community on the northeastern edge of Shanghai. She has two elder sisters and a younger brother. Both of her elder sisters were left behind in rural Anhui because of financial constraints and schooling restrictions. Le felt fortunate to grow up with her parents in Shanghai feeling "spoiled and favored," yet she could not resist the lure of a university education and chose to go back to Anhui in 2009 for eighth grade. Her parents used *guanxi* and paid an extra fee of over 2,000 RMB ($300) to place her in the best middle school in the county. However, Le, quite unexpectedly, returned to Shanghai in the summer of 2010, despite her educational desire and her sense of guilt toward her parents. "I still want to go to an academic high school," she said, "but I do not want to go back to Anhui." Incompatible desires often made her insecure and angry over the year that followed. Only in the summer of 2011 did she finally give up the idea of academic high school and enroll in a vocational school in Shanghai.

When asked why she had returned to the city, Le did not hesitate to describe how "nothing was good" about the year back in Anhui. She lived with her aunt, but she was not used to her aunt's "thriftiness" and how she ate leftovers for breakfast. Homesick and lonely, she also found the school culture restrictive and suffocating. She complained about the low *suzhi* of the teachers and her fellow students back in Anhui: "What low *suzhi* they had! They cursed a lot, and the students did not pay attention to hygiene, spitting and littering in the classroom. I was disgusted at the waste scattered on the floor. Not only the students, but also the teachers would pick their noses in class [*laughter*]!"

Le's refusal to eat breakfasts of leftovers and her disgust at the messiness of her hometown school are emblematic of her visceral rejection of "rural backwardness"—a characterization of difference that migrant students growing up in cities like Shanghai commonly assert as a matter-of-fact observation. Even though a large number of migrant children live in barely furnished, crowded rental places on the fringe of urban Shanghai (see Chapter 1), they are particularly sensitive to the perceived dirty surroundings and uncivil behavior they associated with their home villages and rural schools. Such a double standard can be understood in the hegemonic social mentality that treats the rural as "dirty" and "backward" in contrast to the "clean" and "modern" urban.

Le's adoption of the *suzhi* discourse is particularly intriguing here. As noted, the term *suzhi* has become a value coding system used to make and simultaneously mask differentiation and discrimination in postreform China. Many scholars have pointed out that the term has been used loosely and arbitrarily to devalue rural-to-urban migrant labor in the job market on the assumption that rural migrants lack education and civility. Labeled as "peasant workers' children" in official documents and media reports, migrant students are often associated with "low *suzhi*" in the eyes of urbanites as well. However, Le and other migrant students often use *suzhi* to differentiate themselves from those of their native place who never made the move to the city. Their *suzhi* critique against the rural, of which they are still perceived to be and are forced to remain a part of by the state and in the eyes of the urban public, unconsciously exercises "symbolic violence"—the violence "that is exercised upon a social agent with his or her complicity" (Bourdieu and Wacquant 2002, 167). Such symbolic violence works with the tacit acceptance and complicity of both those who use the *suzhi* critique and those who are subject to it and so naturalize unequal power relations between the rural and the urban.

Ambiguous Socio-Spatial Identities

The lonesome journeys "home" for schooling tend to create heightened sensitivity among second-generation migrant youth to the difference and discord between their adopted cities and their registered hometowns. Far from family but longing to feel at home, these migrant youths are often caught in between and experience great ambivalence in socialization and identification.

Born in 1991, Jiao was taken to Shanghai at the age of three months when her parents migrated from rural Henan to Shanghai. Her parents began making and selling breakfast foods from a small cart and later switched to the more profitable fruit retail and nighttime sidewalk food stall business. Influenced by her entrepreneurial father, who had a senior high school education and shrewd business instincts, Jiao was confident and ambitious. In 2006, she chose to leave Shanghai to pursue her university dream. Her parents had paid 2,480 RMB ($308) per year for tuition to enroll her in a boarding middle school for eighth and ninth grades in rural Anhui near where her aunt lived. They later transferred her to a private boarding school for tenth to twelfth grades in her registered hometown P, a rural county in Henan Province (see Figure 5.1).

Jiao was acutely aware of differences between her and her classmates and observed many socioeconomic and cultural differences between Shanghai and rural Henan. From the moment I arrived at P County in May 2011 to visit her before that year's NUEE, she complained constantly to me about feeling lonely because she could not find true friends there. She realized that the different consumption behaviors and attitudes separated her from others. "Many girls here don't eat breakfast. Even when they eat, they only eat the cheapest plain steamed bun." In contrast, Jiao bought one serving of steamed pork bun (1 RMB for four) in the canteen or packaged bread (2 RMB, about $0.30) from a convenience store. She also drank a bottle of milk every morning. Growing up in Shanghai, Jiao was used to eating rice with dishes. However, the staple foods in Henan were wheat-based steamed buns and noodles, which she disliked and rarely ate. "My classmates seldom order dishes when having meals. It's always plain steamed buns with one spoonful of meat and vegetable in between. When

FIGURE 5.1. Jiao going to a boarding high school in preparation for the NUEE. Photo by the author, May 2011.

I watch them eat with such a small bite, I would . . ."—she pulled a face to express how unbelievable and painful it was for her to watch. Jiao also mentioned several times that "girls seldom [ate] out; even guys [did] not eat out that often." The frugality of her classmates made her a loner who ate by herself. "Even if I go out to eat in a small restaurant, I feel embarrassed to invite along too many people," she said with evident regret and frustration.

Jiao's preference for rice with dishes and her relatively high consumption stemmed from her family's economic success, which was the result of her parents' migration, hard work, and entrepreneurial spirit. She had asked for a 7,000 RMB ($1,060) stipend for one semester. In addition to tuition and rental fees, she spent 300 to 400 RMB ($45–$61) per month on meals, fruit, and milk, plus a few hundred on dining out. This comparatively extravagant consumption was unaffordable for most of her classmates, who came from nearby villages.

In Jiao's view, such economic differentiation also confirmed the regional differences in cultural realms. Jiao found her classmates "very simple and innocent, especially the guys." When asked for evidence, she mentioned her male classmates' acceptance of the idea that men should assume the responsibility for the success of a romantic relationship:

> They all thought they should be responsible for their girlfriends once they start dating and marry them afterward. Upon graduation, my male classmates were all talking about getting married to their girlfriends. They all have a strong sense of responsibility. I asked them how it was possible to stay together after graduation, let alone get married after dating only one person. They found me weird. Therefore, during the one year I studied at P, no guys ever pursued me. Not even one guy would walk me from the classroom to the dorm after class.

Yet even though Jiao did not attract suitors and was regarded by her girlfriends as naive in ways of romantic relationships, her notion of the value of trial and error in romance asserted, in effect, her claim to being cosmopolitan and sophisticated in contrast to the simplicity and purity that her classmates exemplified.

In addition, Jiao encountered in this environment, to her considerable discomfort, much fervid nationalistic patriotism in her classmates. She commented several times that her younger brother, who had been in Henan since seventh grade to prepare for the NUEE, had become "Henanized," by which she meant "brainwashed": "My classmates here are all very patriotic, believing they are contributing to the nation. They like watching CCTV programs. People like me seem very abnormal to them."

In no way opposed to patriotism per se, Jiao felt alienated from patriotic education and mainstream propaganda partly because of her personal encounters with *hukou*-related discrimination. She characterizes herself and her fellow students from P as people with two different value systems. Studies show that identity formation contingent on specific power structures and social contexts (Ghannam 2002; Giddens 1991) is central to one's political socialization (Huddy 2001). This finding applies to the case of migrant youth who are often treated as second-class citizens in their own country and have to constantly navigate through a state of in-betweenness. If in part influenced by alternative channels of information from the internet, Jiao assumed a more critical view of the Chinese political system than her rural classmates due to her liminal status in China's citizenship regime and her resultant ambiguous identity.

The observation that her classmates were "simple and pure" and her disapproval of their blind patriotism revealed Jiao's subtle in-between position in China's geopolitical and sociocultural hierarchies. P, a small county city surrounded by farmland, represents to Jiao the stereotypical rural China: poor, backward, and isolated but simple and pure. The metropolis of Shanghai represents the opposite: rich, advanced, connected, sophisticated, and sullied. In the hegemonic discourse of national development in postreform China, Shanghai stands far ahead of P, as well as the whole province of Henan, on the spectrum of development. When Jiao identified the success of nationalistic education as characterized by her younger brother's "Henanization," she reinforced the perceived backwardness by pinning it on the specific place of Henan and marking its geographic place as equivalent to an earlier stage of development.

The cultural discordance and social alienation experienced by Jiao further convinced her that Henan was not her home and she should *kaochuqu* (literally "test out of," sit a qualification exam to attend university and move out of the place): "Henan people are not very good. I never thought I was a Henanese. 'Henan is my *laojia* [old home].' This is what I would say to explain to others, but it does not mean much to me. [M. L.: Do you consider yourself Shanghainese then?] I am not Shanghainese, but Shanghai is where I grew up and where my home is."

Unfortunately, Jiao failed the NUEE and did not get into university in 2011. After three months of frustration and restless searching for alternatives, she decided to repeat twelfth grade despite her rejection and resentment of the entire NUEE preparation process to attempt one more time to realize her full urban identity by becoming a university student, the key to becoming a legitimate city person. In 2012, she managed to pass the NUEE, but the score only got her into a second-tier university in Henan's capital city Zhengzhou. Unsatisfied with the poor quality of the program and the lack of learning incentives, she made her way back to Shanghai in 2015 through an internship in a microfinancing company and was keen to learn the business in order to keep her job and reclaim her place in the metropolis.

The New Sent-Down Generation

The Chinese state has once before compelled urban youth into rural areas. Shanghai reportedly sent about two million *zhiqing* (educated youth, or sent-down youth) to the countryside during the Cultural Revolution (Bonnin 2013). Few would relate today's rather unnoticed remigration of migrant students, seemingly out of individual ambition, with the top-down rustication campaign under high Maoism. However, the role of the state was prominent in both cases in shaping the causes and experiences of movement to the countryside, though their respective socioeconomic conditions differed.

The stories of these returnees demonstrate how reterritorialization in the "national order of things" (Malkki 1995) via relocation to one's registered place fails to overcome the structural inequality embedded in a highly territorialized citizenship regime as exemplified by China's *hukou* system. Successful or not in the exam, these students' experiences demonstrate how reterritorialization fails to bring "home" close as "symbolic anchors of community" to the returnees. Educational remigration has created opportunities for migrant children to confront, contest, and construct their socio-spatial identity. The "old home," once a distant memory or an abstract notion, suddenly becomes a concrete experience. Yet home trips were not a romantic homecoming for these seemingly long-lost children. Migrant students who grew up on the urban fringes of Shanghai brought with them on home trips their notion of modernity and civility. A strong sense of alienation marks their subjective experiences of the monotonous boarding school life without much family or social support. The seemingly natural return movement, as indicated by expressions like "going back to the old home," turns out to be fraught with discomfort, disorientation, and even despair, contributing to the perpetuation of the sense of in-betweenness among migrant youth moving across the entrenched rural-urban divide.

The stories of hardship during educational remigration have started to serve as precautionary tales for younger siblings, many of whom have shown growing resistance to such journeys. Guan, Huan's younger sister, has resolutely refused to go back to rural Henan for schooling even though she has performed well in school and has been talking about her higher-education dreams since primary school. "Look at my elder sister. She went back to Shanghai after only one year's stay in *laojia*. The school there sounded terrible. I'd rather stay in Shanghai. There will be this or that opportunity anyway."

The low success rate of migrant returnees getting into a first-tier universities also factors into the calculation. "You know how competitive it is in our *laojia*?! If you are not among the top fifty in the top high school [in your home county], it is almost impossible for you to get into a first-tier university!" Jiawen said, cautioning his friend Bei, who was agonizing over whether she should go back to her registered hometown in rural Anhui after seventh grade. The decentralization of school funding, the unequal distribution of university enrollment quota, and the enlarged rural-urban and regional disparities have rendered returnees' chances precarious in the increasingly competitive higher education market.

News reports about the growing difficulty of university graduates finding jobs have exacerbated the perception about decreasing return when it comes to education, which in turn lowers the incentive of remigration. Both Guan and Jiawen, as described in Chapter 4, have reconciled with the option of secondary vocational education to stay in school, wait for job recommendations, and hold out in the metropolis of Shanghai. These who choose to stick it out do so for a variety of reasons and find themselves thrust into a fast-paced, seductive, but often unforgiving urban economy.

6   BUYING BELONGING

"YOU KNOW, even the Coke sold there was fake!" exclaimed Lin, the elder daughter of the vegetable vendors from rural Jiangsu Province. She told me about the time she had bought fake Coca-Cola in her home village during a discussion I was having with her and her parents in the summer of 2011 about why she had refused to return to her home place to take the *zhongkao* and attend an academic senior high school there. Surprised by this abrupt remark as she spoke of her decision, I asked how she could tell fake Coke from the genuine article. Lin asserted that fake Coke had a thinner plastic bottle and a slightly different taste.

To a perceptive soft-drink consumer like Lin, this seemingly minute detail spoke volumes about the undesirability of her registered native place. Lin was taken to Shanghai one year after her parents, Simei and Jianguo, migrated to Shanghai in 1999. Since moving to the city, Lin has only been back for brief visits to her native place three times over the past decade. In addition to being unfamiliar with the rural setting, she decided that her hometown had an inferior consumer market, as evidenced by the presence of fake Coke.

The availability of brand-name household items has become an important factor when migrant students choose between Shanghai and their "old homes." Xian, a classmate of Lin's, also expressed her preference for Shanghai from a consumer's perspective when asked why she refused to go back to her home-town in rural Jiangxi Province for high school:

Fewer choices are available back home: in our village, you can find a lot of dirt-cheap packaged junk food being sold, but I would not be able to find even a decent toothbrush. [M. L.: How can you tell if a toothbrush is not decent?] Well, for instance, the brush I found had uneven colors on its handle; that made me feel uncomfortable using it. Before I went back to my *laojiao* [literally "old home," native place], I had thought that there must be toothbrushes sold, so I didn't bring one from Shanghai. In the end, I could not even find a decent enough toothbrush—that's how poor my home village is!

Migrant youth such as Lin and Xian have a hard time calling a place where only fake Coke and shoddy toothbrushes are available "home." Having grown up with an ever increasing supply of diverse commodities amid the expansion of market-oriented economic reforms, these young people exhibit a high degree of sensitivity to the availability and quality of consumer goods. Their rejection of low-quality goods, expressed in blatant declarations of distaste, represents the increasingly estranged relationship they have with their places of origin.

Migrant youth prefer staying in Shanghai partly because the city is China's supreme marketplace, offering goods of better quality and greater variety for daily consumption. Their preference reflects China's entrenched geopolitical, administrative, and sociocultural hierarchies (X. Liu 1997). Caught between these hierarchies, migrant youth are both empowered and disfranchised in an ongoing "consumer revolution" in urban China.

MIGRANTS, CONSUMPTION, AND CITIZENSHIP

It is axiomatic that postreform China experienced a "consumer revolution" (Davis 2000) after decades of socialist austerity during the Mao era. There has been massive growth in consumer spending on food, clothes, homes, cars, electronics, and leisure activities. Rural-to-urban migrants are no exception to this. However, they are disproportionately underrepresented in media reports and academic research on China's "consumer revolution." The official labeling of migrants as "peasant workers," and their related position as such in the social imagination, objectifies them as merely a source of labor. It is true that rural-to-urban migrants are systematically exploited in workplaces under the *hukou* system, and their purchasing power is often limited because they are underpaid, and in many cases, payment is delayed or even denied. Institutional barriers to employment, housing, education, and social security also repress and delay consumption among first-generation migrant workers (Zhan 2015). The few extant studies of their consumer behaviors emphasize the negative and exploitative effects of China's new consumer culture on low-income migrant workers. Ngai Pun (2003) argues that consumerism is the newest "ruse of capital" that facilitates the exploitation of labor, erodes class consciousness, and deprives migrant workers of empowerment and emancipation. Female migrant workers manning assembly lines in factories in South China, for instance, often found their efforts to refashion themselves into consumer-citizens disappointing and even personally devastating (H. Yan 2002, 2005). Migrants as consumers are portrayed as victims with constrained, minimal agency, whose consumption practices function mainly as a "marker and measure of the negative aspects of economic reform" (Latham 2002, 227–28).

However, the Marxist, labor-centered approach that sees production as the primary site of migrants' identity formation overlooks the complexities embedded in the rich individual experiences and narratives of migrants as consumers. First, it neglects the socioeconomic variation and internal stratification among different migrant groups under the homogenizing label "peasant worker": there are subcontractors, small business owners, and other self-employed migrants who economically attain a level on par with working-class or even lower-middle-class Shanghai natives. They spend more than waged migrant workers in factories and restaurants, especially on dining and social activities for networking to benefit their business. The most successful migrant businessmen own apartments and cars in the city. Any generalizations about the consumer experiences and subjectivities of migrants miss the heterogeneity and reinforce the state-imposed label.

Second, and more importantly, consumer agency, though not necessarily liberating or positive, can be self-transformative. As Baudrillard suggested, in a consumer society, objects are no longer tied to a particular function or defined need but have come to function as substitutable signifiers whose consumption therefore is not to meet needs but to signify differences (Baudrillard 1988, 44–45). In this sense, consumption becomes part of the larger framework of productive forces of identity and class formation. The analytical frame situating the workplace as the primary site of class formation among Chinese migrants misses the crucial role of consumption in migrant identity formation as found elsewhere (Douglas 1996; Miller 1995; Mills 1999; Slater 1997). As Deborah Davis contends, "the structural dynamics and material inequalities of the contemporary late-socialist political economy necessarily frame these narratives, but the consumer culture that individuals create through their personal commentary and social discourse cannot *a priori* be presumed to be illusory or exploitative" (2005, 697).

In particular, consumption has been tied to the empowerment or disempowerment of individuals as citizens in everyday practices. Studies of Chinese middle-class consumers highlight how they negotiate their self-worth and foster a sense of citizenship based on consumer rights (Fleischer 2007; Ren 2013; Tomba 2005, 2009). Some studies of first-generation migrant workers relate how consumption has been embraced by migrant workers as a means to claim their urban membership (Chang 2008; Schein 2001; Xu 2000; Zheng 2009). Following on this scholarship, this chapter focuses on how second-generation migrant youth who have grown up in Shanghai are caught in the pas de deux of consumption and citizenship. Although consumption fails to secure full urban membership for them, citizenship and consumption do enhance each other at times.

Beyond the emphasis on production and subordination in studies of Chinese migrants, the stereotypical representation of migrant children as the "rural Other" in the city (see Chapter 2) commonly renders these young people invisible in consumer studies. This is in sharp contrast to numerous reports and scholarly studies of the consumption of the "only-child" generation from urban households (Davis and Sensenbrenner 2000; Croll 2006; Fong 2004; Jing 2000). When I talked about my research to my Shanghainese friends, who are mostly educated professionals, they were often surprised at my research findings about migrant youths' consuming behavior: "Aren't they *mingong zinü* [peasant workers' children]?" It was difficult for them to associate migrants with consumption, as their image of a migrant is that of a "peasant" who toils in the city—and nothing more than that. However, as the following section shows, consumption is salient in the everyday lives of migrant youth. Unlike first-generation migrant workers, second-generation migrant youth have yet to be fully absorbed into the productive labor force, but even before entering adulthood they have already actively engaged in mass consumption. This experience of consumption, which their parents have worked so hard to facilitate, is an important part of their lives. In terms of youth consumer desire and consumption behavior, migrant youth and their urban peers exhibit more similarities than differences.

POCKET MONEY, PROPER CHILDHOOD

"I cannot keep up with their demands," Simei, the vegetable vendor and mother of Lin and Xin, complained in reference to her children's consumer desires. "They want a good life. When there is the need, we will try our best to give them the money. But our income cannot meet their demands."

First-generation migrants like Simei lead frugal existences to save money. Their lives revolve around making ends meet, raising children, and saving money for retirement. The high saving and remittance rates among married migrants noted by survey studies testify to this frugality (Hu 2012; Murphy 2006). As mentioned in Chapter 1 with respect to housing, most migrants opt for cramped, makeshift dwellings in periurban zones or share apartments with others to minimize expenditures on rent. They seldom shop for clothes, eat in restaurants, or venture beyond their workplace or home for recreation. They may have visited a few signature tourist sites in Shanghai, such as the Pearl Tower and the City God Temple, but only when they first came to Shanghai or when they show around visiting relatives. Their experience of the metropolitan and its urban culture rarely extends beyond these experiences. Few of them have ever visited a movie theater or theme park in Shanghai. The majority of low-income first-generation rural-to-urban migrants remain outsiders to the city both socially and culturally.

Nevertheless, these migrant parents tend to be relatively generous when it comes to their children's expenses. Much like their urban counterparts, they regularly give their children pocket money in addition to money for school fees and clothing. As of the late 2000s, the daily pocket money generally given to my informants was around 5–7 RMB (about $1) for primary-school-aged children, to cover their breakfast and after-school snacks. School lunches were prepaid, so they would not factor into the allowance. The amount usually increased to 10–15 RMB ($1.50–$2.00) when children started middle school. If they went on to secondary vocational schools some distance from home, the amount would increase to 20 RMB ($3) or more per day. In May 2001, Meixia, the only daughter of a divorced construction worker originally from Jiangsu Province, recorded all her expenses on her phone while she was a first-year vocational school student. To her surprise, she found her accrued expenses reached 200 RMB ($30) for one particular week. The lowest daily amount recorded was 17 RMB ($2.50) when she skipped breakfast and had only instant noodles for lunch. Otherwise, she would spend approximately 30 RMB ($4) per day if she had both breakfast and lunch and rode the subway.

One major expense for migrant youth is food. Many parents work long hours or irregular shifts and are unable to cook at home regularly. They also maintain, in a strict sense, a "nuclear family" without help from grandparents, who stay behind in the countryside. The separation brought by migration and restrictions imposed by *hukou* force migrant parents to rely on the burgeoning service economy, with which many are actively engaged, to relieve them of certain household duties such as cooking. Many migrant children buy meals from food carts, convenience stores, and noodle shops.

Migrant youth, like their urban peers, become accustomed to the convenience of cheap industrialized food, such as instant noodles, rice crackers, luncheon and other processed meats, and so forth. Many students consume *yinliao* (flavored beverages) almost every day that cost between 2.5 and 4 RMB ($0.30–$0.50) each. In the summer of 2009, I asked Yang, an outspoken girl originally from rural Anhui, why she would not bring a water bottle along with her, like her parents do, to save money. "It is my habit to have a bottle of *yinliao* in my hand whenever I go out in the summer, or I would feel uneasy." Her answer attributed her consumption of bottled beverages not only to convenience but also to a sense of security, in which she felt she fit in. Such internalization of the high-consumption culture among migrant youth makes for a sharp contrast to the frugal ways of their parents.

Of course, the amount of pocket money varies according to each household's financial capacity. Yang's father once ran a small but profitable cargo transport business in Shanghai. He used the family savings to buy a box truck, hired a driver, and managed to secure subcontracts through his connections with people from the same place of origin to deliver cargo for a larger cargo transportation company. The business went bankrupt in late 2008 because the driver violated traffic regulations and was involved in a fatal accident; the family had to pay hundreds of thousands in the legal settlement. As a result, Yang was given almost no pocket money between late 2008 and early 2010 and ate mostly at home. Her family of two parents and three siblings also moved into a smaller rental unit in an old working-class neighborhood. Later, however, when her father found an accounting job in a transport company and her mother became a daytime housemaid for a well-off expatriate family, Yang, then a vocational school student, started to receive pocket money again—300 RMB ($45) per month in 2010 and 2011. Since she ate breakfast and dinner at home and spent very little on clothes, she saved most of her pocket money to support her social gatherings and leisure activities. In June 2011, for instance, Yang spent over 250 RMB ($40) on her middle school class reunion alone, which included a group lunch at a chain restaurant, followed by going out to a karaoke club.

Spending on leisure and social activities increases significantly after migrant students enter vocational school. Having completed the nine-year basic education, they become "half adults" in the eyes of parents and teachers. They are given more autonomy to hang out after school, which often ends around 3:00 P.M. (see Chapter 5). They also enjoy more free time since they no longer need to study as much as in middle school and the pressure to produce high exam scores is behind them. They have plenty of time to hang out with their peers—playing basketball on campus or computer games in internet cafes, window-shopping, and singing in karaoke bars. Most of them learn to become savvy consumers: going to karaoke bars when prices are reduced, trying on clothes in malls but buying them online at lower prices, and using coupons for discounts in select restaurants.

Most migrant youth, like their urban peers, feel entitled to pocket money and other financial support from their parents even after they have started receiving pay from internships. Those from lower socioeconomic backgrounds are not immune to the saturation of consumerism. I record below part of a June 2011 group discussion with the students of Class Five of the ninth grade at the Bridge School, two years after they graduated from middle school:

M. L.: Do you still ask for pocket money from your parents?

MING: Yes. My expenses are too much—far beyond what I earn.

JUNJIE: The money I earn is not enough at all. Usually I run out of money. I feel there's never enough money.

JUN: I feel the same way. I spent 1,000 RMB [$140] these last two days. A pair of Nike sneakers alone cost me over 600 RMB [$80]. I also bought new pants from Printemps Department Store [*Bali chuntian*, literally "Paris Spring," a midtier joint-venture department store in Shanghai].

M. L.: Do your parents put limits on your pocket money?

JUNJIE: Money for clothes should not count toward pocket money.

MING: I don't ask for pocket money that often. My parents pay for school fees. I use the monthly subsidy from the vocational school for rural-*hukou*

> students for my small purchases. Actually I didn't ask for one penny from
> my parents this semester.
>
> JUNJIE: Once you hang out, you need to use money. Once friends ask me out, I
> need to spend money.
>
> MING: Mainly for group meals. I spend most on eating out.
>
> JIANXIN: I have to ask for money from my parents.

Except for Ming, whose parents are economically less well off than the others,
the students take it for granted that their parents should support them after
they turn eighteen, the legal age of adulthood in China, even after they take
internships.

Of course, internships and training programs pay these young adults barely
enough to meet their consumer needs (see Chapter 7). Ranging from almost
nothing to 1,000 RMB ($120), the payments are far from giving migrant youth
enough to enjoy city life and maintain social relations. Hence many vocational
school students, especially the men, who are expected according to the gender
stereotype to foot the bill when out with women, find it difficult to afford dating and other social outings.

These students' sense of entitlement to this financial assistance from their
parents has a lot to do with the changing social value of children in late-
socialist China. Although the powerful *suzhi* discourse emphasizes the improvement of population quality through scientific child bearing and discipline
(Greenhalgh 2005), there is an equally influential discourse that emphasizes
children's unique nature and distinct developmental requirements—including
the requirement that they experience a "joyful, stress-free childhood" (Naftali
2010, 591). The extension of childhood seen in Western industrialized societies (Pufall and Unsworth 2004; Zelizer 1985) has also gained institutional
support in the Chinese legal and educational systems. Children become economically less valuable but emotionally more precious to parents as they spend
more years in school and enter the job market at an older age. This emergent
idea of childhood is part of an ongoing transformation in the construction of
personhood and social order in urban China. Such a prolonged childhood consequently increases parents' responsibility to satisfy their children's everyday
needs even after they reach age eighteen.

Three decades of birth-control policies have also driven up the stakes of
having "only one or two children," putting children at the center of the family and
making Chinese parents more receptive to the redefined notion of childhood.

Although most rural-to-urban migrant families were not subject to the stringent one-child policy like their urban counterparts because of their agricultural *hukou* (see Chapter 2), they are caught in the process of redefining childhood and parenthood nonetheless. These migrant parents came of age between the 1970s and 1980s before the economic reforms had made substantial changes in the countryside. Their childhood was characterized by material scarcity and physical hardship. They moved to the cities for higher income and a better livelihood. They also strove to provide their children with easier and happier childhoods than their own. The recognition that their children "want a good life" among migrant parents, such as Simei, serves as a projection of their desires as well. Since consumption has become crucial to childhood experience, they want to be supportive of their children's daily expenditures within their means. They delay their own personal consumption in the city to enable their children to have a proper childhood like their urban peers.

TIERED MARKETS, STRATIFIED CITIZENSHIP

Consumer goods, such as a bottle of Coke and a Colgate toothbrush, as quotidian as they are, symbolize modernity and urban prosperity. The brand names give migrant youths a sense of assurance derived from the global nature of these brands, which reinforces the metropolitan appeal of Shanghai. They have become important references for migrant youth to locate their sense of belonging in the city. In contrast, fake and poor-quality goods represent rural poverty and backwardness. The visceral rejection of goods of inferior quality as seen in the attitudes of Lin and Xian signifies and justifies their subjective alienation from their rural origins.

Shanghai's unique position as China's largest industrial and commercial city makes the rural-urban, backward-modern divides an even more entrenched part of the migrant youth's consumer experience. Shanghai is categorized as a "first-tier city," together with Beijing and Guangzhou, in marketing terminology. Shanghai's long history as a treaty port open to the West since 1843 contributes to its prestige in the consumer market.[1] Nicknamed the "Paris of the East," the city was famous for its vibrant entertainment industries, consumer culture, and global cosmopolitanism in the late nineteenth and early twentieth centuries (Bergère 2009; L. O. Lee 1999; H. Lu 1999; Wasserstrom 2009; Yeh 1997, 2007). Although the city suffered dearly from Mao's socialist policies that ideologically antagonized consumption and bourgeois culture, local Shanghainese often prided themselves on being savvy consumers and shrewd homemakers who could keep a decent living with very limited resources (Cochran 1999; Gerth 2013). Since Deng Xiaoping's 1992 trip to South China to speed up market-oriented economic reforms, Shanghai has reemerged as China's financial center and commercial haven. Today the city boasts the highest GDP per capita in China and some of the world's tallest skyscrapers. It hosts regional headquarters of multinational companies, flagship stores of luxury brands, and trendy entertainment venues. The city abounds in supermarkets and convenience stores competing to offer a great variety of quality household products. New products and services often appear first in Shanghai, whose residents are believed to be more receptive to novelty.

The hierarchy of consumer markets in postreform China closely parallels the hierarchy embedded in the *hukou*-based citizenship regime.[2] The Shanghai municipal government, which is at the provincial level in China's administrative hierarchy,[3] possesses much more political and fiscal power than regional city and county governments. Consequently, a Shanghai *hukou* grants its local citizens access to much better social benefits, including public education and medical service, than what a small-town or regional-city *hukou* can offer. Equally important is that having a Shanghai *hukou* empowers people to feel entitled to high-quality goods. By contrast, the countryside—poor, backward, and lacking—is flooded with cheap packaged foods, obscure domestic brands, and knock-off products (Lai 2016). If a rural *hukou* has already subjected migrant laborers to a high degree of exploitation in production, it has also severely restrained rural youth from a high-quality consumption experience. This is not only because of economic disparity but also market stratification and the distributive hierarchy of the consumer market.

In the tiered logic of consumption, consumers situated lower in the market hierarchy, such as those in second-tier cities, small towns, and the country-side, emulate the lifestyles of those higher up to acquire social prestige (J. Wang 2005). Although migrant youth are, in general, perceived as belonging to the underclass in Shanghai, they are simultaneously privileged consumers superior to their country fellows in villages and small towns. The social prestige that comes with geographic proximity to quality goods and convenient shopping experiences makes migrant youth in Shanghai feel strongly attached to the city. After her short trips to Beijing, Sichuan, and Fujian sponsored by NGO J in the summer of 2012, Lin shared with me her impressions: "After traveling back and forth and seeing things elsewhere a few times, I find Shanghai is still the best by every means of comparison." She added that there was fake Coke for sale even on the Tiananmen Square in Beijing. The superior status of Shanghai helped to reaffirm her decision to forgo her university dream and remain in the city.

This partly explains why a recent survey shows that the relaxing of policies regarding small-city and township-level *hukou* conversions for migrants has not been met with enthusiasm. In July 2014, the state council issued a *hukou* reform plan dubbed the "National Plan on New Urbanization 2014–2020." It largely reinforces the socioeconomic hierarchy of Chinese citizenship, fostering the growth of small cities and towns by making it easier for migrants to change the locale of their *hukou* to the towns and small cities where they work and thereby gain local urban citizenship. However, the study showed that migrants displayed a lukewarm response to this policy change. Since the *hukou* conversion is not irreversible, migrants show great hesitance (C. Chen and Fan 2016). Many still want to cling to the collective land ownership granted by their rural *hukou* as a security guarantee in case they encounter a severe economic downturn.

More importantly, 69 percent of migrant informants expressed their preference for working and living in the big and mega cities, among which the four provincial-level municipalities, including Shanghai, are most popular (C. Chen and Fan 2016, 26). Big and mega cities offer not only more job opportunities but also a more exciting urban life, consumption being an important part of it. As consumption has become a crucial technology of the self in China today (Rofel 2007), consuming in mega cities like Shanghai instead of a regional city or small town confers an opportunity of self-realization and a sense of achievement. However, the 2014 *hukou* reform specifically tightens *hukou* conversion policies in big and mega cities, raising the qualification criteria for migrants to obtain formal residential status. This tightening, implemented in the name of preventing overpopulation, allows the hierarchy and inequality intrinsic to the *hukou* system to remain largely intact.

Whether this sense of privilege derived from proximity to the first-tier market in Shanghai can help override dissatisfaction with the *hukou*-based bias against migrant youth still treated as "outsiders" remains an open question. The following sections probe the ambivalence and anxiety facing migrant youth as consumers in Shanghai and reflect on China's ongoing contention over urban citizenship and social stratification.

FAIR SKIN: AESTHETICS, PLACE, AND IDENTITY

While male migrant youth often feel burdened with having to pay the bills for social gatherings, female migrant youth, influenced by commercials and their peers, spend a large portion of their pocket money on skin-care and makeup products. Yang noticed that many of her classmates started to wear light makeup in the summer after graduation from middle school. After finishing middle school in 2009, she herself spent around 200 RMB ($30) to fill her dresser with face wash, toner, moisturizer, suntan lotion, eye shadow, and mascara from a foreign chain supermarket. She chose Garnier, an international brand, which she found affordable but of sufficiently high repute among youth users influenced by television ads. The well-advertised skin-care routine, which includes at least the three steps of using face wash, toner, and moisturizer, has been widely accepted among these young women. Wearing makeup also necessitates the use of skin-care products to protect the skin.

Given that migrant students could only attend secondary vocational school in Shanghai regardless of their academic performance and preference (see Chapter 4), Yang saw such investments in beauty products necessary for her to fit in at the vocational school where dress codes are more relaxed than those in exam-centered high schools. For female vocational students, knowing how to dress smartly and apply makeup is also considered to be important skills for preparing for and succeeding in future jobs. They are encouraged to participate, first as consumers and later as workers, in the continued growth of China's beauty economy, which emphasizes "feminine beauty" (Croll 2006, 335).

The major interest in using skin-care and makeup products of Yang and her friends is the pursuit of a light or whiter skin tone. Having light skin is widely considered across China and Asia to be more beautiful and hence more valuable than darker skin: female stars on magazine covers almost always appear highly polished with pearl-white fairness (Yu 2014). Women often use umbrellas and sunscreen diligently to guard their skin from sun exposure. Many Western brands have also introduced their whitening products specifically to appeal to their Chinese customers. Fair skin is also one of the top criteria that men on Chinese dating websites look for in their wives.

Although female migrant students may not have yet become regular consumers of skin-care products, they clearly have bought into the aesthetic value of fair skin. When they buy such household items as body wash and moisturizers, they often choose those that claim to have whitening benefits. On a hot summer afternoon in 2010, a few of these girls gathered at NGO J's office around Le, a tall ninth grader originally from rural Anhui. They looked attentively at Le's imitation of a recent Olay whitening body wash commercial. Amid giggles, Le ardently repeated the advertised benefits and shared beauty tips she had learned from talk shows on how to whiten skin: use a sponge, scrub hard to exfoliate the skin, wash the face with milk, eat fruit every day, and so on. Knowing about whitening skin-care products and applying them has become an exercise of choice and control that earns self-respect for these young women.

Such beauty consciousness is not uncommon among first-generation migrant women, especially migrant mothers with daughters. When I accompanied Yan to her parents' food vending booth on a late morning in July 2010, Yan's mother noticed that we did not bring umbrellas. She vehemently disapproved: "If you get tanned, you will get ugly." She reminded us that dark-skinned girls would have a hard time finding husbands. Her appreciation of fair skin suggests a gendered bias in favor of domesticated beauty protected from the outdoors and hardship. She herself would consciously wear a pair of white over-sleeves and a worn white shirt on top of her t-shirt to keep away the sun even when she was busy with making egg crepes for customers. During casual conversations over the years, she often commented on how much damage she had sustained being in the street-vending business day and night, how it had darkened her fair skin and given her freckles. Fair skin signifies both the youthful beauty and urban comfort that she now feels she has lost or been denied.

Of course, the preference for fair skin can be found throughout Chinese history, in which poems, novels, and plays repeatedly described porcelain-like fair skin as one main feature of feminine beauty. Yet the fixation on light skin tone has been reinforced by an urban-oriented, Western-worshiping evaluation system of beauty in the global market system (Adrian 2003; Leong 2006; Miller 2006). Fair skin today is often associated with being in the city and doing indoor mental work. In contrast, dark skin is associated with belonging to the minorities, being in the countryside, and having to do outdoor manual labor, thus being of lower socioeconomic status.

The evaluation of skin tone epitomizes the hierarchy of urban citizenship. Shanghai and the prosperous lower Yangtze River delta is often perceived as the place that breeds fair-skinned beauties. This urban myth has been widely circulated and accepted by local residents and migrants alike. Although many migrant girls are born with relatively fair skin, the perception that Shanghainese have lighter skin persists. When Yang talked about her decision to take better care of her skin, she half-jokingly said that she was a woman after all, and it was time for her to be feminine, especially when hanging out with female Shanghainese friends. Yang used to pride herself on her tanned skin and outgoing, boyish manners. As she entered adulthood, however, she started talking about adapting to the norms of femininity in Shanghai, including having fairer skin. Partly out of girlish anxiety over her femininity, she internalized the hierarchy of the aesthetic value regarding skin tone and elected to apply whitening moisturizer and suntan lotion as a part of her daily routine.

Guan shared a similar anxiety over her skin tone and expressed explicitly the association between light skin and Shanghaineseness. She has grown up in Shanghai since the age of five when her parents took her and her two siblings with them when they moved from rural Henan to Shanghai (see Chapter 1). She has not been back to her home village since. When I asked, during my June 2011 visit after she had finished seventh grade, whether she thought of herself as "Shanghainese," she immediately lamented that her dark skin marked her as an outsider.

> GUAN: My skin is too dark [*hei*]. They always say my skin is dark. It looks OK now [at the beginning of the summer break]. But during the school terms, my skin was so tanned because I lived far away from school and had to ride my bicycle to school for three years.
>
> M. L.: So you want to have fair skin?
>
> GUAN: Of course! [*Nodding eagerly*]
>
> M. L.: Do you find fair skin more beautiful?
>
> GUAN: Of course [it is] more beautiful. The celebrities all have very fair skin.
>
> M. L.: Do you think people with dark skin are *waidiren*?
>
> GUAN: Yes, just about [*chabuduo ba*]. I find Shanghainese have light and soft skin [*baibai nengneng*].

Guan's abrupt shift on the issue of fair skin with respect to her identity puzzled me. I tried to challenge Guan's generalization by asking her what she thought of my rather dark skin even though I am Shanghainese. Guan tactfully avoided my question by complimenting my eyes. When pushed, she defended herself by saying, "Aiya, you are an exception." By categorizing me as an outlier, she preserved her belief in the stereotype intact. The cognitive equation between the place of Shanghai and fair skin remains valid and powerful to her.

The valuation of light skin tone shows an intimate manifestation of social hierarchy that puts local Shanghainese on top: fair skin belongs in the metropolis of Shanghai, a symbol of urban modernity in China, while dark skin belongs in the rural hinterland. The preference for fair skin even helps shape preferences among migrant youth to working indoors as clerks, beauticians, and accountants, even though many outdoor blue-collar jobs pay much more (Lan 2014). Behind the desire for fair skin and the efforts to obtain it among migrant youth lies their aspiration for urban identity with the city of Shanghai and its associated Western-influenced modernity and sociocultural superiority. The obsession with fair skin via whitening and anti-UV products hence reflects and reifies aesthetic values and cultural sensitivities shaped by the hierarchical structure of urban membership.

"SLUM BRANDS" AND "MINI CK": YOUTH, FASHION, AND DESIRE

"Hey, wear something nice when you come. Don't be too *tu* [literally "earthy," unfashionable]." Yang woke me up in the early morning with this last-minute call in June 2011 when I was again to visit her family in Shanghai for lunch. Somewhat embarrassed by her direct, half-joking request, I was left reflecting on my fieldwork dress code: Was I really that *tu* in the eyes of my informants? I did consciously dress to "blend in" with the students: plain T-shirts, pullovers, jeans, sneakers, and straight long hair or ponytail, in the belief that my student-like outfit would help me fit in better in the environment and avoid unnecessary attention in the middle of my participant observation. I thought about how the students did often cautiously tease me a bit for the way I dressed, saying it was *tu* or *pusu* (plain). They expected me to assume a more dressed-up, more mature look that was appropriate for my age and level of education. To them, I was presumed to have "a bright future" because of my educational credentials from leading universities in both China and the United States. They thought I could wear something more stylish and glamorous. Once I wore a nice summer dress, and the students, especially the girls, immediately noticed it and complimented me warmly. It turned out that wearing better clothes did not distance me from them. They preferred hanging out with someone well dressed, and they themselves aspired to "look good" like the well-educated, white-collar professionals who are their role models.

Yang's request for me to put on nicer clothes deserves further exploration of taste and fashion among migrant youth. I may have been subconsciously dressing down without fully recognizing that these migrant students have been saturated with the imagery and inculcated material desires of Shanghai's consumer culture. Limited resources have constrained their purchasing power but not their consumer desire. Yang's using *tu*, the most emblematic everyday term that articulates the rural-urban distinctions, also reminds me of the embrace of urban taste among migrant youth. They grow up in a fashion-conscious society filled with billboards, store signs, magazine stands, and television commercials. They avidly watch soap operas from Taiwan and South Korea featuring well-dressed pop idols. Media influence, in addition to peer pressure and urban identification, contributes to their sensitivity to how not to be *tu*.

China's increasingly segmented consumer markets enable migrant youth to realize their desires for beauty and fashion without having to spend too much. Large low-end wholesale markets flourish in low-rent settings on the urban outskirts. They offer bargain clothes, shoes, textiles, and accessories of the latest fashions, including imitation items. Migrant businessmen in the garment-production business and retail industry play a crucial role in the formation and operation of such markets. Many migrant parents purchase clothes in these wholesale markets because of the low prices and geographic proximity, as they also live on the urban fringes.

Big chain supermarkets offer another important venue for migrant youth to buy quality goods, such as food, stationery, clothes, household items, and personal care products. Given that most migrant families have very limited living space, it has almost become a form of recreation for migrant families to take a stroll in air-conditioned, brightly lit supermarkets on a summer night. These sorts of fundamental shopping spaces for daily necessities reinforce migrant youth preferences for Shanghai as the right place for consumption and belonging.

Like their urban peers, migrant youth have become accustomed to the sense of freedom to choose and consume from an early age.[4] As a savvy consumer, Yang knew how to haggle for a pair of jeans from the listed 120 RMB ($17) to 30 RMB ($3) in a wholesale market and to find a cute matching T-shirt for 10 RMB ($1.50). Many have been browsing magazines and mail-order catalogs that target adolescent consumers since middle school. With the rapid development of business-to-customer websites, such as the leading giant Taobao.com, online shopping and discussion forums have become the most important venues for purchasing goods, as well as for consumers to inform themselves about fashion trends. Although most of my informants could not open bank accounts and were ineligible to apply for credit cards in the late 2000s, when they were still students, a variety of payment methods that do not require credit card have now made online shopping easy and accessible for them.

Within their own defined limits, school-age migrant youth carefully construct practical youthful styles. They usually accept that compromise has to be made between quality and a bargain price, but footwear is an exception: most migrant students wear sneakers in and outside of school nearly every day and tend to be pickier about them than anything else; school rules also tend to be more lenient when it comes to footwear. As elsewhere around the world, sneakers are particularly associated with teenage fashion under the influence of global hip-hop culture (Swain 2002; Wilson and Sparks 1996). In Shanghai, migrant students in this study also exhibited strong preferences for high-quality, brand-name sneakers. Many of them make sure that they or their parents purchase brand-name sneakers from standard supermarkets or franchise stores instead of buying imitation products from low-end wholesale markets. The most common brands are major Chinese domestic brands, such as Anta, Li Ning, and 361°, priced between 100 and 300 RMB ($12–40) and targeting working-class and lower-middle-class youth. The few male students who wear Nike or Adidas, predominantly basketball shoes, are from the better-off entrepreneurial migrant families. These international brands, known for premium designs and coveted as a fashion statement, usually cost three times as much as domestic ones. Brand-name consciousness aside, these students also defend their choices on the basis of practicality: one genuine, brand-name pair can last a whole year, whereas imitation products wear out easily and last only a few months. The emphasis on durability coincides with what Bourdieu has observed about the choice of the "value for money" clothes made by working classes for substance and functionalist use out of economic necessity (Bourdieu 1984, 377–78).

Fashion is class specific, and the ways commodities are purchased and used contribute to social stratification. However, the class distinction between migrant and local students is not as pronounced as between adults yet, and youth tend to see clothes and footwear more as a personal statement of style than of social status. Two reasons may explain this lesser degree of class distinction: First, students have to wear uniforms and follow strict rules on clothing, posture, and personal grooming, such as nail length and hair color, especially in Chinese primary and middle schools; the intention is to impose conformity and prevent peer competition. Second, most migrant students attend nonelite schools in Shanghai's suburbs (see Chapter 3), where their local classmates generally come from working-class or lower-middle-class families that are no better off than they are. Class differentiation is not felt especially acutely at school.

Fashion is also age sensitive. Migrant youth and their local peers internalize the normative life stages and the associated dress codes. Because I was in my late twenties during my dissertation field research, they constantly asked me about my marital status and future career. For Yang and many other migrant students I hung out with, my casual out-of-fashion outfits matched neither my age nor my status. Similarly, teenagers who are too eager to dress like an adult or wear brands associated with mature styles also invite derision from their peers. The imperative to find and keep a balance between showing one's self-worth and conforming to social expectations in consumer behavior creates space for individuals to lessen the competitive tendency.

Both Western and Chinese media have focused on the frenzied pursuit of luxury brands, such as Chanel and Louis Vuitton, by the new affluent Chinese as evidence of China's rapid social stratification. Those brands nevertheless remain largely irrelevant to these migrant students. First, they are sold in flashy downtown shopping malls and department stores that migrant teenagers and their parents seldom visit. Moreover, migrant students' take on youthful style that emphasizes age appropriateness and affordable coolness enables them to feel self-righteous and content as nascent consumers. "Chanel looks way too old on us, and many of its clothes don't even look pretty," Yang once commented in a rather dismissive tone. Such somewhat defensive judgments enable them to prescribe a style appropriate to their age and position themselves according to their own economic calculations.

When migrant youth start working in the urban centers or are far away from the periurban shopping areas in which they feel at home, they have to confront blatant class differentiation. Both Yang and Jiao are from families engaged in small business and were comparatively lax with their pocket money. In the summer of 2010 when they went to Beijing for a TOEFL cram course sponsored by NGO J, they wandered into downtown Beijing to shop for clothes. To their disappointment, they could not find any of their favorite, familiar brand names.

> YANG: Yes, my classmates care about brands, but they don't often buy brand-name products.
>
> JIAO: And what we consider "brand names" is not what you would think. When we went brand shopping in Beijing, we were told that we were looking for slum brands. We were looking for Tebu, Mester Bowne, Lanse Tiankong, Yichun [all domestic clothing brands targeting youth], and so on. They thought these were all slum brands.

M. L.: Who are "they"?

JIAO: Our "big boss" [nickname for a Beijing-based journalist who hosted them]. She once said that these brands are not to be found in Xidan [an upscale commercial center in downtown Beijing]. The brands there are not seen in the places where we used to go. We were looking for clothes we can afford, say, from 100 to 200 RMB, but all clothes in Xidan cost at least 1,000 RMB!

YANG: Damn expensive.

The girls were used to the domestic brands targeting late teens of lower to middle socioeconomic conditions. Their limited brand-name consciousness keeps them content within their comfort zone. Once they ventured out of familiar settings, however, they had to confront their inferior position in the larger, more hierarchical consumer market. The rather insensitive and condescending commentary about "slum brands" from the generous, university-educated journalist and host illustrates the naturalization of social stratification in postreform China. In comparison with urban professionals, migrant youth like Yang and Jiao become second-class consumers from the "slums."

Of course, the consumer market has been evolving rapidly in response to demographic changes and social demands. Embarking on jobs, many migrant youths forego copycat or brandless clothes sold in crowded supermarkets or wholesale markets frequented by their parents on the city's outskirts. Instead they embrace fast-fashion brands to put together a certain appearance and a style of their own. Chain stores selling fast-fashion clothing, footwear, and accessories, such as Zara and H&M, have boomed in Chinese cities since the 2000s and replaced many domestic brands to become the new fashion standard for urban youth, migrant youth included. These international fast-fashion brands offer a global touch to their products and shopping experiences.

Lin and several of her close friends, for instance, after they graduated from vocational school and started working, preferred buying purses from what they would refer to as "mini CK" in daily conversation: Charles & Keith, an international footwear and accessories brand based in Singapore. Its retail stores are situated in popular midtier shopping complexes and use eye-catching decor to appeal to urban youths' brand consciousness. Lin once posted on WeChat a picture of the mirror-filled interior design of a new Charles & Keith store she visited, calling her friends' attention to the cool design. This brand resembles the chic urban styles of the better-advertised American brands, such as Calvin Klein and Kate Spade, with slight twists and often at one-third of the prices. Unlike low-end imitation products, fast-fashion brands like Charles & Keith, H&M, and Zara invest heavily with global capital in advertisement and retail store decoration to build brand images so that they can appeal to young consumers who are fashion sensitive and status conscious. "It is not fake and has its own name," Lin said of her Charles & Keith handbag. She insisted on the brand's authenticity even though she acknowledged that the initials of Charles & Keith intentionally resemble those of Calvin Klein. The idea of sporting brand-name style at a fraction of the price without compromising the consumer experience and public recognition sells well to young professionals like Lin, who strive to enjoy the sensation of consumption and embody urban chic with limited resources.

While a fake Coke represents rural backwardness to Lin, wearing "mini CK" satisfies her desire for affordable fashion and showing she is au courant with global trends. Her belief that Shanghai is the place for her to become a metropolitan consumer-citizen is thus confirmed. Yet it remains an open question whether migrant youth can remain content and avoid disillusionment as they grow older and shoulder increasing financial pressures to establish families amid rising income disparities in urban China.

"BMW": CARS, MOBILITY, AND SOCIAL STRATIFICATION

Migrant students generally show little interest in high-end fashion brands that are remote from their daily needs and considered inappropriate for their life stage. However, they do fancy automobile brand names, the most familiar and popular of which are Mercedes-Benz and BMW. They often point out expensive cars on the road with excitement. The following summer 2011 group discussion that spontaneously shifted from the topic of dating to cars captures this enthusiasm, especially among young men:

YUQIANG (M): Those who drive BMWs are usually *xiaokai* [children of rich people]. Those who drive a Mercedes are successful professionals.

FANZHE (M): In China, a Mercedes-Benz is more expensive.

YUQIANG: Actually the difference is not big. It all depends on which series.

M. L.: What are considered upscale car brands?

VARIOUS SPEAKERS SIMULTANEOUSLY: Porsche, Bentley, Lexus!

JIXUE (F): I like Bentley. I also like Rolls-Royce!

M. L.: What are the even more high-end brands?

VARIOUS VOICES JOINED: Lamborghini! Maserati!

YANG (F): One series of Volkswagen is also superexpensive; plus Hummer and Land Rover.

LIN (F): My brother Xin said he wanted to buy ten Lamborghinis for his wedding.[5]

JIXUE: OK, so when we get married, we'll just borrow Xin's Lamborghinis.

FANZHE: Once I saw a wedding with a Porsche in front followed by four Audis. At that time, Xin said to me, "I don't want Audis. I want Lamborghinis of different colors. Ten colors!"

YUSI (M): Listen, in our village in Fujian [Province],[6] people get all kinds of cars. Families with average wealth would use a dozen Benzes and BMWs for a wedding car parade. A long line! Usually the order goes Rolls-Royce, Mercedes-Benz, and Land Rover.

JIAWEN (M): Why not use an F1 [race car] for weddings in the future? Ten F1 race cars!

FANZHE: Even a regular Lamborghini costs more than three million.

YUSI: We should go green and go with low-carbon options: three-wheel carts. One hundred carts, ha ha! They will make great noise, and you can even save the money for firecrackers.

JIAWEN: Ride a donkey! Oh, just ride a "grass-mud horse" [caonima, an internet pun for "fuck your mother"]![7]

This animated discussion suggests the kind of "imagined community" (Anderson 1983) that these migrant students fantasize themselves to exist within—that of fast, modern, and metropolitan car users. None of the participants of this conversation drove or owned an automobile of any kind. None of their family members owned one, except Yusi's father, who had a good income from trading construction materials through his native-place networks in the early 2000s. Few of them have ever taken a taxi before. However, the lack of financial means and direct experience of driving or owning cars has not prevented them from knowing, talking, and dreaming about cars, especially new luxury cars. Nor do they have to deal with the practical aspects of owning a car, such as gas prices, registration, tax, license plates, parking, and maintenance and insurance. A luxury car to them is a symbol of a lifestyle and social position they aspire to. Luxury cars in China today, as Barthes observed about the new Citroën model at a car show, "are almost the exact equivalent of the great Gothic cathedrals . . . conceived with passion by unknown artists, and consumed in image if not in usage by a whole population which appropriates them as a purely magical object" (Barthes 1972, 88). The glitter in these migrant students' eyes reveals their deeply felt desire for a transcendent experience through the image of brand-name cars in late-socialist China.

The physical mobility and social status associated with cars have stirred a widespread desire for cars across all walks of life in postreform China. Both the production and consumption of cars have been considered the paramount symbols of and means to modernity in postreform China (J. Zhang 2009, 2019). In addition to political, economic, and international trading concerns, the Chinese obsession with the automobile follows the logic of which China as a developing country emulates the United States' mobile lifestyle to cement its acquisition of developed-nation status. The myth goes that in the United States even the poor on welfare drive cars. To catch up with the developed world means to drive like the Americans. China's participation in the "system of automobility" (Urry 2004), which includes not only car production and consumption but also related infrastructure (e.g., superhighways and energy supply), technology, and images, grants both individuals and the nation-state a ticket to join the first world and obtain a position in the global order. The Chinese state at both the central and local levels has actively promoted the development of the indigenous automobile industry. The governments have issued a series of directives and preferential policies to support the "pillar" industry of the automobile. Joint ventures of automobile makers top foreign direct investment lists. On the consumer side, Chinese newspapers have run regular columns on car models and user experience since the early 2000s. China's rising middle class proudly demonstrate their newly acquired cars in the streets, on blogs, and in wedding ceremonies (J. Zhang 2019).

Migrant youths' sensitivity to and excitement over car brand names exemplify the shared aspiration for social status through consumption of mobility via automobiles in postreform China. Chinese social life is "irreversibly locked in to the mode of mobility that automobility generates and presupposes" (Urry 2004, 227). Yet not every member of society will be able to enjoy the ride, so to speak. The differentiation among car brands reifies China's ongoing social stratification. BMW has become in internet terminology acronyms for both "business, money, woman" and "*bie mo wo*" (literally "don't touch me"), signaling simultaneously success and arrogance. There were several high-profile car accidents in the 2000s in which luxury car owners, some of whom were BMW owners, did not follow traffic rules and behaved irresponsibly after causing serious damage and even death. BMW thus has become the acronym of *bie mo wo* to mock the arrogance of luxury car owners and China's socioeconomic stratification and inequality in general.[8]

The glamour of luxury cars, so removed from everyday necessity as they are, ignites more enthusiasm in these migrant youths than the practical image of a condominium unit. The young men and women who joined the lively conversation I witnessed were not even considering that it would be unlikely for them to be able to afford a Mercedes anytime soon. The conversation ended with an abrupt shift from their luxury car fantasies to the mocking of the rudimentary three-wheeled carts that exposed the anxiety felt deeply among migrant youth about the affordability of such dreams. Jiawen, the elder son of a construction worker and a janitor originally from rural Anhui, evoked the popular internet pun of "grass-mud horse" to close the conversation. His dark humor suggests a sense of disillusion lurking beneath the consumer desire and metropolitan aspiration. Luxury cars, in effect, have become a sign of both desire and exclusion.

CONSUMER CITIZENSHIP'S CONSTRAINTS

Shanghai has been transformed from a site of production under Maoist socialism to a place of commerce and consumption after market reforms. Its skyscrapers, neon lights, shiny malls, and glittering shop windows create not only spaces of exchange but also aspirational landscapes of metropolitanism. The rapid development of commercial centers as multifunctional spaces filled with stores, restaurants, theaters, cafes, supermarkets, and karaoke bars across the city also enables those with limited spending capacities to engage in the consumption of the space itself. Living in Shanghai grants its residents both tangible and intangible consumer benefits, such as access to the greatest varieties, latest trends, and most exciting shopping experiences in China.

Second-generation migrant youth have embraced consumption as a means of constructing their identity and claiming their membership in Shanghai. They have grown up in the urban consumer culture and are not yet burdened with the financial duty of supporting a family. With financial assistance from their parents, they have become accustomed to certain urban comforts and conveniences. Mass production and market segmentation also enable them to afford brand-name household items and fashionable clothing at low prices. Such practical youthful styles help migrant youth express individuality and, more importantly, claim urban membership.

However, it remains to be seen whether migrant youth will be content with their relative lack of consumer power when they eventually work full-time and expand their interactions with other social groups. While they enjoy the advantages of a first-tier consumer market in Shanghai, they also face the increasing challenges resulting from China's rising socioeconomic disparity. The denial of full urban citizenship (i.e., a local Shanghai *hukou*) to migrants remains an impediment for them to rise above the category of both second-class citizen and second-class consumer. Discrimination against nonlocal residents in housing, schooling, employment, and social security policies makes it more difficult for these migrant youths to acquire economic security in the city, which may render their consumer desires unattainable in the long run. When they step out of the low-end market segment that they have become used to, they will have to live with the notion of "slum brands." They will also have to confront consumer desires that are mostly unfulfilled, such as for a car and an apartment of their own. This leaves them anxious and sometimes disillusioned as they enter adulthood and shoulder ever more family responsibilities. In addition, as migrant youth internalize the market hierarchy, they reinforce the underlying geopolitical and sociocultural hierarchies that place the rural hinterland and rural-*hukou* holders on the low end. Their acquired taste for urban modernity through consumption paradoxically pronounces the inferiority of rurality that they are tied to despite their identification with the city. In this sense, consuming in Shanghai is simultaneously empowering and alienating for migrant youth in China's place-specific citizenship regime.

7 "NO GOOD PROSPECTS IN SHANGHAI!"

BEI MOVED TO HER registered hometown in Anhui Province in 2009 for eighth and ninth grades, where she boarded in a local middle school. Those two years of hard work nevertheless failed to yield the result she wanted: she scored much lower on the HSEE than she had hoped for and would not get into the key academic high school in her home county. This meant it would be very unlikely for her to test into any good university after three years of high school education.[1] Disappointed and unsure of what to do next, she went back to Shanghai in June 2011 for the summer vacation and eagerly sought advice from her friends who had stayed in the city for vocational school. Bei asked them whether she should remain in Anhui in a non-key academic high school or return to Shanghai for secondary vocational education. A spirited discussion on the pros and cons of schooling in Shanghai ensued:

> JIAWEN: Which vocational schools do you think are better, the ones in your *lao-jia* [old home] or in Shanghai? Well, of course, the ones in Shanghai are better! After all, Shanghai is Shanghai.
>
> MEIXIA: Shanghai has much better conditions, much better facilities.
>
> JIAWEN: Yeah some [Shanghai vocational] schools have really good conditions. I think, in general, it's better to stay in Shanghai if you can get into a Shanghai vocational school. But let me tell you, actually we who stay in Shanghai are also facing a big problem!
>
> YANG: There aren't any good prospects in Shanghai!

JIAWEN: Right, there are no good prospects even in Shanghai. After we graduate, we are going to be stuck with jobs that pay 2,000 RMB or so per month. What good is that? [*Sighs*] Aiya, come to think of it, you'd better go home. Look at us. We study in vocational schools in Shanghai. We all seem to make choices, but the truth of the matter is that we never had any options in the first place.

YANG: Actually, staying in Shanghai and going back to the old home are not so different in the long run. But you are going to learn more in Shanghai than you would back home because you gain more social experience and there are more opportunities here. Even if you go back to Anhui and enroll in vocational school there, eventually you will still come back to Shanghai to work; the difference is you will readjust to Shanghai now rather than later.

This discussion reveals a deep frustration among migrant youth over their future after attending vocational schooling in Shanghai. Yang, Jiawen, and Meixia all seem to be convinced that Shanghai offers better educational opportunities, yet they concede that there are "no good prospects in Shanghai." What are the sources of their anxieties? How do they navigate the job market in Shanghai after they graduate? These migrant youths' school-to-work transitions illuminate how they experience the gap between youthful dreams and work experience and reconcile the two.

BETWEEN AVERSION AND ASPIRATION

As Chapter 4 demonstrates, Shanghai's educational policies have channeled migrant students to secondary vocational schools to become semiskilled workers to relieve the labor shortage in the manufacturing and service industries. Government subsidies and scholarships since 2008 have made the socially and culturally inferior vocational training more appealing and viable than it would have been otherwise, prompting a growing number of migrant students who remain in Shanghai to give up their desire for a university education and take up the free-of-charge yet socially stigmatized vocational education.

From 2011, the migrant students in this study embarked on practical training in the manufacturing and service industries through the recommendation, at no cost, of the vocational schools they had attended. Conversations about internships and future job placements become central to vocational student life in their second year. In June 2011, a group of migrant students studying in a relatively reputable technology school discussed jobs and expected salaries in the classroom:

QI: I don't know what we are going to do exactly with our *zhuanye* [specializations].

JIAWEN: I heard that chemical technology [*huaxue gongyi*] leads to front-line industrial jobs. But if your specialization is chemical analysis [*huaxue fenxi*], you get a job in the lab. That's better than a front-line job.

ML: What's your expected starting salary?

JIAWEN: 3,500–4,000 RMB. My dad makes around 3,000. He is supporting a family of four—that's a bit tough. So I would like to make a bit more than him.

QI: Now the minimum taxable wage is 3,000, so I hope to make 3,000.

MEIXIA: I think the salary of your first job is your "first bucket of gold" [*diyi tong jin*, initial capital]. Whatever it is, it's your starting point. If the job is not difficult, you get at least 1,500. The starting salary can't be a few hundred.

LIN: Ideally, I would like 5,000. I won't accept anything below 1,500.

These migrant youths were more conscious and concerned about their future incomes than they were about what jobs their majors might lead to eventually. Having grown up in the city, they are fully aware of the high costs of living in Shanghai. Even though most of them tried to cultivate realistic expectations about their starting salaries, the lowest figures were still higher than the minimum wage set by the Shanghai government, which was 1,280 RMB/month ($250/month) or 11 RMB/hour ($1.70/hour) in 2011.

Gender plays a role in income expectation. Young men who internalize the differentiation of gender roles feel more pressure to make more money not only to support themselves but also to purchase an apartment, find a partner, and establish a family. Jiawen's family came from rural Anhui and was financially constrained due to his parents having an unplanned second son. When I asked him about his ideal starting salary, his answer immediately associated his expectation with gender difference: "For girls, the family is like a warm harbor where they find comfort. For a man, the family is where you bring money to. At least my dad thinks a daughter belongs to another family, while a son is one's own and should shoulder more pressure." His female classmate Meixia agreed with him instantly: "Male students have more pressure. See, he [Jiawen] needs to find a wife, but girls can marry themselves off. For girls, the pressure is a lot less and it is less important for them to support a family."

Both Jiawen and Meixia naturalized the principle of patrilocal marriage that emphasizes a man's financial obligations to a conjugal relationship and a woman's integration into her husband's family. The sexist differentiation in marital practices partly explains Jiawen's stronger anxiety about his starting salary. Young women experience much less financial pressure because of the patriarchal subordination of women in marriage. Hence, they seem to be more willing to accept a salary that barely exceeds minimum wage even though their ideal income might be twice as much.

Young migrant men, under the pressure for men to earn more in order to establish a family, often entertain the idea of entrepreneurship. During a group discussion in June 2011 with the graduates of Class Five from the Bridge School, Junjie and Yalu discussed their anxiety over the gap between expected salary and desired income:

> YALU: My expected starting salary is around 3,000. But, you know, it is impossible to afford an apartment by *dagong* [doing work for others]; you have to *ziji dang laoban* [be one's own boss].
>
> JUNJIE: If you *dagong*, it would be an infinite number of years before you could afford an apartment. I need to earn my "first bucket of gold" to do business. Yet there are a lot of uncertainties. Who knows? [*Laughter*]

Both young men realize the difficulty of accumulating enough savings and acquiring home ownership in Shanghai through regular salaried work. Their evocation of the catchphrases the "first bucket of gold" and "being one's own boss" demonstrates how persuasive the capitalist logic of capital accumulation and labor exploitation has become in postreform China. Deng Xiaoping, the mastermind behind China's economic reforms, famously coined the slogan "it is glorious to get rich" (*zhifu guangrong*) to push for more drastic marketization measures in the mid-1980s. The mass media regularly disseminates stories of how Chinese billionaires earned their "first buckets of gold" and were thus rewarded for their entrepreneurial efforts. The self-made newly wealthy have become role models for Chinese youth, including second-generation migrant youth. Being a boss to have control over the gains of one's own labor and even exploit others' labor value has been implicitly hailed as a desirable means to realize self-transformation and national development in postreform China.[2]

Having experienced the life in a family-operated small business also contributes to many migrant youth's aspiration for self-employment and entrepreneurship at an early stage. Yalu's father runs a kiln that makes bricks in Jiangsu Province and sells them in Shanghai; Junjie's father is a subcontractor who makes money on construction projects in Shanghai. Both are examples of migrant entrepreneurs who have succeeded in transforming themselves into "bosses" and disengaging themselves from heavy manual work during China's rapid urbanization. In this study, more than half of the migrant families engage in small business for a living, working as subcontractors, traders, storekeepers, and street peddlers. Most of them are not as financially successful as the fathers of Yalu and Junjie, but they nevertheless tend to believe that they are better off being self-employed than being a salaried worker in a factory.

For migrant youth, "being one's own boss" has its appeal particularly as it stands in stark contrast with *dagong* (literally "working for others"). Because of rural-urban disparity and labor exploitation, rural migrant workers have been suffering from extremely exploitative labor conditions for more than two decades (C. K. Lee 1998; Pun 2005a, 2005b; Pun and Chan 2012, 2013; Pun and Lu 2010, 2007; Solinger 1999; Swider 2015; H. Yan 2003, 2007, 2008). Although the term *dagong* carries a sense of autonomy when compared to *mingong* (peasant worker), *dagong* is widely viewed as an inferior and unpromising option for migrants who have no better alternatives in the city.

Ironically, averting waged manual work among second-generation migrant youth is reinforced by first-generation migrants' avoidance of discussing the hardship of *dagong*. Xian, the elder daughter of migrants from rural Jiangxi Province who run a small packing business inside their rented courtyard house, learned about what *dagong* could entail from *Last Train Home*, a well-acclaimed 2010 documentary film on the internet.[3] The documentary records the struggles of a migrant family; the parents of the family migrated to Guang-dong Province for jobs in a garment factory, leaving behind two children in rural Sichuan for many years. What Xian saw in the documentary shocked her, causing her to vow to never *dagong* in the future: "I grew really upset. I thought to myself: this is what *dagong* is like! I would rather die than *dagong*! I have never thought living in a factory dorm would be like that, having to wash my own clothes every day, on top of all the exhausting work."

Xian's emotional response to the documentary stems from her ignorance of the typical *dagong* life. Though labeled "peasant workers' child" on official documents and media, she has nevertheless grown up in relative ease. Although her family's financial situation has not been great by any means, and, unlike urban only children, she must compete with her younger brother for her parents' attention (see Chapter 2), she has been sheltered from the hardship and volatility of the migrant livelihood her parents went through. Her relatives also seldom told her what *dagong* life was like.

> All my cousins *dagong*, including one cousin who is only one day older than me. Of course, my parents wouldn't let me *dagong*; but I thought *dagong* was fun. . . . My eldest cousin went to *dagong*, and every time she came back home, she would have a lot of new pretty clothes. So I thought *dagong* was nice and fun. When my other cousins came back, they would not talk about *dagong* either. We would play, watch and chat about TV dramas together. So I didn't know about their *dagong* life.

The collective silence or refusal among migrants like Xianjing's cousins and other relatives to talk about their *dagong* experiences is not uncommon. The silence suggests a subconscious effort to forget or hide the hardships, frustrations, and boredom of migrant work and life. They instead watch TV dramas and buy new clothes to embody urban modernity. Hairong Yan's study of migrant women from Anhui who work as domestic servants in Beijing finds that many migrant women feel compelled to erase any traces of migrant work experience and "fashion a respectable self-image through consumption when they return home" (2008, 180). Their untold experiences become "subterranean experiences" generated in the market economy but are "not justly accounted for by the mainstream discourse of market development" (H. Yan 2005, 4).

To make things worse, the mainstream discourse in postreform China is a story of success: the market economy offers opportunities for success as long as one tries hard to acquire the right "human qualities," or *suzhi*, the amorphous term referring to one's innate and nurtured physical, psychological, intellectual, and moral qualities. Individuals are solely responsible for their own *suzhi* and achievements in the prevailing logic of (self-)development, where public discourse subdues and even erases individual struggles and personal suffering. This represents an ethos of "subsumption," in which "the extraction of the surplus value of labor is hidden and suppressed by the overvaluation of consumption and its neoliberal ideologies of self-transformation" (Pun 2003, 469). However, such conscious erasure and self-representation often obscure, even misdirect, the expectations and understandings of *dagong* of second-generation migrant youth. The following sections on migrant youths' work experiences during state-mandated internships and first full-time jobs illustrate the resultant ripple effect of disappointment.

ON-THE-JOB TRAINING

China's secondary vocational school curriculum requires its students to have at least one semester of on-the-job training (*shixi*, internship) in a factory or company before they can graduate. The rationale is to help vocational students gain both the technical and social skills necessary for the real working environment so that they can be immediately employable upon graduation. However, the presumed school-to-work transition is fractured because of the incongruence between its stated aims and the actual practices.

Several vocational school staff in charge of student job placements admitted to me that such on-the-job training is impractical at best. They saw it as an inevitable outcome of socioeconomic changes and educational reforms in the postreform era. The structural shift from a socialist planned economy to a market-oriented one has made the pursuit of profit the undisputed goal for companies. The former "iron rice bowl," which linked practical training directly with long-term full-time employment, has been broken, reducing the incentive for companies to invest in student interns, most of whom will leave for other jobs or further education. It has become a challenge for administrators of vocational schools to have enough companies interested in taking in and mentoring vocational students. Meanwhile, the expansion of university admission since 1999 has pushed secondary vocational education further down the hierarchy in China's education system. Those who fail to get into academic high schools but are unwilling to start working immediately enter secondary vocational schools. Those students are often perceived as "bad students," lacking intellectual capacity and self-discipline (see Chapter 4). The teaching and training they receive in secondary vocational schools also fall short of rigor. This also makes it acceptable for companies to treat vocational student interns as cheap temporary labor instead of prospective employees.

Students majoring in rather specific, technical subjects, such as mechanics, cooking, lathe operation, and automobile repair are more likely to be recruited by companies requiring those particular skills. Due to the lack of skilled workers and technicians in Shanghai, manufacturing companies generally have stronger incentives to recruit and retain student interns with the hope that qualified ones might stay on as full-time employees after their internship. However, the companies often fail to provide sufficient incentives for senior workers to mentor interns. Many internships become more about familiarizing vocational students with the menial work conditions they are expected to face upon graduation than about honing their professional skills.

Although practical training tends to be less demanding than full-time jobs, most students find their jobs boring and meaningless. Junjie, a male student from Class Five at the Bridge School who majored in automobile repair in vocational school, commented dispassionately on his first training stint at a truck manufacturer: "*Shangban* [going to work, taking work shifts] is just tedious; you do the same thing every day." Such a sense of boredom has been widely reported among vocational students. Gong, Junjie's classmate from Class Five, specialized in computers in vocational school because of his interest in computer games. He was assigned to an internship in an electronics company that packaged and stored Apple iPhones. His job was to stack packaged iPhones in a warehouse. He complained about his sore arms and said he felt like a robot. He quit the internship after a month. The monotonous nature of manual work and often poor social relations with senior workers aggravates the students' aversion to manual labor. Contrary to the state's intention to train migrant youth to be "new generation peasant workers" (see Chapter 4), the on-the-job training reinforces the appeal of becoming one's own boss.

A large percentage of internships are in low-skill service sectors, bearing little resemblance with vocational majors. Vocational students specializing in accounting, finance, logistics, business English, and other "soft" subjects usually end up working as cashiers at McDonald's, receptionists in call centers, servers in hotels, salespeople in supermarkets, and so forth. Min, a female student who was born in 1996 in rural Sichuan but grew up in Shanghai with her factory-worker parents, majored in hotel management. In the spring of 2016, she spent half a year interning at a five-star hotel through her vocational school's recommendation. Although this arrangement was considered to be a good match for her major, she still complained how her internship was irrelevant to her major. "I thought hotel management was about management, but I found during my internship that it was merely about holding plates." She also noticed that the hotel had many interns, and "even the college interns were working just as servants."

Min's disappointment over the incongruence between her major and her internship experience is common among vocational students. The misleading names of the majors and lack of career counseling in middle schools and vocational schools contributed to her misunderstanding of the major. However, as Min herself admitted, her vocational school did teach her how to fold napkins, place plates, and other service skills. She felt unprepared for what her internship required her to do largely because of her unrealistic expectation. These students' expectations of work life, which were higher than what the job market could offer, inevitably resulted in disappointment. Several job placement officers and employers also complained to me how youth in Shanghai, both locals and migrants, are "spoiled" and have unrealistically high expectations. "What other work could they do?" asked one vocational school teacher in frustration during a 2015 interview.

China labor scholars argue that a "student labor regime" in postreform China has emerged through which local states channel vocational students toward work as cheap labor for private companies (J. Chan 2017; J. Chan, Ngai, and Selden 2015; Koo 2015; Pun and Chan 2012). In the face of higher labor costs and increased mobility, local state agents, such as labor and education bureaus, work together to attract investment and boost local economic development by sending students to work as interns. Foxconn, the world's largest electronics manufacturer, for instance, receives tens of thousands of "student workers" every year in its factory compounds. These "student workers," many of whom are under the legal minimum working age of sixteen, endure long working hours, harsh labor conditions, and little personal freedom for several months to a year to get an internship certificate so that they can graduate from vocational school. The collusion between local states and global capital in turning vocational school students into slave-like labor in the name of practical training exposes one of the particularly dark sides of China's "state capitalism."

School-recommended internships in Shanghai are not as repressive as those situated in factories in South China. Unlike the Foxconn student workers, who are mostly from rural areas and study in vocational schools in job-scarce hinterland locales, Shanghai students, both locals and migrants, are better positioned to negotiate their internship options. Shanghai offers many more work opportunities in the manufacturing and service industries in the first place. The fact that vocational students have grown up in China's most prosperous city and enjoyed better living conditions also makes it harder for vocational schools and companies to coerce them and their parents into agreeing to harsh terms. In addition, the strict implementation of the one-child policy in Shanghai has made the notion of a prolonged childhood more firmly established than in rural areas (see Chapter 2). Secondary vocational students, between the ages of fifteen and eighteen, are widely considered too young to work full-time and too immature for substantive tasks.

Knowing the strong parental preference for keeping their only child in Shanghai, the city's public secondary vocational schools would not send their students to intern outside the municipality. Rather, most schools offer their students an alternative called "self-administered employment" (*zizhu jiuye*) in addition to "school-recommended internships." Students that opt for "self-administered internships" obtain internships through their family or personal networks. So long as they can produce some proof issued by a company of having been engaged in internship endeavors, they can earn credits for practical training to graduate. Local students with strong family networks tend to take advantage of this option. Migrant students, whose parents have much weaker local connections in Shanghai, can also make use of this alternative if they quit school-recommended internships but find other part-time jobs through classmates or job-search websites.

However, the relative ease of finding an internship cannot override the disappointment experienced by these students. Besides internships being tangential to the students' majors, internships pay much less than regular full-time positions. The compensation ranged mostly from 500 RMB to 2,000 RMB ($70–$310) per month in the 2010s. In some cases, no salary was paid at all, and interns were reimbursed for meals and transportation only. They could barely support themselves during the internship and have to rely heavily on their parents to support their accommodation, food, and personal consumption. Min, who interned in a five-star hotel, received a monthly paycheck of slightly over 1,000 RMB (around $150), which she considered "very, very low." Her salary was far below Shanghai's minimum wage, which was 2,190 RMB ($318) in 2016. Min was neither spared from nor compensated for overtime work.

> I was new there, knowing little as a student. I had to stand in high heels for a dozen hours every day. I found it exhausting. Since it was a five-star hotel, high-ranking officials like the city mayor often came and we had to stand to *yingbing* [welcome guests]. We seldom had any days off. Sometimes there would be no off days for months. I worked every day. And there was no overtime pay, not even for extra work during holidays.

To a large extent, the criticism against the "student labor regime" that uses students as cheap labor continues to be valid.

EMBARKING ON FULL-TIME JOBS

After completing practical training, vocational school students may sign a formal contract with their current employers and become full-time workers; those who do not want to stay on can return to their schools for new recommendations, unless they prefer to look for employment on their own. The vocational schools no longer guarantee job placements (*baofenpei*) since the late-1990s market reforms shattered the socialist "iron rice bowl" and the lineal school-to-work transition. However, the responsibility continues to belong to public vocational schools to help their graduates find job placements and meet the expectations of both parents and local governments, thereby solving the problem of youth (un)employment. In other words, the schools still serve as paternalistic labor agents. The logic behind such endeavors is market oriented, though: a high job placement rate is key for the vocational schools to recruit enough students and secure stable revenue. The staff in charge of student recruitment, stationed in a "student recruitment and placement office" (*zhaosheng jiuye bangongshi*), manages graduate placement as well. Nearly every vocational school's recruiting brochure (*zhaosheng jianzhang*) boasts a "99.99%" job placement rate. Whether this figure is inflated or not, it testifies to the centrality of placements to a vocational school's survival and success in Shanghai's increasingly competitive education market.

Academic performance remains the most important criteria in school recommendations of students for a job, even though academic learning is no longer emphasized in secondary vocational education. There is no systematic résumé submission or standardized recruiting process; placement officers usually inform homeroom teachers whenever they are contacted by liaison companies and ask the teachers to recommend students for interviews. The teachers act as gatekeepers, screening students for prospective employers. "Good" students who have performed better academically, obeyed school rules, or have maintained good relations with the teachers get interviews with the more desirable companies that offer higher salaries and more job security. As to students that have average to poor academic performances or conduct, the teachers usually follow the principle of geographic proximity, recommending students to companies that are close to their residences. If a student is unsuccessful at an interview, the school will try to arrange another interview until the student finds a placement, unless the student opts out of the school recommendation system.

Lin, the elder daughter of a migrant vendor couple from rural Jiangsu Province, enrolled in a well-reputed secondary vocational school on the west side of Shanghai in 2011. She majored in chemical analysis, which her family believed would teach her some "hard" skills and could lead to some office work. She performed well in examinations and received scholarships from the school. She also served as a student assistant to help her homeroom teacher to manage student affairs. Lin was, thus, recommended for an interview with a Fortune 500 international chemical corporation for on-the-job training. She did well in the interview and interned as a clerk in its production planning unit for a full year. Upon graduation in 2014, Lin was offered a three-year contract to continue working in the same unit. At that time, the plant had just expanded the work floor that her unit oversaw, and the unit manager was able to arrange a new full-time position for her so the unit could meet the rising production demands. She felt very lucky to get the job, which was widely considered to be one of the best placements any of her classmates had attained. The company offered a good benefits package, including a transportation subsidy of 500 RMB ($70) and free lunches and dinners for overtime work. More importantly, the position was a "cleaner" job in an air-conditioned office on the second floor, unlike jobs in the polluted workshops on the first floor. Dan, another intern from Lin's school, was assigned to the plant's laboratory. In addition to breathing in plastic particles dispersed in the air on that floor, Dan had to take on three shifts and navigate a more than an hour-long daily commute by bus. She thus left the plant after completing her internship. She was immediately hired by a smaller private company as a chemical analyst because of her internship experience with the big plant.

Lin and Dan represent the minority who get decent on-the-job training and stay in full-time posts in an industry closely related to their chosen majors—unlike most vocational school graduates, who end up working jobs that bear little relevance to their specializations. As mentioned in Chapter 4, many students lacked sufficient knowledge when choosing their specializations in the first place. After graduation, these specializations, in any case, rarely made any difference to their career development. Most available entry-level jobs look uninteresting to these aspiring graduates, who still entertain the prospects of getting higher degrees or becoming their own bosses. Poorly administered, highly exploitative on-the-job training experiences exacerbate the students' sense of disappointment with the promised practicality and future prospects of their vocational training. After interning in a five-star hotel, for instance, Min decided to enter junior college and switch her major to administrative management, which she thought would allow her to "at least sit in an office and have an easier job."

Clean, less-laborious office work is equally preferred by male students. Fan, a young man whose parents came from rural Anhui, went to study auto repair in vocational school in 2010. His parents, who sold fruit in a market, thought that this major would guarantee Fan a job in Shanghai's rapidly growing auto retail and repair industry, since car ownership in the city had skyrocketed. In 2013, he was recommended by his vocational school to intern in a 4S ("sales, service, survey, and spare parts") car shop under the Buick franchise. Fan learned electrical and mechanical skills in the workshop in the rear of the 4S store. His on-the-job training lasted a year and paid 800 RMB ($130) per month with meager transportation subsidies. Afterward, Fan signed a full-time three-year contract, with his monthly wage increased to 3,200 RMB ($515), including transportation and meal subsidies. However, Fan stayed on only for six months. He complained about how tiring the job was and expressed his concern about the high risk of injury in the workshop. He was equally upset that his hands were always dirty after work. To make things worse, the constant disputes between the business department at the front and the workshop at the back wore him out.

> The receptionists sitting out front care too much about the customers and not enough about us. For instance, no orders can be taken thirty minutes before the workshop closes, according to company policy, yet the receptionists take orders as they come, completely disregarding the rule. We at the back end up having to work overtime while those in the office get off work as usual. And we are often underpaid for our overtime work.

The conflict between the front and the back of the 4S store exemplifies how manual labor has been pushed to the bottom of the value chain in global capitalism. Working-class jobs have become increasingly mechanic, repetitive, and demeaning. Being a worker has lost its socialist revolutionary appeal in postreform China, where doing business and making money dominate daily conversations and the social milieu.

Fan decided that he would not just accept becoming a manual worker for life, like he was expected to, as his destiny. In spring 2016, he joined a former classmate to become an insurance salesman. His company was located in one of Shanghai's major commercial centers in Pudong. After the first two days of training, Fan was required to show up at work only from 11:00 A.M. to 1:00 P.M. to study policies and make phone calls; for the rest of the day, he was on his own, expected to go out and make sales. Fan found this arrangement of flexible working hours and lack of supervision refreshing at first. Soon, however, the pressure to find customers and fill quotas began to mount. He managed only one sale during the three months. Seeing no future in that position, Fan quit, along with his friend, who was not having much success either. Fan searched for jobs online but fell victim to an employment scam that lured him and his friend all the way to Shandong Province. They narrowly escaped but couldn't recoup the 6,000 RMB ($850) deposit paid and travel costs. In the end, Fan returned to Shanghai and through a former colleague joined a 4S store under the General Motors franchise in late summer 2016, once again becoming an auto mechanic.

As of the summer of 2017, Fan had remained in that mechanic position out of practical needs. Rarely do Fan and his male classmates show much pride in their manual labor work. Masculinity has been delinked from manual labor partly because of the feminized assembly lines in Chinese export-oriented manufacturing plants (Pun 2004, 2005b). These young men also see heavy manual work, especially jobs in construction and auto repair that do not pay much, as obstacles to their fashionable pursuit of fair skin and slim figures, a style they first embraced in middle school through watching East Asian romantic dramas and hip-hop music videos. The migrant youths' aversion to suntanned skin, heat, and dirt contributes to their preferences for clean indoor jobs (Lan 2014). They try to avoid as much as they can the "3D" (dirty, dangerous, and demeaning) jobs that first-generation rural-to-urban migrants like their parents often take on for a living, although as shown in Fan's case the alternatives for them are often limited.

CONFRONTING LABOR MARKET SEGMENTATION

In addition to low wages and undercompensated overtime work, migrant youth have to face outright discrimination in getting internships and jobs particularly because of their *waidi* (outsider) status. As the labor market segmentation theory (Piore 1979) points out, it is common for migrants to be channeled into secondary or informal sectors of the labor market. What makes the case of Chinese migrant youth stand out is "the central role of the state in channeling and constraining peasant migrants to specific sectors and jobs" (C. Fan 2008, 8). Although the labor market in China has transformed from being centrally administered to more market oriented, and a local urban *hukou* is no longer necessary for holding a job in the city, *hukou*-related discrimination continues to segment the job market (Cai, Park, and Zhao 2008; K. W. Chan 2010; C. Fan 2002). Local urbanites, considered to be more stable and connected, are preferred for well-paid professional and administrative jobs. Big state-owned enterprises and state agencies employ migrant youth only as temporary workers and bar them from those contracted positions that come with the possibility for promotion. The Beijing municipal government once issued a list of 103 job categories for which migrants are not legally eligible (Eckholm 2000). In Shanghai, only 8.7 percent of the migrant population was employed in state enterprises according to a 2005 survey (Ruan 2009, 37).

The relative ease of securing job placement through a vocational school's network is often undermined by the *hukou* restrictions and social biases against *waidiren*. Junjie learned that one local classmate got an internship at a profitable General Motors joint venture in Shanghai. The internship later turned into a full-time job as an auto repairman paying a starting salary of 4,000 RMB ($600) per month and increasing to over 8,000 RMB ($1,150) after two years. This elicited much envy from Junjie. He had hoped to get a position in the joint venture as well, but his Anhui *hukou* prevented him from even securing an interview: "That company selects people on two criteria: first, a Shanghai local *hukou*—they do not take *waidi* students. Second, you have to be over eighteen. I meet neither criterion."

Ming, Junjie's middle school classmate, confirmed Junjie's observation of *hukou*-based discrimination when speaking of his own job interview experience:

> That factory [a foreign company in one of Pudong's industrial zones] is disgusting. It made me feel that there is *guijian zhifen* (explicit difference between the rich and the poor). We all got in the first round, and we were all waiting in the conference room, but then, out of nowhere, we were told that we came from *waidi*, and we were taken outside to somewhere like a canteen. Only the Shanghai students stayed in the conference room for the examination. They treated us really badly.

The indignity experienced in such cases of explicitly targeted discrimination against them as migrant students is particularly upsetting and demoralizing. The spatial separation along the *bendi-waidi* binary that Ming and his Class Five classmates had already experienced in middle school (see Chapter 3) has, they find, followed them into the job market.

Local and migrant workers are also subjected to differentiation regarding rights and benefits within their places of work (F. Wang 2008; F. Wang, Zuo, and Ruan 2002). A survey by Yu Chen and Caroline Hoy (2008) found that in 2005

rural migrants earned around 44 percent less than local workers in the manufacturing sector in Shanghai, and discrimination explained about 45 percent of
the cases of such wage differences. Because of *hukou*-based differentiation in
employment and welfare policies, private enterprises actually may prefer migrant employees to reduce labor costs. They exploit the migrants' lack of legal,
political, and social supports, offering them lower wages and withholding from
them full employee benefits. An experienced student recruitment and placement officer at the Newtown Vocational School complained about such skewed
employment practices while lamenting the difficulty of finding placements for
his "spoiled" local students after the 2008 global financial crisis:

> Nowadays all private factories want to employ *waidiren* and people from
> Chongming Island [Shanghai's last rural county located at the mouth of the
> Yangtze River]. First of all, they can "eat bitterness" [*chiku*, endure hardship).[4]
> Second, they have fewer alternatives so that they don't easily quit a job. Third,
> they cost less, as the company only needs to get the lowest "nonlocal worker
> insurance" for outsiders, about 200 RMB [$30] per month, whereas for the
> *bendiren* [local residents], the cost of insurance per person is about 600 RMB
> [$90] per month.

When asked whether locals have any advantage, the officer pointed out the
perceptions of *waidiren* as the inferior "rural Other": "They are dumb, slow at
learning and adapting. Their hygiene and mind-set are also problematic." The
urban-oriented perception that equates rurality with a lack of intelligence and
civility resonates with the *suzhi* discourse, which disparagingly puts Chinese
peasants at the bottom of the human quality scale (Jacka 2009; Murphy 2004;
Sigley 2009). It helps to attribute the devaluation and exploitation of migrant
labor to some presumably innate personal deficiencies. Such sociocultural
prejudice, in addition to institutional discrimination, reinforces employment
discrimination and wage discrepancies. Although migrant workers still bear
the label of a "floating population" from the 1990s, employers in Shanghai think
that migrants are more committed than their local peers to stay in low-level
positions because they lack resources in the city. The belief that migrants as the
"rural Other" can put up with hardship unlike local people is used to justify
smaller insurance payments, in turn weakening the migrant workers' socioeconomic security, forcing them to swallow more bitterness. This contributes to a
vicious circle that deepens the social perception that migrant workers are the
inferior rural Other.

INVESTING IN CONTINUED EDUCATION

Out of their unrelenting encounters with educational and labor segmentation pinned on their nonlocal status, migrant youth grow increasingly anxious and discontent as they become more embedded in the labor market. Even though she had a full-time office job in a Fortune 500 company, Lin complained frequently and at length about her low salary after two years of full-time work. She was paid about half of what her colleagues made for the same position because of her low educational credentials.

> I talked to the head several times [about my salary], but in vain. They can only give me this much because of the ranking system. But I think I am doing no less than anyone else. Because of my low educational qualifications, my base salary is lower. There are huge differences. University graduates at the production lines start at 4,000 RMB, and many get higher than 5,000 RMB. There's little I can do about it. Many of my colleagues in the office told me that I am already lucky to work in the office despite my educational background. "Just finish the three-year contract and you can look for other jobs," they say.

Like many of her friends and other migrant students in Shanghai, Lin sought a way out of her precarious position by pursuing a higher degree. Forced off the formal higher-education path of *gaokao* because of *hukou* restrictions, Lin and her former classmates feel insecure and disadvantaged in the job market. "I feel that nowadays almost everyone has a college degree. I've read in a newspaper that even a subway driver job asks for at least a college degree." Yalu, the only son of a kiln owner from rural Jiangsu and graduate of Class Five at the Bridge School, also noted with dismay the phenomenon of degree inflation. He felt obliged to obtain extra certificates to make up for his limited formal education.

Secondary vocational schools embrace this "certification fever" (*wenpinre*, avid pursuit of educational qualifications) in urban China. They offer an alternative to on-the-job training for their seniors: senior students who enroll in a full-time *gaofuban* (prep classes for academic high school students who do not perform well in the NUEE or vocational students who want to take the NUEE to get into university) can be excused from the on-the-job training requirement. The schools count any students taking *gaofuban* as graduates "having a placement" (*youchulu*); such is their way of justifying offering *gaofuban* and boosting their overall "job placement rate."

Many schools have profited from students' and parents' insecurities by offering their own *gaofuban* on campus. Offering such classes becomes a profitable business: the quality of teaching is kept very low, but tuition fees are high. A full-time yearlong *gaofuban* easily costs 6,000 to 10,000 RMB ($900–$1,400). *Gaofuban* is designed to drill students on Chinese, English, mathematics, and other academic subjects that are examined in *sanxiaosheng gaokao* (the college entrance examination for secondary vocational students). However, since the requirements for these subjects for vocational schools are much more relaxed than in the academic track, vocational students often have a hard time coping in *gaofuban*, which are crash courses. Hardly any of the student's genuine learning needs are addressed. Both Junjie and Yalu enrolled in full-time *gaofuban* instead of on-the-job training in the last year of their vocational education. They found experiences with *gaofuban* very unfulfilling. "The teachers would highlight all the content to be examined. It was all rote memorization. It is very meaningless," recalled Junjie. Disorganized, lacking substance, and ineffective, the curriculum gave him the impression that he was on an "expensive vacation."

In recognition of the profit-driven nature of continuing education, both Junjie and Yalu enrolled in adult junior colleges (*chengren dazhuan*) part-time after taking the *sanxiaosheng gaokao* with the support of their parents. By then they had lowered their expectations for education, cynically regarding it as merely utilitarian.

> JUNJIE: *Shangban* [going to work] is just tedious. You do the same thing day in, day out. *Shangxue* [going to school] is also boring, but at least you get to take different courses.
>
> M. L.: So would you prefer *shangxue*?
>
> JUNJIE: No. I feel I am no longer of that age. Even if I were allowed to study [in an academic senior high school], I'm afraid I would not have enough motivation [to study]. You need to have specific goals to study, or it would be meaningless. I take adult junior college only because I want to have a higher degree to improve my job prospect. Anyway, it does not take much time—one day per week, from 9:00 A.M. to 2:00 P.M., 20,000 RMB for tuition in total. I think even if you learn a lot in university, the knowledge might be useless. Many jobs asking for university graduates can be done by any junior middle school graduate after two or three days' training. The key is to have *guanxi* [connections, network].

More than two-thirds of the interlocutors in this study either attended *gaofuban* to attend a junior college as full-time students or enrolled in part-time junior college courses while taking up an internship or a full-time job. The latter option is appealing to those who have worked but nevertheless want another degree in order to switch jobs or get promoted. They only need to attend classes during weekends at a registered junior college and take examinations administered by the colleges. Once they pass all the exams, which usually take two to three years depending on individual capacity and commitment, they would obtain an adult junior college degree. Those who are ambitious can pay for another round of courses and tests over two to three years to achieve *zhuanshengben* (an upgrade from a junior college degree to a university degree).

Detailed cost analysis reveals the internalization of the market logic of human capital investment among these students. As seen in Junjie's comment, most of them take a practical and even cynical approach to their pursuit of a junior college degree. They refuse to romanticize the power of knowledge as the state did in the early reform era. Tertiary education has been losing both prestige and appeal due to its high costs and low returns since the marketization and expansion reforms took effect in 1998. That many university graduates cannot find well-paid jobs in the late 2000s has fueled social disappointment with higher education. Junjie's emphasis on *guanxi* also shows migrant youths' disillusion with the ideal of meritocracy that is believed to be central to China's examination-oriented education system.

The cynical attitude toward *gaofuban* does little to curb or slow migrant youths' pursuit of certificates, which still have practical allure. The belief that they can *tiaocao* (hop over or switch to another job) with more ease after getting a college degree lures them and their parents to invest money and time in this highly commercialized subset of tertiary education. After all, it offers migrant students who are forced off the *gaokao* path a chance to meet the minimum criteria to compete for office work in the credential-based society that urban China has become.

LOOMING PRESSURE OF ADULTHOOD

Though better off in both absolute and relative terms than the older generations, Chinese youth born in the late 1980s and 1990s—migrant youth included—often call themselves "Alexanders," as the name sounds very close to the Chinese phrase *yali shanda* (literally "mountain-like pressure"). For them, China's integration into the global capitalist market has brought not only enormous economic development and rapid wealth accumulation but also escalating competition in education, employment, consumption, and marriage.

Migrant youth feel even more pressure, and they feel it sooner than their local peers in Shanghai. Barred from taking the HSEE in Shanghai, migrant students embark on an earlier transition into work and adulthood. Those who gain a cushion period in secondary vocational school and junior college with the support of their parents also have to think about their future before long.

> JUNJIE: Now there is not a lot of pressure yet; but life will become fatiguing soon after we have jobs.
>
> M. L.: Do you have any concerns now?
>
> JUNJIE: The biggest concern is whether I can support myself in the future. I am worried that my spending will be limited and it will be humiliating to go back to my rural home if I cannot make big money. . . . If you go back to [your] rural home, people would say: this kid moved to Shanghai at the age of three, now look at him.
>
> M. L.: Do you often go back home?
>
> JUNJIE: I go back on Chinese New Year's. There, people compare. Everyone compares, right? They mainly compare which household has more money. It is hard to hide the smell of money. If you have money, word spreads fast in the village. Most villagers who have energy migrate out to *dagong*.

A major concern for the future among these second-generation migrant youth is their earning capability in comparative terms. Not only do they compare and compete with urban peers, but they also face social expectations back in their home villages, where most capable laborers migrate to the cities for a better living. Migrants often invest tens of thousands of renminbi to rebuild their houses in their home villages as a statement of their wealth and success in the cities. The assumption that migration brings both money and self-improvement is embedded in the metadiscourse of development and leaves little room for migrants to afford or admit failure.

The difficulty of settling down in Shanghai exacerbates migrant youths' anxiety over their earning power. Being fully aware of the skyrocketing housing prices in Shanghai and their limited job opportunities and prospects for good salaries, migrant youth often turn bitter and sarcastic about their future. Jiawen, who claimed that there were no good prospects in Shanghai in the opening conversation, was once asked to talk about the dream of buying an apartment in Shanghai during the shooting of a popular TV reality show *Good Professional*. The show featured people from different walks of life competing for jobs in front of potential employers and a dozen commentators. With a recommendation from NGO J, to which Jiawen had grown very attached after joining its free tutorials and extracurricular activities, he and his mother applied to compete on the show for a part-time milk delivery job after he finished the first year of vocational school. When the show was in preparation, the TV director suggested to Jiawen that he play up his desire to settle down in the city in order to gain the audience's sympathy:

> The program producer said to me, "You should talk with exaggerated emotions, crying while smiling. You should say that your mom has been working in Shanghai for years; she worked hard to make money and to pay off debts because your family built a house back home and owed money. Now, though the debts have been paid off, she still needs to support her two sons' schooling. She came to apply for the job in the hope that she would help you settle down in Shanghai, to help buy an apartment." [*Laughter*] I thought that was too much. [The rest of his friends in the room joined in the laughter.] Even if I sold my dad for money, it would not be possible for me to buy an apartment in Shanghai. But the producer said, "It doesn't matter; you don't need to mean it; you just need to say it." [*Hysterical laughter*]

Jiawen could not help but laugh at the suggestion of selling the dream of buying an apartment in Shanghai to garner public sympathy. He found it difficult, almost ridiculous, to think like that. His family relied on his father's meager salary from odd jobs, which was around 3,000 RMB ($400) per month at that time. The family of four had been sharing a single room for almost a decade to save on rent. Jiawen would likely work as a lathe operator after graduating from vocational school, earning 3,000 RMB per month. It was not feasible for the family to plan to buy an apartment, which could easily cost 1 million RMB ($140,000) in Shanghai.

After Jiawen started his on-the-job training in 2015, he rode his bicycle for over an hour to work in order to save money for his younger brother's schooling fees. In 2016, his parents pulled together all their savings of the past two decades to purchase a two-bedroom apartment in their hometown in Anhui for retirement. When asked what his plans were for the future, Jiawen often sounded evasive. He would sometimes claim that he would not stay in Shanghai in response to living costs in the city; as a young man, he is particularly concerned with the difficulties involved with setting up his own family, given that social norms foster the expectation that men pay for or contribute more to an apartment purchase, which is seen as, ideally, necessary for him to get married.

However, he seldom visits his home village, and he does not see himself living with his parents in the newly purchased apartment either. He has been study-ing to be certificated as an accountant while also pursuing a part-time junior college degree in Shanghai. The pressure to support himself and his younger brother compels him to remain invested in developing a Shanghai future and maintaining his social network; yet it also alienates him from the city.

Not only the children of waged migrant workers but also those of migrant businessmen share Jiawen's conflicted relationship with Shanghai. Yusi and Yuqiang, two brothers hailing from rural Fujian, where there is a long history of migration and most villagers are engaged in trade, are acquaintances of Jiawen and Lin. Their father used to trade construction materials through an extensive home-origin network, making a living through speculating on the stone and steel markets across China. Financially, the brothers were much more confident about settling down in Shanghai because of their parents' fi-nancial support. Their parents purchased an apartment for them in Jinshan, an island under the jurisdiction of Shanghai where housing prices were still low, about 5,000 RMB per square meter in 2015. Nevertheless, they still felt uncer-tain about the future. According to the brothers, their home village was flooded with brand-name cars and "false" money because the businesses of the locals involved predatory high-interest loans.[5] They are aware of the risks involved with such financial operations because China's economic structure and finan-cial policies are fundamentally suspicious of and restrictive to the small-scale private sector (Yasheng Huang 2008).[6]

Instead of following in their father's footsteps and going into the trading business, the brothers embarked on a brand-new path into the high-tech ser-vice industry, which had only recently emerged during Shanghai's economic restructuring. Avid video gamers, the brothers seized an opportunity in the early 2010s to make money by playing online games for long hours and trading their earned points for cash during their free time at vocational school. Upon graduation, they obtained driving licenses and with family support purchased a sedan to drive for Uber (China) and Didi Taxi (the Chinese version of Uber), both of which were just starting to become popular in urban China. Like many, the bothers took shifts and kept their car on the road for more than twelve hours a day to maximize profit. When Uber and Didi competed fiercely by subsidizing drivers with kickbacks to gain market share in 2014 and 2015, Yusi and Yuqiang easily made more than 20,000 RMB ($3,100) per month because they were adept at using smartphones and social media. Yet after Didi acquired

Uber (China) in August 2016, the brothers' earnings dropped significantly, though making 8,000 RMB ($1,230) per month was still possible if they worked hard. The long hours on the road also began to prove taxing, especially for Yusi, who had a steady relationship with his girlfriend and was considering marriage in 2016. They began wondering, once more, what they could do next to fulfill the dream of being their own bosses in Shanghai.

STILL *WAIDIREN*

The subordination of rural nonlocal *hukou* holders in the job market forces second-generation migrant youth to confront the discrepancy between their aspirations and reality. Of course, local students who only obtain middle school certificates or attend secondary vocational schools in Shanghai also face difficulties, especially as they often come from lower socioeconomic backgrounds. Yet these local students have more family supports and connections in Shanghai as compared to their migrant peers, and more importantly they are not subject to state-imposed *hukou* barriers against migrants in the job market. In the household registration system and in the eyes of local Shanghainese, migrant youth remain *waidiren*, even though they grew up in the city and share much more in common with local youth than with their rural peers. They find themselves in an awkward position between first-generation rural-to-urban migrants and local urban youth when they compete for jobs in the city. The assumption that migrant students are more willing and able to put up with hardship and low pay is deeply flawed. However, labor agents, human resource departments, and government policies often fail to exercise discernment, categorizing and treating migrant youth as the rural Other and trying to channel them to low-end, menial jobs as "new-generation peasant workers."

Most jobs available to migrant youth upon graduation from vocational schools are at the entry level in the manufacturing and service industries. They find their on-the-job training and full-time work experiences tedious and the money they can make meager. Frequent job hopping is common among these restless young men and women who are anxious to find a better way to stay in Shanghai and fulfill their consumer desires. Many who are aware of their weak position in the job market acquire extra certificates in hopes that a college degree can help them transcend the labor market segmentation. Many also expressed and tried to fulfill the aspiration to become their own boss, seizing on opportunities in the emerging sector of e-commerce to gain increasing autonomy and control over their own time, labor, and earnings. They aspire to entrepreneurship, hoping to defy the state design of reproducing "new genera-tion peasant workers."

Since their life chances have been largely shaped by their formal education, migrant youth who have had their formal schooling cut short must confront and cope with the pressures of adulthood much earlier than their local counter-parts. Most of them suffer from long daily commutes and continue to live with their parents and siblings in crowded rented places on the city outskirts. Many migrant youths in this study claim to be *yueguangzu* (literally "moonlit tribe," people who save little from monthly income), spending most of their income on outings, group meals, and personal items to enjoy city life and maintain their social relations. With limited resources and opportunities, these young men and women appear unlikely to ever escape a life of *dagong*; and the hand-ful of job options genuinely available to them means their aspirations for eco-nomic independence and an urban lifestyle are in considerable jeopardy. This produces deep anxiety about the future in them, especially in the young men. "There are no good prospects in Shanghai," they lament. Having grown up in the city, migrant youth identify Shanghai as *the* place for them to work, to make a living, and to aspire to better opportunities but not without recognizing that their yearning for a comfortable metropolitan life is often curtailed.

CONCLUSION

Next-Generation Shanghai

IN TODAY'S WORLD of the unprecedented global movement of people, capital, goods, and information, the struggles for living spaces, job opportunities, legal entitlements, public services, and symbolic resources among different groups have intensified. The resultant differentiating and discriminating practices, intentional or not, have also become more pronounced. The drowned body of a Syrian toddler on a Turkish beach in 2015 symbolized the refugee crisis in Europe. The repeated efforts to impose travel bans on specific groups of foreign nationals by the Trump administration testified to the rising nativist sentiments against (im)migrants across the globe. It has never been more urgent to unravel how the politics of citizenship play out in policy making and, more importantly, in everyday practices to understand anti-(im)migration populism on the ground.

The notion of a universal "right to the city" (Harvey 2008), which reminds us of the "collective power to reshape the processes of urbanization" (23), may be politically and morally appealing. In practice, nevertheless, one group's right and access to urban resources often "become[s] another's source of exclusion" (Harms 2016b, 46). The perception that cities can only accommodate and be used by so many people has been widely accepted and intimately validated as social fact by both urban residents and city governments. Spatial density, especially in densely populated megacities like Shanghai, Mumbai, and Rio among others, makes the subjective fear of overcrowdedness and disorder even more tangible. Instead of dismissing such perceptions as false and parochial, it is important to examine the social effects of such perceptions on real people in everyday lives in ethnographic detail.

China's resilient socialist *hukou* system makes its internal migration experience a unique but important case for understanding the politics of citizenship. After three decades of massive internal migration, the accommodation and management of this growing second-generation migrant population, treated as economically indispensable but sociopolitically undesirable, represents one of China's greatest challenges. This book has clarified how recent policy modifications of the *hukou* system have gradually and selectively aimed to achieve a desired urban population for economic development and social stability rather than addressing fundamental issues of equality and social justice. Migrant youth remain in an ambiguous condition and disadvantaged in both the administrative system and the sociocultural order.

The experiences of migrant youth in Shanghai demonstrate the "intersection of multiple modes of exclusion" (Harms 2016b, 55), which include "paperwork, money, violence, environment, space, and civility" (46). Migrant youth are subject to regulatory exclusion by household registration papers that frame their educational and, to some extent, employment eligibility. Short-notice demolition and relocation projects resulting in the tearing down of their rented homes without any compensation represent forceful exclusion, in effect "violence," inflicted by state agents and private developers out of the combined interests in profit and social order. When told by urban elites that the fast-fashion clothing they like and identify with are "slum brands," migrant youth experience subtle market-based exclusion. Although they pride themselves on being practical and youthful, they experience a growing awareness of social disparity in the city. Spatial exclusion embedded in the construction of the *waidiren* categorization intertwines with sociocultural exclusion resulting from the moralization of fertility control and child-rearing practices under the one-child policy in Shanghai, in which migrants are contrasted to the new middle class and labeled undesirable citizens, who fail to act as self-disciplinary subjects in the new mode of urban governmentality.

This study highlights how discursive practices have intertwined with institutional measures to create powerful ordering parameters for socioeconomic life on the ground. Under the official label of "peasant workers," rural-to-urban migrants are categorized as a transitional social group, caught between the ideal binaries of agricultural and industrial, rural and urban, inside and outside, and past and future, along a unilinear developmental axis. Institutional restrictions imposed on the migrant population endorse and encourage social discrimination against rural-to-urban migrants in the urban job market. In addition to labor market segmentation, the denial of local *hukou* status and its accompanying right to public services places extra burdens on migrant workers for reproduction. Their precarious conditions result in minimum living expenses and high savings rates, as exemplified by cramped, makeshift rental housing arrangements on the city outskirts. In addition, schooling barriers raised against migrant children in the cities force millions of migrant parents to leave their children behind in the countryside, so they may receive a basic education free of charge. Such structure-induced family choices and parenting styles are nevertheless often interpreted and criticized by urbanites as evidence of migrants' lack of responsibility and civility. Stereotypical representations in the media of "peasant workers" as being coarse and stupid facilitate the social construction of migrants as the Other among local urbanites. The state-imposed liminal status of "peasant workers" hence becomes a collective social fact and even necessity that substantially affects policy implementation and everyday urban social interaction.

The making of migrant children as liminal subjects in Shanghai enables and justifies the practice of segmented inclusion of its sovereign subjects within national boundaries. Although the state has had to relax *hukou* restrictions because of massive migration and socioeconomic transformation, it manages to endow rights and services selectively to different social groups in different time frames. Shanghai recruits only a relatively small number of highly educated migrants, being professionals or well-off entrepreneurs, as talents to enjoy its local residential status and full urban citizenship. By contrast, the remaining majority of migrants of lower socioeconomic strata, who are labeled as "peasant workers," remain disqualified for the prestigious Shanghai *hukou* and hence barred from full access to pensions, medical insurance, and public schooling.

According to the market logic of human value, selective policies of endowment articulate an ideal modern citizen to help achieve the desired composition of urban subjects. The segmented inclusion of migrant students into urban public schools, a key site of struggles to make Chinese youth into appropriate modern subjects, is only one clear example. The removal of blatant spatial segregation by closing down migrant schools and opening up public schools in Shanghai does not necessarily foster inclusion for migrant students. Seemingly minor yet intimately felt acts of differentiation affect temporal, spatial, pedagogical, and emotional aspects of schooling experiences of migrant students.

In particular, the negative impacts of the systematic closure of higher-education opportunities to migrant students cannot be overemphasized. Deprived of the right to participate in the high school and university entrance examinations in Shanghai—a widely accepted rite of passage for most local youth—migrant students are forced off the normative path of adolescence. Their presence in junior high school is void of purpose since their schoolwork and performance on examinations are discounted in the evaluation system and are presumed not to lead to a higher academic degree. Many migrant students thus just find ways to pass the time in and out of the classroom. When this sort of ennui comes together with the passivity of school administrators and teachers, a vicious circle takes shape and leads to a decline in academic performance among a large number of migrant students. This, in turn, contributes to establishing their inferior status in the view of the qualification-oriented society.

The segmented inclusion of migration students in urban public schools contributes to the perpetuation of migrant youth as liminal subjects to ensure the stability of a semiskilled labor supply for the booming urban service economy. When the municipal government blocked the path to a university education for migrant students through academic senior high schools, it opened up the alternative of secondary vocational education. The state at both the central and local levels sponsors migrant youth to receive formal vocational training in certain preprofessional specialties. In addition to the social stigma associated with vocational schools, the channeling of migrant students to specializations that are concentrated in low-end manufacturing and service industries adds to their disadvantages as compared to local peers.

For those who returned to their hometowns, where they are registered to attend academic senior high schools, the path to higher education proves equally difficult, despite the removal of *hukou* barriers. The entrenched disparities in educational resources between the urban and the rural, the east coast and the hinterland, big cities and small towns, prevent most migrant youth from entering desirable four-year universities. In turn, such low success rates reify social prejudices against rural migrants in China's prevalent *suzhi* discourse which deems "peasants" inferior to urbanites in terms of intellectual capacity and civility.

Hereditary *hukou* status prevents second-generation migrant youths who grew up in their adopted cites from translating their urban residence and experience into formal urban citizenship. Their ambiguous status caught between dichotomous categories greatly affects their personal lives. Their upward mobility is deeply circumscribed. The official label of "second-generation peasant worker" hints at the state's intention to reproduce cheap labor for urban development and national modernization. The reproduction scheme goes far beyond the labeling practice and permeates everyday practices that contribute to the making of "second-generation peasant workers" as the state intended. This study shows how persistent structural inequality in the education system and nuanced everyday practices in and out of the classroom continue to differentiate and discriminate against migrant students to their disadvantage.

The journeys of these migrant youth in Shanghai illuminate comparable processes faced by young generations of migrants elsewhere, who also confront dichotomous categories and live in in-betweenness in religious, political, and sociocultural realms. Migration across national borders needs to be seen in the larger context of migration from economically underprivileged areas cordoned off by governmental boundaries and controls to economically prosperous mega urban areas that are dependent on migrant labor but enforcing controls that fix them in unstable, dehumanizing second-class citizenship status. By exposing the structure of power and its exercise in everyday life that maintains inequality amid rapid economic growth and high social mobility in Shanghai, this book cautions against the intensification, rather than relaxation, of segmented and stratified citizenship in today's increasingly polarized world.

Yet migrant youth are by no means passive recipients of the state-led reproduction scheme. Although schools are primary sites for reproducing social hierarchies, the "field" of school does not entirely determine the reproduction of dominant power structures to the exclusion of human agency. As this book has shown, a new kind of subjectivity that transcends the rural-urban, local-nonlocal binaries has been forming during the segmented process of urban inclusion, although the implications for class formation in postreform China remain unclear given the heterogeneity of migrant subgroups and the absence of class consciousness. Living on the periurban edge, migrant families maintain their native-place-based networks and embedded economic opportunities. In their passing-time activities, migrant students begin to reject the false promises of meritocracy in the formal education system, which, in fact, simultaneously perpetuates and undermines their status as failures. Many of them concede that academic qualifications are desirable but not necessary for success in China's market socialism where practical knowledge and social connections are essential. Having been spared the exacting tasks of taking tests and producing a certain standard of numerical examination scores, they put their time and energy into making friends, having fun, and preparing themselves to take advantage of the booming urban economy whenever opportunities arise.

Growing up in Shanghai's periurban zones, migrant youth lead a life "in between," building ambiguous relationships to rural and urban, inside and outside, past and future. They embody "social edginess," seizing opportunities arising in relation to their ambivalent position with respect to the *hukou* system. They combine the insight of the insider with the distanced view of the outsider and, thus, become the bearers of an in-betweenness that is deeply imbricated in China's long quest for development and modernity. As the landscapes and social constituents of both the rural and the urban constantly change around them, these young people's oscillation between different positions and categories brings both flexibility and uncertainty, from which they can successfully negotiate for resources in spite of structural binaries and policy constraints.

The lives of the young migrant men and women in this study are still unfolding, sometimes in unexpected ways. Their trajectories (see Appendix 2), deeply entangled with China's ongoing economic restructuring and sociopolitical transformation, demonstrate how these "liminal subjects" have been redrawing boundaries, forming networks, and acting on new possibilities. A few of them took advantage of the resources of NGO J and were admitted to an international university preparatory school on full scholarship. They have circumvented the *hukou* barriers and fulfilled their educational desire by getting scholarships to attend universities in Canada and the United States. As exceptional as these success stories are, they are suggestive of the mostly untapped potential of these migrant youth, much more of which might well be realized if institutional restrictions were removed, dichotomous categories rejected, and social support put in place. Yet, presently, as most of the migrant youth considered here remain in Shanghai and search for their way forward— marrying, having children, seeking better jobs, higher pay, and happier lives—it remains an open question whether the hereditary *hukou* status and discriminative practices will and can continue to channel the third generation into the restricted category of second-class citizens. The answer matters greatly to this generation, their parents, and their children, to the city of Shanghai, to China as a whole, as it should to all of us who are concerned about the inequality of segmented inclusion for migrants around the world.

APPENDIX 1

China's Policy Changes over Migration Management

Main Stage	Policy Initiatives	Major Events	Migrant Population in Millions (Year)
1979–1983 Restricted Flow	• Grain rationing • Household contract responsibility system, allowing rural households to control and dispose of surplus agricultural production after meeting state quotas	• Third Plenum of the Eleventh Central Committee (1978), which announced economic reforms • Establishment of special economic zones in Shenzhen, Zhuhai, Shantou, and Xiamen	30 (1982)
1984–1988 Permitted Flow	• Self-supplied food grain *hukou* • Temporary residence permit • Compulsory detention and repatriation of migrants without temporary residence permits	• 14 coastal cities opened up to overseas investment	70 (1988)
1989–1991 Controlled Flow	• Work permit system • Employment registration system	• June 4, 1989, Protest	80 (1994)
1992–2003 Channeled Flow	• Blue-stamp *hukou* (urban residential status via real estate purchase)	• Deng Xiaoping's "Southern Trip" in 1992 • 1997 Asian financial crisis	100 (1997)

(continued)

Main Stage	Policy Initiatives	Major Events	Migrant Population in Millions (Year)
2003–2008 Assisted Flow	• Abolition of the forced detention and repatriation system (2003) • State council's "Solutions to the Problem of Peasant Workers" (2006) • New Labor Contract Law (2008)	• Death of Sun Zhigang, a college graduate who was beaten to death in a detention center in Shenzhen for not producing proper identification in 2003 • High-profile visit of Premier Wen Jiabao to a migrant family in 2003 • 2007 CCTV New Year's Gala featuring migrant students in Beijing • 2008 global financial crisis	140 (2008)
2008—present Segmented Inclusion	• State council's "Opinions on Improving Mandatory Education for Peasant Workers' Children Living in Shanghai" (2008) • State council's "Opinions on Planning Further Rural-Urban Development and Strengthening the Base for Agricultural and Countryside Developments" (2010) • Shanghai Residential Status Management Policy (2013) • National Plan on New Urbanization (2014–2020) issued in July 2014 to announce limited *hukou* reform by gradually removing agricultural-nonagricultural *hukou* distinctions and providing local *hukou* in small cities and towns for 100 million rural migrants • State council's "Opinions on Improving Service for Peasant Workers" (2014)	• Serial suicides in Foxconn (18 attempted suicides by migrant workers, resulting in 14 deaths) in 2010 • 2010 Shanghai Expo with the theme of "Better City, Better Life" • Debate initiated by Zhan Haite via social media over migrant students' right to sit in high school entrance examinations in Shanghai in 2010 • 2011 CCTV New Year's Gala featuring three performances by migrant workers • Shanghai became the first Chinese city to apply the *jifen* (point accumulation) system to all nonlocal residents in 2013 • Expulsion of thousands of migrant workers after a deadly fire in a building crammed with migrant workers in Beijing in November 2017	253 (2014)

APPENDIX 2

Brief Biographies of Migrant Youth
Mentioned in This Book

Below is a list of the pseudonyms of migrant students mentioned in this book, along with brief descriptions of their trajectories, which I came to know about over the past decade. I have not included all the informants I met and interviewed during this study. The listed ones represent slightly less than half of the total informants. During field research, I addressed many people, especially migrant parents, not by name but by their relationships to the students I knew. This appendix hence lists some parents under their children's names.

Huan (female), born in 1993 in Henan, was taken to Shanghai in 1998. Huan's mother, Aidi, has worked as a janitor, and her father, Dalu, takes odd jobs on constructions sites, collects recyclables, and drives a motorized pedicab at night. Huan attended a migrant primary school and a public middle school before enrolling in a secondary vocational school in Changning District in 2009. She took the specialization Western-style pastry making. In 2011, she got, through a school recommendation, an internship in a state-owned hotel's cake shop and later worked full-time there for over two years. After quitting her bakery job, she started working first as a volunteer and then as full-time staff for an educational foundation through the NGO J network. In 2015, Huan married a local Shanghai man, whom she had met through her part-time job and dated for one year and a half. Huan moved out of her parents' rental place and lived with her husband in a furnished two-bedroom apartment inside a gated community with the financial support of her in-laws. She enrolled in a part-time vocational college program in early education while working for educational organizations.

Huan has two younger siblings, Guan and Chuan.

Guan (female), born in 1995 in Henan, is Huan's younger sister. She has had strong academic grades since primary school and attended a public middle school free of charge. She enrolled in a vocational school in Zhabei District in 2011, specializing in business English. Through the help of NGO J, she got admitted into an international prep school for two years with full scholarship. She has been studying at a university in Canada since 2015 with a full scholarship.

Chuan (male), born in 1999 in Henan, is Huan's younger brother. He went to a migrant primary school and a public middle school. He chose to study automobile repair at a vocational school in Baoshan District and has participated in several city-level technical skill competitions. In 2016, he enrolled in a full-time, three-year vocational college program, specializing in automobile engineering.

Yan (female), born in 1993 (1994 according to her birth certificate) in Anhui, was taken to Shanghai as an infant with her mother but was sent back to Anhui at the age of six to stay with her paternal grandparents and be schooled there through sixth grade. She joined her parents in Shanghai in 2006 and attended a public middle school by paying extra fees. Yan's parents have been working as street food vendors in Shanghai since 1986. They ran a small restaurant, a food stall, and a stationery store in the 2010s. Yan enrolled in 2009 in a trade school in Yangpu District, specializing in finance. Yan took several office jobs in small private trade companies between 2012 and 2013. Unsatisfied with the low wages and lack of autonomy, she started helping out in her parents' restaurant. Later in 2015 she helped her boyfriend, a Fujian native who grew up in Shanghai and attended Yan's middle school one year ahead of her, open a noodle shop. Her boyfriend owns a compact car with the support of his parents. Yan enrolled in a part-time college program in 2016 and took driving lessons to get a license. In 2016, Yan got married to her boyfriend and rented a two-bedroom apartment in an urban neighborhood. In 2017, Yan gave birth to a son and started retailing clothes and skin-care products on WeChat social media, while staying at home to take care of the baby. They have been decorating their new apartment in Kunshan, Jiangsu Province, which was purchased in the early 2000s—before the real estate prices there skyrocketed—by the groom's parents, who made a fortune in construction material trading in the 1990s.

Yan has two siblings: a younger sister, Tan, and a younger brother, Gan.

Tan (female), born in 1994 (1996 on paper) in Shanghai, was sent back to Anhui for grades 1–3. She returned to Shanghai in 2005 and studied in a migrant school for grade 4 before transferring to a public school, although she was put in an "outsider class." She could not enroll in her preferred major of aviation in vocational school because of her nonlocal *hukou*, so she chose international business instead. Slim and fair, Tan has been modeling part-time for publicity events since vocational school and helped out in her parents' restaurant after graduation. In 2016, she started a retailing business on social media and later partnered with Yan.

Gan (male), born in 1997 (1999 on paper), spent most of his childhood in Shanghai. His parents put him in public primary and middle schools by paying extra fees until 2009. In 2013, Gan was sent to a boarding high school in Anhui to prepare for the national university entrance examination. He did not perform well on the 2017 exam and could not get into a four-year university program. His parents sent him to serve in the army in the hope that he would get disciplined and have better job opportunities after leaving the army.

Jiawen (male), born in 1994 in Anhui, grew up in Shanghai. He has a brother twelve years younger than him. His father takes odd jobs on construction sites and drives a motorized pedicab at night. His mother used to work as a janitor but has been staying at home since 2006 to care for her newborn second son. Jiawen went to a migrant primary school and a public middle school. He was in good academic standing and enrolled in a vocational school of good reputation in Putuo District, specializing in digital lathe operation. Because of his nonlocal *hukou*, he could not get his preferred internship in a big international company. In 2013, through a teacher's recommendation, Jiawen got a job as a panel operator in a factory in Pudong and stayed for almost two years. Tired of the mechanic work, he joined the NGO J as a program coordinator and treasurer in 2015. He has been studying part-time and taking tests to obtain a vocational college degree in accounting.

Le (female), born in 1994 in Anhui, grew up in Shanghai. Le's parents have made a living by running a bathhouse, a game room, and later a restaurant in their migrant community. Le has three siblings, including two elder sisters who grew up and were schooled in rural Anhui with paternal grandparents, and a younger brother. Le attended a migrant school and chose to go back to

Anhui in 2009 for eighth grade in the hope of attending high school and obtaining a university degree. However, she did not adjust well and returned to Shanghai after one year. In 2011, she enrolled in a secondary vocational school in Yangpu District, specializing in business English. She took an internship in a private English-tutoring company in 2015. After graduation, she took several office jobs and enrolled in a part-time vocational college program. She got married in 2018 and has been staying at home after giving birth to take care of her daughter.

Lin (female), born in 1994 in rural Jiangsu, joined her parents in Shanghai in 1999. Lin's father, Jianguo, and mother, Simei, have been working as vegetable vendors in Shanghai for over two decades. Lin was schooled in a migrant school for grades 1–4 and in public middle school for grades 5–9. She decided against going back to Jiangsu despite her passable academic performance. Lin enrolled in 2011 in a secondary vocational school in Putuo District, specializing in chemical analysis. In 2014, she obtained through a school recommendation a one-year internship in an international chemical plant in Pudong. She was offered afterward a full-time, three-year contract in her department. Lin has been enrolled in a part-time vocational college program affiliated with Shanghai University, specializing in graphic design. In 2016, Lin's parents purchased an apartment in a satellite town in Jiangsu, which is connected with Shanghai via an extended subway line.

Xin (male), born in 1996, is Lin's younger brother. He is less interested in academic learning and majored in Japanese at a vocational school in Xuhui District in 2013 because of his interest in Japanese computer games. He took some time off after graduation and started working in a trade company in 2017.

Meiyun (female), born in 1993 in rural Chongqing, joined her parents in Shanghai in 2000. Her parents migrated to Shanghai in 1998 and have since worked in a privately owned rubber parts manufacturing plant in Pudong District. Meiyun attended a migrant school before transferring to a public one in Pudong. She ranked top in academic performance and debated for years whether she should go back to Chongqing to prepare for the high school entrance examination. In 2011, she enrolled in a vocational school in Putuo District, specializing in chemical analysis. In 2014, Meiyun got an internship through a school recommendation in an international chemical group in Pudong but for personal reasons did not stay for a full-time job after graduation.

Between 2015 and 2016, she tried three jobs in different industries while studying on her own for a vocational college degree in administrative management. Since 2016 she has been working as a chemistry lab assistant at an international high school through recommendation. In 2017, Meiyun received her vocational college degree and got married to her long-term boyfriend from vocational school, who is a local Shanghainese from Jinshan, an island under Shanghai's administration. They then moved into their apartment, a wedding gift from the groom's parents. Meiyun's parents also purchased, with their life savings, a small apartment in Jinshan.

Yang (female), born in 1992 in Anhui, was brought to Shanghai in 2002. Yang's father moved to Shanghai to work as a math teacher in a migrant school. With a high school education, he managed to become a treasurer in a brick kiln in suburban Shanghai and later joined his friends in the cargo transportation business. Yang's mother started working as a janitor in a public hospital when the family business went bankrupt in 2008 because of a traffic accident. Yang studied grades 3–5 at a migrant school in Shanghai but went back to Anhui for grade 6 in the hope that she could get a university education in the future. She moved back to Shanghai one year later because of personal reasons. Yang was placed in a public middle school through the efforts of NGO J. Yang studied well and was reluctant to go to vocational school. She eventually enrolled in a private high school in Baoshan District in 2009. In 2010, through NGO J, Yang found out about an opportunity to apply for an international nonprofit prep school. In 2011, she passed the interviews and won a full scholarship to study at the prep school. Since 2013, Yang has been studying on full scholarship at a Canadian university. She went back to Shanghai in 2017 for internships but returned to Canada to finish college studies and has been working there after graduation.

Yang has a younger brother, Fanzhe, and a younger sister, Jixue.

Fanzhe (male), born in 1994, specialized in business English at a secondary vocational school in Xuhui District after graduating from a public middle school. Inspired by his elder sister, he managed to get into the international prep school in 2014 after trying for two years. In 2016, he started his university life with a full scholarship in the United States.

Jixue (female), born in 1996, also had a strong academic record from primary school and followed the path of her elder siblings. She managed to pass the interviews and got admitted into the international prep school's Canadian campus in 2016 after three years of studying Japanese at the same vocational school Fanzhe attended in Xuhui District. She has been studying in an American university with a full scholarship since 2018.

Zhihui (female), born in 1992, grew up in rural Anhui before joining her parents in Shanghai in 1999. Her parents moved to Shanghai in 1997, helping fellow migrants sell fruit at first and later switching to the bicycle and motor-cycle repair business. After eight years of schooling in Shanghai, Zhihui went back to Anhui in 2007 and attended a private boarding school for grades 8 and 9. She got accepted into a top high school in the county, but she did not score as high as expected in the NUEE in June 2011 and enrolled in a major university in Anhui instead of a top university in Shanghai as she would have preferred. Zhihui majored in sociology and got interested in social work. She has been working as a full-time employee at NGO J in Shanghai since 2015.

Zhihui has an elder brother, who got into a secondary vocational school in Shanghai and served in the army afterward for two years before joining his parents' motorcycle repair business. He got married in 2015 and has a daughter. His parents purchased a small apartment in Shanghai before his marriage, and they live together.

Jiao (female), born in 1991 in Henan, grew up in Shanghai from the age of three months. Her parents migrated to Shanghai in 1991 and have been self-employed as street food and fruit vendors. Jiao attended a migrant school in Yangpu District. She left Shanghai in 2006 to study first in Anhui, where she stayed with a relative, and later in a boarding high school in Henan in the hope of pursuing a university education. In 2011, Jiao failed the NUEE. She later took *gaofuban* in Henan to cram for the exam and passed the NUEE in 2012. She enrolled in a small college in Henan's capital city, Zhengzhou. In 2015, Jiao went back to Shanghai for an internship in a microfinancing company and has been working there full-time. Jiao has two elder sisters who grew up in rural Henan and joined their parents to work in Shanghai after graduating from middle school and a younger brother who went back to Henan for middle and high school and got admitted into a second-tier university in Shanghai. Jiao's eldest sister got married to a local Shanghai man and had twins in 2016.

Meixia (female), born in 1994, grew up in Shanghai with a nonagricultural *hukou* from Jiangsu. She lives with her father, who is a construction worker, after her parents got divorced when she was very young. She has no siblings. Meixia can speak the Shanghai dialect, as she has relatives in the city. Meixia went to a migrant primary school and a public middle school. She enrolled in a vocational school in 2010, specializing in chemical analysis. With little interest in the chemical industry, she took an internship at one of China's largest travel service providers in 2014. After a three-month trial period with little salary, she got a full-time position as a customer service assistant, taking phone calls and dealing with complaints. In 2016, she got a better-paid, less stressful position in a smaller travel agency and has been working there since.

Qi (male), born in 1993 in rural Sichuan, grew up in Baoshan District in Shanghai. His parents both work in a joint venture company that makes soy sauce and other condiments. Qi attended a migrant school and later enrolled in a public vocational school in Putuo District free of charge because of his agricultural *hukou*. He majored in chemical analysis and in 2014 got, through a school recommendation, a yearlong internship at a research institute affiliated with a state-owned enterprise in Putuo. He worked full-time for one more year before quitting the job. He got interested in photography and apprenticed with a freelancing documentary maker. He has been working full-time for NGO J as a program coordinator and photographer since 2016. He also enrolled in a part-time self-study vocational college program.

Mi (female), born in 1993 in rural Sichuan, is Qi's twin sister. Mi dropped out of school in the middle of ninth grade partly due to tension with teachers. She tried to learn hairstyling in a salon but later leased with her parents' financial support a clothes retail booth in a garment wholesale market, which did not make any profit after a year. In 2015, she joined her elder brother to become a real estate agent and worked there for two years. Mi got married in 2017 and moved to Anhui where her husband's family came from.

Qi and Li have an elder brother named Peng.

Peng (male) was left behind in Sichuan for schooling and only joined his parents in Shanghai after finishing high school. He found an apprenticeship making metal frames in Suzhou, thirty minutes from Shanghai via the high-speed train, and years later went back to Shanghai to work as a real estate agent.

Bei (female), born in 1994 in rural Anhui, grew up in Shanghai. She was sent back to Anhui at the age of six for primary school but returned to Shanghai after three years. She attended a migrant school in Baoshan District. At grade 11, Bei was put in a boarding school in Anhui in order to get into high school. She did not perform well on the high school entrance examination and instead enrolled in a self-financed 3 + 2 program (five-year program that offers a vocational college degree) in a private vocational college in Hefei, the capital city of Anhui. Bei majored in accounting but was sent with her classmates to Beijing by her college for an internship, which semiforced her to work as a waitress in a golf club in suburban Beijing between March and September 2013. In October 2013, she found a six-month accounting internship in Shanghai with the help of NGO J. After graduation in 2016, she moved back to her parents' rental place in Baoshan and took a gap year, trying different part-time jobs and volunteer work.

Bei's father (born in 1968) moved to Shanghai at the age of eighteen. He first worked as a laborer unloading stone and sand bags on the wharf. Later he partnered with his relatives and friends, pooling their savings to purchase subleases of unused warehouses and rent the spaces to businessmen and migrant tenants. Bei's mother is a housewife and helps out the business.

Bei has three siblings. Her elder sister, born in 1992 in Anhui, spent a few years in Shanghai before going back to Anhui for schooling. She completed vocational education in Anhui and then went to Suzhou for work. She joined her parents one year later and has been working as a shopping guide in a department store in Yangpu District. Her younger sister (born in 1996 in Anhui) and youngest brother (born in 1998 in Anhui) stayed in the countryside and attended school together for grades 1–12. They both took the 2016 NUEE. The younger sister got an offer from a second-tier university in Tianjin, while the youngest brother failed the exam and could not get into any college.

Xian (female), born in 1994 in rural Anhui, was brought to Shanghai when she was in second grade. Her parents operated a small wood packaging company in Baoshan District for over a decade before moving to Jiangxi in 2010 for better business opportunities in mining. Xia chose to stay in school in Shanghai when her parents left for Jiangxi and spent most of her after-school time at NGO J. After graduating from a public middle school in 2011, she enrolled in a vocational school in Xuhui District, specializing in business English. For the school-recommended onsite training, she worked as a managing assistant, organizing name cards and helping out with office work. In the summer of 2014, after graduating, she found an internship through the internet in a start-up company, working as a secretary. She also enrolled in a part-time vocational college program in architecture. Since 2015, she has been working full-time in a nonprofit orphanage through the recommendation of NGO J. She has a younger brother.

Dan (female), born in 1994 in rural Henan, was brought to Shanghai at the age of five. Her parents have worked as meat vendors in Pudong District for over two decades. She has a younger brother. Dan went to a migrant school and later a public middle school. In 2011, she enrolled in a vocational school in Putuo District, specializing in chemical analysis. She was classmates with Lin and also got a school recommendation to interview with an international chemical group in Pudong. She got in and was assigned to the plant's laboratory. Dan had to take three shifts and commute more than an hour by bus between home and work each way. She left after completing the internship and got a job in a smaller private company in Yangpu District as a chemical analyst.

Fan (male), born in 1996 in Henan, grew up in Shanghai. His parents have been working as fruit vendors in a market for almost two decades since they migrated to Shanghai. He has an elder sister. Fan went to a migrant primary school, a public middle school, and then a vocational school in Baoshan District in 2010, specializing in automobile repair. In 2013, he was recommended by his vocational school to intern in a 4S car shop under the Buick franchise that provided "sale, service, survey, and spare parts." After a one-year internship, Fan signed a full-time, three-year contract but quit the job after six months. In the spring of 2016, he joined a former classmate to become an insurance salesman. He quit after three months without making much money. Afterward Fan fell victim to an employment scam that lured him and his friend all the way to Shandong Province. He narrowly escaped but lost much of his savings. Back in Shanghai, through a former colleague's recommendation, he took a job in a 4S store under the General Motors franchise and has been working there since the late summer of 2016.

Yuqiang and **Yusi** (males), born in 1992, are twin brothers originally from Fujian Province. Their father has been involved in trading construction materials in Shanghai, especially steel and stone, through his hometown networks, since the early 1990s. Their mother stays at home as a housewife. The brothers grew up in Shanghai and attended a private vocational college in Yangpu District after graduating from public middle school. They chose the computer studies as their specialization. They started to make money by playing online video games and selling their scores to other game players. After graduating in 2014, they purchased a car with their parents' money and joined the booming car-sharing business via social-media-based Didi Taxi and Uber (China). They live in an apartment purchased by their parents in the early 2000s on the southeast edge of Shanghai.

Gong (male), born in 1994 in Bridge Town in Pudong, was one of the ninth-grade students in Class Five in the Bridge School. His parents ran a small street-facing shop in Bridge Town, making and selling aluminum-alloy windows and doors. He has two elder sisters. Gong enrolled in a public secondary vocational school in Pudong. He chose the specialization of computer studies because of his interest in computer games. He was assigned to an internship in the fall of 2011 in an electronics company that packaged and stored Apple iPhones. His job was to stack packaged iPhones in a warehouse. He complained about his sore arms and said he felt like a robot. He quit the internship after a month. After finishing vocational school, he helped out in his parents' shop while taking part-time vocational college courses on weekends.

Yalu (male), born in 1994 in rural Jiangsu, grew up in Bridge Town with his parents. He has no siblings. His father runs a kiln that makes bricks in Jiangsu Province for sale mostly in Shanghai. His mother stays at home taking care of housework. His family lives in a self-purchased, well-decorated three-bedroom apartment in a middle-class neighborhood built in the early 2000s on the east edge of Bridge Town. Yalu, frail and shy, did not have strong academic records and enrolled in a nearby vocational school after graduating from the Bridge School. He specialized in computer studies. With the support of his parents, Yalu enrolled in a full-time *gaofuban* instead of on-the-job training in the last year of vocational education. He took the *sanxiaosheng gaokao* and enrolled in an adult three-year college (*chengren dazhuan*) part-time while working for his father's company.

Min (female), born in 1996 in rural Sichuan, grew up in Shanghai with her factory-worker parents. After graduating from a public middle school in Yangpu District, she studied hotel management in a secondary vocational school. In the spring of 2016, she spent half a year interning at a five-star hotel through her vocational school's recommendation. Unsatisfied with the menial hotel service internship, she enrolled in a vocational college in the fall of 2017 as a full-time student, specializing in administrative management.

Ming (male), born in 1994 in Bridge Town, Shanghai, holds an agricultural *hukou* in Anhui. His parents are self-employed meat vendors in a market in Bridge Town. He has an elder sister, born in 1990, who went back to Anhui in eighth grade for high school. Ming's sister was admitted to a teacher's college in Nanjing, the capital city of Jiangsu, in 2009, and later got into a master's degree program in northeast China. Ming attended a local public primary school before enrolling in Bridge School. He stayed in Shanghai and enrolled in a vocational school in Pudong in 2009, specializing in computer studies. Upon graduating in 2012, Ming joined the army at his parents' suggestion and served as a seaman near Shanghai for two years. After retiring from the navy, he worked as a salesman for a financial company. In 2015, he partnered with a former comrade to start a garment retail business in Yiwu, where the world's largest small commodities market is. In 2016, he decided to end the unprofitable business and tried to sell insurance in Shanghai.

Jia (female), born in 1994 in Bridge Town, grew up in the town. She holds an agricultural *hukou* in Zhejiang Province. Her parents have operated a small logistics company in Bridge Town since the early 1990s. She has no siblings. Jia attended a public primary school before enrolling in Bridge School for her middle school education. She enrolled in a secondary vocational school in Yangpu District and majored in business English. Upon graduating, she took an internship in an aviation company in Beijing and met her present husband, whom she married in 2015. She has been living with her husband in Chengdu in Sichuan Province, where her husband came from, and raising their first child with the help of her in-laws.

Limi (female), born in 1994 in Bridge Town and raised there, holds an agricultural *hukou* in Jiangsu. Her father, Xiaming, went to Shanghai in 1989, first working as a watch repairman and then an eyewear retailer. Her mother helps manage the retail store. Limi has no siblings. Limi attended a public primary school before enrolling in the Bridge Middle School. She enrolled in a secondary vocation school in Pudong District in 2009, specializing in business English. She dropped out of vocational school after two years. She later took a self-financed training program to become a certified optometrist. In 2014, her father leased a big counter in a new shopping mall and put Limi there to manage the eyewear and cell phone retail business.

Junjie (male), born in 1993 in Anhui but raised in Bridge Town, holds an agricultural *hukou* in Anhui. His father works as a subcontractor for a local construction company, and his mother is a housewife. His family lives in the apartment he bought on the edge of Bridge Town. Junjie attended a local public primary school and the Bridge Middle School. He has an elder sister who stayed in Anhui to complete high school and got into a second-tier university in Anhui. Although his parents wanted Junjie to get a university education, they finally decided to put him in a vocational school in Pudong District. Junjie majored in automobile repair, but instead of taking on-the-job training, he took *gaofuban* classes in the last year of his vocational education and enrolled in a part-time vocational college program. Junjie started a kitchen decoration and appliance retail store with the support of his parents in 2013, but closed the business after two years because of low profit.

Bing (male), born in 1993 in Anhui, was brought to Shanghai when he was three years old and grew up in Bridge Town. He has two elder sisters. His father works as a truck driver for a small private logistics company and his mother has stayed at home taking care of children and housework. After graduating from the Bridge School, he enrolled in a vocational school in Pudong, specializing in computer studies. He quit vocational school after one year's study and started working in a restaurant partly because of his family's financial constraints.

Jianxin (male), born in 1994 in Shanghai and raised in Bridge Town, holds an agricultural *hukou* in Anhui. He has an elder brother. His father makes a living by leasing and managing the parking lot for bicycles inside a public housing compound. His mother works in the kitchen of a restaurant. He attended a migrant primary school before enrolling in the Bridge Middle School. In 2009, he enrolled in a vocational school in Pudong, specializing in computer studies. He dropped out of school after one year and started working in a factory in the economic zone adjacent to Bridge Town. He got married in 2016 and has a son.

NOTES

INTRODUCTION

1. In 2010, Shanghai's natural population growth rate of native residents (i.e., population increase or decrease caused by birth and death instead of immigration and emigration) was −0.6 percent, which means the number of deaths was bigger than the number of births in that year. The city's natural population growth rate of native residents has been negative since 1993. "Outlander Population Grew Close to Local Hukou Population," *Xinmin Evening*, September 22, 2011, accessed May 6, 2012, http://news.xinmin.cn/t/xmwbtj/2011/09/22/12157438.html.

2. Ibid.

3. See also Howard W. French, "Shanghai Moves to Close Private Schools for Migrants," *New York Times*, January 24, 2007, accessed July 12, 2007, http://www.nytimes.com/2007/01/25/world/asia/25iht-china.4335146.html?pagewanted=all.

4. The 2010 National Census, the National Bureau of Statistics of China.

5. The term "floating population" is nevertheless still in use occasionally, which shows the resilience of the binary sedentary-versus-mobile framework in the *hukou* system. Two Chinese academic conferences held in December 2008 in Shanghai and in June 2009 in Beijing used *liudong renkou* and *renkou liudong* frequently without much reflection on the term itself.

6. There are several Chinese variations in use. For instance, *nongmingong tongzhu zinü* (children living together with peasant workers) and *wailai renkou suiqian zinü* (children who move with the outsider population) are also used in news reports and official documents.

7. The so-called left-behind children (*liushou ertong*)—22 million migrant workers' children—were estimated to have stayed in villages under the supervision of grandparents, relatives, or boarding schools. See "As China Booms, Millions of Children Are Left Behind," *Wall Street Journal*, January 24, 2007, accessed March 3, 2019, http://online.wsj.com/article/SB116959002141185426.html.

8. China's administrative hierarchy contains central level (*zhongyang*), provincial level (*shengji*), city level (*shiji*), region level (*diji*), county level (*xianji*), district level (*quji*), and basic levels (*jiceng*), including rural county (*xiang*) and town (*zhen*) levels, plus grassroots administrative units, villages (*cun*), and neighborhoods (*shequ*).

9. These municipal cities, including Beijing, Shanghai, Tianjin, and Chongqing, enjoy the administrative rank of provincial-level governments and report directly to the central government.

10. The geo-administrative hierarchy in the Peoples' Republic of China (PRC) parallels the tiered marketing system proposed by G. William Skinner, which seeks to map out the interconnections between villages, towns, cities, and regions to explain how Chinese society remained integrated and unified to various extents in spite of vast regional variations and poor communication and transportation technologies in late imperial times (Skinner 1964, 1965a, 1965b). However, scholars argue that the rural-urban divide and articulated hierarchies favoring cities have been largely constructed in the twentieth century, especially through the *hukou* system in the PRC era (Brown 2014; Siu 1990; Whyte 2010).

11. There are more specific native-place identities based on provincial or regional names, such as Henan *ren* (people from Henan Province), Anhui *ren* (people from Anhui Province), and Liu'an *ren* (people from Liu'an County in Anhui Province) that suggest certain geographic, linguistic, occupational, or cultural characteristics and stereotypes. However, such references of native-place identities are more used among migrant groups. It is not easy for most local Shanghai residents to tell such differences, especially when referring to second-generation migrant youth, the majority of whom are Han Chinese, have grown up in Shanghai, speak Mandarin, and sport urban styles that defy regional distinctions.

12. Sun Zhigang, a college graduate and fashion designer who had gone to Guangzhou for work, was beaten to death in a detention center for not carrying proper ID in March 2003. His death received massive attention in Chinese newspapers and on the internet, which led to the suspension of the detention system months later.

13. Many Chinese cities issued "blue-stamp *hukou*" (*lanyin hukou*) to nonlocal investors and home buyers in the 1990s and early 2000s, partly to boost the then lukewarm real estate markets. Holders of blue-stamp *hukou* keep their original *hukou* and may petition to transfer to permanent local *hukou* years later if they meet criteria set by local governments in terms of age, education, and work skills. The blue-stamp *hukou* entails more social benefits than "temporary residence cards," the most important of which is access to local public schools. Concerns of overpopulation and real estate bubbles resulted in the end of the policy in Shanghai in April 2002.

14. I see the designation "late-socialist" more appropriate than "post-Mao," "post-socialist," or "postreform," to describe the current conditions in China. Late socialism, as argued by Li Zhang (2001b), is not to predict the demise of the socialist regime but to capture the transformations brought by the capitalist developments mixed with the legacies of Maoist socialism.

15. Bourdieu (1984) points out how temporality is woven into people's ability to navigate fields of power on an everyday basis. His emphasis on social reproduction as a set of complex games and his reference to the importance of timing and a feel for the game are instructive to understanding how such structural inequalities and sociocultural discriminations channel migrant youth to substandard education and low-end work in urban China.

16. Bourdieu (1984) has illustrated how routine success instills in people an ability to project their lives into the future, which is itself a form of capital.

17. See Bernard 2006 and Falzon 2009 on multisited ethnographic research.

18. The Bridge School, like other public schools, enrolled a small number of migrant students before 2007, but it used to charge extra fees (*jiedufei*). The Shanghai government's subsidies since 2008 enabled the Bridge School to enroll more migrant students without tuition charge.

19. According to a survey conducted in 2010 by the Shanghai Education Commission on language usage among Shanghai students of different ages, only 45 percent of Shanghai families, in which both parents and children were born and raised in Shanghai, use Shanghai dialect at home.

20. Some studies reported incidents in which local students disdained migrant peers, and migrant students tended to identify other migrant children as close friends in primary and middle schools (Kwong 2011, 876; Lan 2014, 13).

CHAPTER 1

1. In most Chinese public schools, one class of students stay in one assigned homeroom throughout the school day for a whole academic year, while teachers of different subjects move between classrooms from one period to the next. Each class is assigned a homeroom teacher, usually someone who teaches the class on certain subjects.

2. Teachers are not supposed to inform students in advance of such visits so that they can observe genuine, nonstaged family situations and behaviors at home; it is in this context that Huan's teacher was unable to reach the family home.

3. The government creatively separated land use rights from land ownership in the late 1990s to allow the trading of land use rights to develop the real estate market and generate revenues. When urban residents purchase apartments, they obtain property ownership and the limited lease of land use right; the state and its apparatus maintain the absolute power over land ownership. Please see Hsing 2010 for a detailed analysis of the evolution of Chinese land politics.

4. The 2015 Shanghai Statistic Yearbook, like most Chinese censuses, underregisters rural migrants by only counting migrants who live in Shanghai for more than six months and have proper temporary residence permits as "nonlocal residents." It is hence reasonable to suggest that the majority of migrants, especially those from lower and middle economic levels, live in the exurbia and outer exurbia districts (including Pudong) that are periurban in nature.

5. The administrative categorization and naming of towns and counties in Shanghai in the Qing dynasty and the republican era are too complicated to detail here. To put it simply, Chuansha was part of Huating County, Shanghai County, and the Chuansha Civil Center during the Tang (618–907), Yuan (1271–1368), and Qing dynasties (1644–1911), respectively. After Republican China was founded in 1912, Chuansha became a county of Jiangsu Province. In 1958 Chuansha officially became a county under the jurisdiction of the Shanghai municipality. See http://english.pudong.gov.cn/2017-07/21/c_85558.htm (accessed July 20, 2018).

6. China's Fourth National Census, 1990, and Sixth National Census, 2010. Pudong merged with Nanhui County in late 2009, but its population in the 2010 census did not count Nanhui's.

7. It is beyond the scope of this book to recount the complex history of Shanghai's urban development since the mid-nineteenth century. The Virtual Shanghai Project, directed by Christian Henriot, documents the city's spatial transformation via rich textual and visual resources. See http://www.virtualshanghai.net.

8. The street committee was very cautious about giving out exact data to outsiders. I asked one informant who used to help the committee conduct the survey to accompany me during the visit. Only through long conversation did the staff reveal the rough number to me and suggest that even the committee has no accurate account of the total population.

9. I do not intend to suggest that the term *penghuqu* does not suggest disparity, as the term does effectively translate to "shanty area or town" and has a long, historic reference to displaced internal refugees camping out on the edge of cities at times of famine, natural disaster, war, or severe weather (J. Chen 2012). Yet *penghuqu* does not expressly refer to poverty like *pinminku* does in the Chinese context.

CHAPTER 2

1. When the PRC was founded in 1949, the Chinese government adopted a pronatalist approach of "more people, more strength" and issued public "Glorious Mother" commendations for women who had more than four children. Yet the government had concerns over rapid population growth as well and established China's Birth Planning Commission within the state council in 1964, shortly after China's population growth recovered from the Great Famine (1959–61), which claimed millions of lives after the Great Leap Forward, a Maoist campaign that tried to aggressively industrialize and collectivize the agrarian economy. Some high-level officials perceived a Malthusian crisis, in which population growth outpaces food production and exhausts natural resources, and pushed for more restrictive birth-control policies (Greenhalgh 2008; White 2006).

2. In the post-1970 family-planning campaign, "later" refers to late marriage after age twenty-five for brides and twenty-seven or twenty-eight for grooms in the city, and after twenty-three for brides and twenty-five for grooms in the countryside. "Longer" refers to greater intervals between permitted births, at least four years. "Fewer" means no more than two children for urban families and three for rural families. Scholars have shown that the coercive enforcement techniques that became notorious during the one-child-only campaign had already been employed during the mild "later, longer, fewer" campaign, resulting in rapid increases in female sterilization, induced abortions, and IUD insertions in the 1970s. See Whyte, Feng, and Cai 2015.

3. Of course, scholars have shown that the rapid decrease in fertility rate in China occurred in the 1970s prior to the one-child-only campaign. See Whyte, Feng, and Cai 2015; Whyte and Gu 1987. Yet mass media and even many scholarly works tend to attribute such fertility decrease to the one-child-only policy.

4. Scholars studying migrant workers living in special economic zones in South China suggest a semiproletariat class has been emerging amid a growing number of labor conflicts and collective actions (C. K.-C. Chan and Pun 2009; J. Chan and Selden 2014; Pun and Lu 2010). However, the dormitory-based workers' solidarity and working-class consciousness are not applicable to migrants working in big cities, who are much more diversified and less organized.

5. The original interview transcript was published on ifeng.com on June 12, 2016, the website of Phoenix New Media, a multimedia company headquartered in Hong Kong. A complete version was obtained from a repost at http://www.wenxuecity.com/news/2016/06/11/5284631.html (accessed October 11, 2017).

6. Recent studies, such as S. Li, Zhang, and Feldman 2010 and Y. Shi and Kennedy 2016, show that delayed registration and unreported births, in addition to sex-selective abortion and infanticide, have contributed significantly to the SRB imbalance.

7. *Xinmin Evening News*, originally founded as *Xinmin News* (*Xinmin bao*) in 1929 in Nanjing, has become one of China's major regional newspapers, based in Shanghai since 1952.

8. The number is a conservative reflection of real income based on Simei's initial reluctance when she answered the question about income. There is a tendency to under-report family income in China during interviews, especially among small vendors and businessmen who have little legal protection and are often harassed by municipal administrators. See Bramall 2001; Heimer and Thøgersen 2006.

9. Since the early 2000s, China has witnessed a rising inflation rate, especially in the prices of consumer goods, including food. In the Chinese media, there were numerous reports and discussions about how the government should control inflation and cool down the overheated economy. During my field research, the feeling that living in Shanghai is getting more and more expensive was prevalent in everyday conversations among different social groups.

CHAPTER 3

1. Local families may also use *guanxi* or pay extra fees to put their children in better schools that are located outside of their neighborhoods; this type of "school selection" (*zexiao*) is nevertheless of a different nature from migrants' paying extra fees to enroll in nonelite public schools. Local students are at least guaranteed seats in public schools in their registered neighborhoods.

2. In January 2008 the Shanghai government issued a document entitled "Opinions on Improving Mandatory Education for Peasant Workers' Children Living in Shanghai." See "Shanghai Issued Plan to Enrol All Migrant Children into Public Middle Schools by 2010," *Jiefang Daily*, January 22, 2008, http://news.aweb.com.cn/2008/1/22/5118200801221059320.html.

3. About 26 percent of the migrant students in Shanghai enroll in these schools at no costs, for which the schools receive subsidies. In 2008, for instance, the Pudong Education Bureau subsidized privately run schools 1,000 RMB for each migrant student they admitted. In 2009, the subsidy was 1,500 RMB per student.

4. The option of public secondary vocational school in Shanghai only became available in the mid-2000s. In 2008 the Shanghai government started to open dozens of public vocational schools to migrant students and subsidize migrant students enrolled in certain majors. See Chapter 4 for more discussions on migrant students' experiences in vocational schools.

5. At the Bridge School, Class One and Class Two were the "good classes" reserved for students with higher entrance scores and children of school faculty, hence a higher percentage of local students; the other four classes have local and migrant students (see Table 3.1).

6. One male student was from a local family, but his grandparents were sent to the countryside during the Cultural Revolution and lost their Shanghai *hukou*. For some reason, they could not transfer their *hukou* back to Shanghai, and the student thus inherited a non-Shanghai *hukou*.

7. Public schools receive two kinds of state funding from local governments: *bangong fei* (school operation fee in a lump sum) and *shengjun shiye fei*. Schools tend to calculate expenses in class units.

8. The Shanghai Municipal Education Commission has recategorized fifty-five city-level "key-point schools" as *shiyanxing shifanxing gaozhong* (literally "experimental high school for demonstration") since 2005. Pudong New District had eight such elite public schools as of 2012.

9. For instance, nonblack teachers are found to have, often subconsciously, lower expectations of black students resulting from racial stereotypes (Gershenson et al. 2016).

10. The interlocutors generally went back home for dinner and stayed indoors at night as required by their parents during ninth grade. To my knowledge, none of them were involved in high-risk activities, such as using drugs, motorcycle racing, shoplifting, paying for sex, or drunken group fighting, which are often reported among marginalized youth groups in Western societies. A study comparing age-crime patterns in Taiwan and the United States between 2008 and 2010 also finds that "peak ages in Taiwan are consistently much older, in the mid-20s to early 30s, as compared with the late teens in the United States" (Steffernsmeier, Zhong, and Lu 2017, 391–92). Greater parental involvement and control, stronger attachment to school and education, and socially sanctioned activities surrounding adolescence in Taiwan are considered to be major factors that discourage deviance and delinquency among teenagers. Similar patterns could be found in Shanghai. Strong state efforts to maintain social order and crack down on crime in Shanghai may also partly explain the lack of common delinquent youth behaviors. Another explanation for their rather placid activities is that this study chose to focus on migrant students remaining in ninth grade in public schools, which indicates relatively better socioeconomic conditions and stronger parental support for education.

11. The municipal government requires legal internet cafes to admit adult customers with valid IDs only. Underage students resort to illegal ones hidden in small alleys to chat online and play computer games.

12. In most cases, it is the teacher that assigns seats to students according to their height, special physical requirements (such as near-sightedness), and for discipline

purposes. In Class Five at the Bridge School, the students were left to rearrange their own seating twice in ninth grade.

CHAPTER 4

1. China's Criminal Law Code included the loosely defined crime of hooliganism as Item 160 in 1979, subjecting behaviors that disrupt public order or social morality, such as group fighting and homosexual behavior, to severe punishment. Although this item was replaced with better-defined subcategories of minor offenses and criminal activities in 1997, the term *liumang* remains widely used in everyday discourse.

2. The criminalization of migrants has been in practice since the early reform era. See L. Zhang 2001a, 201–22. In the 2000s, there is an emerging discourse in the mass media criminalizing second-generation migrant youth for social unrest.

3. The paid work as *liyi xiaojie* (ceremony girls) has emerged since the 1990s and tends to exclusively recruit young attractive women. These women typically have to dress in outfits that emphasize their bodies and are expected to pose in public to greet guests, hold ceremonial ribbons, serve as ushers, etc. See K.-M. Wu 2018 on the sociopolitical implications of *liyi xiaojie*.

4. Although survey studies tend to conclude that *hukou* barriers negatively affect students' academic performance, my field research shows that a significant percentage of migrant students who chose to remain in Shanghai fare reasonably well academically, and teachers often see migrant students as hardworking, especially in contrast to local children of families recently granted urban *hukou*. See Yi 2011, 313–30, for similar findings.

5. The legal age for employment is sixteen according to China's Labor Law as revised in 1994. This coincides with the end of nine years of basic education. But the improvement of living conditions, expansion of college enrollment, and consequent degree inflation have pushed up schooling duration and educational attainment, especially in big cities.

6. Local residents who are unemployed, have lost their ability to work, or are earning less than the minimum wage (1,280 RMB in Shanghai in 2011) can apply for *dibao* welfare. About 5 percent of Shanghai's local population receives *dibao* welfare (450 RMB/month per person in 2011).

7. There are also students who come from better-off families but fare badly academically and have little incentive to attend private prep schools and pursue higher education. They nevertheless represent a small percentage in vocational schools.

8. The three types are *jixiao* (technical school), *zhixiao* (professional school), and *zhongzhuan* (specialist school). *Zhongzhuan* and *zhixiao* are administered under the Ministry of Education; *jixiao* is under the Ministry of Human Resources and Social Security. No major differences exist among the three types, and their certificates are equivalent in the job market, although there might be subtle stratification between individual schools in terms of funding, size, faculty, and reputation.

9. "TMD," an online abbreviation for *ta ma de* (Chinese phrase for "fuck"), is often used in casual conversations among Chinese youth to express anger or excitement without being too vulgar.

CHAPTER 5

1. As discussed in Chapter 2, China's family planning policies have been more lenient with agricultural *hukou* families, allowing them to have a second child if the first one is a girl after certain number of years (depending on provincial policies).

2. *Daxue* in colloquial Chinese may include both *benke* (four-year university education) and *zhuanke* (two- to three-year college education). However, when talking about educational desire, people usually refer to *daxue* as a four-year university education acquired after passing the annual NUEE. *Dazhuan* is of much less prestige, and students can acquire *dazhuan* degrees through various means, such as long-distance learning courses or part-time college programs, after graduating from either academic high school or vocational school.

3. In 1905, the Qing imperial government ended the civil service examination system believing that the exam bred rampant corruption, focused too much on rotation, failed to foster scientific learning, and was thus no longer instrumental for national survival in face of Western intrusion. See Spence 1999.

4. The numbers of candidates who could sit for the *gaokao* exams in the 1980s were quite circumscribed, as were university places. Yet stories of individuals overcoming difficulties, succeeding in *gaokao*, and changing life trajectories were widely publicized. This contributed to the rapid rise of mass interest and investment in *gaokao* when the tertiary education system reforms took place in the 1990s. See Kipnis 2011.

5. The other means include marriage with urban residents and serving in the army and getting urban job placement after discharge.

6. Urban elites have always been overrepresented in Chinese universities, even during the Maoist era when political performance and family class were also considered in school admissions (C. Li 2012; C. Liang et al. 2012). Although good-class (workers, peasants, revolutionary cadres) children benefited from the political agenda, urban children of the former middle classes "held the greater chances of entering the better equipped schools" and thus better chances to acquire university education (Unger 1982, 18). When the NUEE was reinstituted in 1977, news reports tended to emphasize the success stories of rural youth and sent-down youth through the NUEE, resulting in a myth of educational opportunity and its purported nexus with upward mobility.

7. I only knew of two cases of both parents and children moving back to their registered hometown for schooling. In both cases, the parents were small vendors and did not see much economic prospect of staying in Shanghai. The remigration of their children for schooling offered a reason to relocate and start over.

8. Only nine-year basic education in the public school system is free; high schools charge tuitions of a few thousands per semester and fees for textbooks, canteen food, and so forth.

9. The wall facing the street was replaced with roll-up shutter doors so that the store is fully open for customers to come and go easily. Against the walls, shelves that reach up to the ceiling contain every kind of bicycle and motorcycle part imaginable for repair and retail. The couple sleeps at night in a small garret above the cashier's desk. A hole-in-the-wall kitchen and an equally tiny bathroom are carved out with planks in the back

of the store. Above the kitchen and bathroom is another small attic for Zhihui to sleep. The pedestrian lane and the dead-end road outside the store are utilized as outdoor space for repairing motorcycles and bicycles.

10. The middle schools returnees attend are mostly located in towns and counties whose surroundings are still largely rural (e.g., those that have crop fields within the vicinity). This is why I still use the term *rural* to indicate the contrast subjectively experienced by migrant students grown up in Shanghai.

11. By 2014 China had become the biggest source of foreign students studying in the United States.

12. Fei Xiaotong (1910–2005) was China's best-known anthropologist and sociologist. He attended Yenching University (whose campus is now that of Peking University), Tsinghua University, and the London School of Economics for his BA, MA, and PhD.

CHAPTER 6

1. Shanghai was one of the first four southeast coastal cities forced to open as treaty ports, where foreign traders were allowed to conduct business in China, after the Qing Chinese government lost its battles to Britain in the First Opium War (1840–1842) and had to give up its monopoly over foreign trade.

2. China's tiered marketing system has a long history. G. William Skinner's (1964) tiered marketing system delineates a hierarchical series of economic and administrative centers, which formed a web of commerce and governance in late imperial and modern China. According to his model, a standard market town at the lowest level serves the daily needs of nearby villagers, while local cities and regional cities have larger and more sophisticated markets serving a larger region and population with more varieties of goods and services.

3. Shanghai, Beijing, Tianjin, and more recently Chongqing are the four *zhixiashi* (municipalities under the direct control of the central government). Shanghai's status is equivalent to that of China's twenty-two provinces and five autonomous regions. In practice, the municipalities' political status is usually higher than the normal provinces.

4. While the belief in the "freedom" to choose can be strong and real, it is of course another matter whether such freedom is actually so in light of the taste-making industries and online key opinion leaders in hypercommercialism. See Horkheimer and Adorno (2002 [1944]) on the "culture industry" and the capitalist production of needs. Thanks to Jan Kiely for pointing this out to me.

5. Since the 1990s the traditional practice of *yingqin* (sending a party to escort the bride to the groom's house) across China has commonly come to involve a wedding caravan composed of six to twelve luxury cars. In the 2010s in Shanghai, it cost several thousand renminbi to rent luxury cars in a single color (usually in white or black) for a wedding caravan.

6. Fujian, the province where Yusi came from, has a long history of migration (both internal and international). The province is on the southeast coast north of Guangdong Province. In the Ming and Qing Dynasties, many Fujianese migrated to Southeast Asia

and North America to find better livelihoods. After economic reforms started, Fujian saw new waves of emigration. According to Yusi, most of the villagers in his home region migrated to the cities in the 1990s, and many succeeded in investing in and speculating on the construction material markets. Many villagers became rich, rebuilt their village houses, and purchased brand-name cars to show their wealth back in their home communities.

7. "Grass-mud horse" is a popular online euphemism for the Chinese curse of "fuck your mother," which also sounds like *caonima* in Mandarin Chinese. The phrase gained popularity on the internet in 2011 when China's internet censorship escalated and Chinese netizens created many puns, including "grass-mud horse," as a gesture of protest and mockery.

8. *Bie mo wo* (don't touch me) as an acronym for BMW became popularized after the blockbuster Chinese comic movie *Crazy Stone* (2006), directed by Ning Hao, used this acronym to mock nouveau riches riding in BMWs.

CHAPTER 7

1. High school students in populated provinces such as Anhui face much more severe competition because of the university admission quota system (see Chapter 5). It is widely acknowledged among local teachers and students that only those who get into key academic high schools will have the chance to score high on the NUEE and succeed in getting into first- and second-tier universities.

2. Of course, the Chinese media has been careful to avoid any Marxian critique of wealth accumulation through labor exploitation since the party-state still holds socialism as its official ideology.

3. The documentary, directed by Lixin Fan, an independent filmmaker, has won international awards and acclaim since its release in 2009. It documents the struggles of a migrant couple from rural Sichuan to get train tickets to get home during the Chinese New Year and improve their estranged relations with two left-behind children, one of whom ultimately went to Guangdong Province for work before completing middle school. See N. Li, Lin, and Wang 2012, on the documentary and its social context.

4. The phrase "eating bitterness" is commonly used in daily conversation to describe individuals' tenacity and grit. China scholars have pointed out how "eating bitterness" was promoted in the Maoist era as a form of embodied patriotism and self-denial in service of collective interests (see Woronov 2009). In the postreform era, "eating bitterness" has been often associated with peasants and migrant workers and used to help justify the subordination of these underprivileged groups in low-paying, labor-intensive sectors with discriminative policies.

5. Many private businesses in China routinely use unregulated, underground lenders because the government-run banks typically lend only to big, state-run corporations. When China's economy slowed slightly after the 2008 financial crisis, there were an increasing number of scandalous cases in which bosses could not make debt payments, with interest rates often running as high as 70 percent in the underground loan system, and so committed suicide or fled. See David Barboza, "In Cooling China, Loan Sharks

Come Knocking," *New York Times*, October 13, 2011, http://www.nytimes.com/2011/10/14/business/global/as-chinas-economy-cools-loan-sharks-come-knocking.html.

6. The high-profile, controversial case of Wu Ying, who was sentenced to death in 2009 (reconfirmed in the second instance in January 2012) for allegedly "raising funds illegally" among friends and kin is telling. Wu, born in 1981, held a vocational training certificate and started with a beauty salon and later expanded her multimillion-dollar businesses into foot massage, car rental, real estate, hotel management, and the futures market. She has been involved in high-interest loans worth billions and accused of "fraud in financing." Some Chinese legal and financial experts criticized the death sentence while debating the structural flaws and confusions within China's current financing regulation system.

GLOSSARY

baibai nengneng	白白嫩嫩	fair and tender (complexion)
baichi	白痴	idiot
baimao	白猫	"white cat," nickname for policemen
bangong fei	办公费	school operation fee
banzhuren	班主任	homeroom teacher, teacher responsible for supervising class affairs and coordinating student-related issues
baofenpei	包分配	guaranteed job placement
bendiren	本地人	local resident
BMW (bie mo wo)	别摸我	a pun for "don't touch me"
cao ni ma	草泥马	"grass mud horse," a pun for the Chinese curse "fuck your mother"
chai	拆	to demolish
chabuduo ba	差不多吧	kind of true
chaosheng youjidui	超生游击队	literally "overquota birth guerrilla," meaning couples who migrate to have more than one child and avoid state supervision and penalty
chasheng	差生	bad student, student of poor academic performance or behavior
chengguan	城管	"urban management," referring to the informal policing force of city governments, which is notorious for treating street vendors violently

chengren dazhuan	成人大专	adult vocational college
chengxiang jiehebu	城乡结合部	city-country convergence zone
chengzhongcun	城中村	"village in the city," urban village or city enclave
chiku	吃苦	literally "eat bitterness," meaning to endure hardship
Chuansha	川沙	literally "river sand," Chuansha County, one of Shanghai's rural districts
chuang zong jie dai	传宗接代	continuing the blood line through male heirs
dagong	打工	doing paid work for others
danqin	单亲	single-parent families
danwei	单位	a work unit
daxue	大学	university
dazhuan	大专	a three-year college
dibao	低保	government subsidy for lowest-income households
dibaohu	低保户	lowest-income families
difang fuze	地方负责	local funding responsibility
diyi tong jin	第一桶金	"first bucket of gold," initial capital
feinongye hukou	非农业户口	nonagricultural household registration
gaofuban	高复班	prep classes for people without high school education to prepare for tests to get into college
gaokao	高考	national university entrance examination (NUEE)
gaozhong	高中	senior high school
gongfang	公房	urban public housing projects mostly built by socialist work units since the 1950s to accommodate employees
gonggong	公共	common, public
gongmin yu shehui	公民与社会	"Citizen and Society," a course taught in middle school

gongzhu minban xuexiao	公助民办学校	"publicly sponsored, privately run schools," referring to private migrant schools that receive subsidies from local governments
guan	管	manage, monitor, care
guanxi	关系	social network, connections
gui jian zhi fen	贵贱之分	difference between the rich and the poor
haoban	好班	"good classes," classes hosting students of good academic standing
haohao dushu	好好读书	study hard
hei	黑	black, nonexistent in record
hei hukou	黑户口	"black" or void household registration
heimao	黑猫	"black cat," nickname for policing staff of urban management who are notorious for treating street vendors violently
hen nongcun, hen xiangxia	很农村，很乡下	very rustic, very rural
huaxue fenxi	化学分析	chemical analysis
huaxue gongyi	化学工艺	chemical technology
hukou	户口	household registration
huji leibei	户籍类别	type of household registration
huji suozaidi	户籍所在地	place of household registration
huan wo zhongkao quanli	还我中考权利	give back one's right to the high school entrance examination
hui	回	return
hui laojia	回老家	going back to one's hometown
huikao	会考	junior high school graduation test
huizhan	会展	exhibition
huli	护理	clinical care
hun	混	muddle (along); get by with minimum efforts
hushi	护士	nurse

jiben gonggong fuwu	基本公共服务	basic public services
jifenzhi	积分制	point accumulation system
jixiao	技校	technical school, one type of secondary vocational school
jianzhu mianji	建筑面积	construction area
jiedu fei	借读费	"borrow-study fee," extra fee paid for studying in schools
jiudian fuwu guanli	酒店服务管理	hotel service management
jiuli	旧里	old alley house
jiujin ruxue	就近入学	getting into a school in the vicinity
jinjiao	近郊	inner exurbia
jixiao	技校	technical school
juweihui	居委会	neighborhood committee
kao daxue	考大学	to pass the test to get into a university
ku	苦	bitter, hard
lanyin hukou	蓝印户口	blue-stamp residential status
laojia	老家	"old home," hometown, native place
laoxiang	老乡	a person of the same home origin
liangpi	凉皮	a type of seasoned cold noodle made from gluten and mixed with cucumber slices
liudong ertong	流动儿童	children of parents who are among the "floating population" (see below)
liudong renkou	流动人口	floating population, or people who leave their rural homes to seek work in the cities
liumang	流氓	hooligans
liushou ertong	留守儿童	left-behind children, referring to children left behind in rural areas while their parents seek work in cities
liyi xiaojie	礼仪小姐	"miss etiquette," a female master of ceremony
luan	乱	messy

mangliu	盲流	literally "blind flow," derogatory reference to migrants
mingong	民工	peasant workers
mingong zinü	民工子女	peasant workers' children
modi	摩的	motorcycle taxi
nongmingong	农民工	peasant workers
nongmingong tongzhu zinü	农民工同住子女	peasant workers' children who live with their parents in cities
nongye hukou	农业户口	agricultural household registration
penghuqu	棚户区	shack settlement
penghuqu gaizao	棚户区改造	shack settlement transformation or regeneration
pinminku	贫民窟	slum
pinde yu shehui	品德与社会	"Morality and Society," a course taught in public primary school
Pudong	浦东	a district in Shanghai, on the east side of the Huangpu River
Pudong Xinqu	浦东新区	Pudong New District
pusu	朴素	plain
putong gongban xuexiao	普通公办学校	ordinary public schools
Puxi	浦西	west side of the Huangpu River
quanrizhi putong zhongxue	全日制普通中学	nonelite full-time public secondary school
qunzu	群租	group renting
rencai	人才	"talent," referring to a well-educated laborer
roujiamo	肉夹馍	a Chinese hamburger with stewed, shredded pork between a baked bun
san bu guan	三不管	"three no management," no supervision or management from the local government, the real estate market, or the local residents
san xiao sheng	三校生	students studying in three kinds of secondary vocational schools

sanxiaosheng gaokao	三校生高考	the college entrance examination for secondary vocational students
seqing fuwu	色情服务	erotic service
shangban	上班	going to work, taking work shifts
Shanghai ban	上海班	Shanghai classes
shangmian de ban	上面的班	a class on the upper floor
shangshan xiaxiang	上山下乡	"up to the mountains and down to the countryside," referring to China's campaign during the Cultural Revolution that sent millions of urban youth to the countryside
shangxue	上学	going to school, attending school
shehui jixu jinque hangye	社会急需紧缺行业	urgently needed professions that are in short supply of laborers
shengjun shiyefei	生均事业费	subsidy for operational expenses per student
shiqu	市区	downtown districts
shishi xianfa, baozhang renquan	实施宪法, 保障人权	to implement the constitution, to guarantee human rights
shiyanxing shifanxing gaozhong	实验性示范性高中	literally "experimental high school for demonstration purposes," elite high school
shiqu	市区	urban districts
shixi	实习	internship
shukong	数控	literally "numerical control," numerical control lathe or machine operation
sifang	私房	privately owned houses
sixiang pinde	思想品德	"Ideology and Morality," a course taught in public middle school
sixiang zhengzhi	思想政治	"Ideology and Politics," a course taught in public high school
suzhi	素质	quality
suzhi jiaoyu	素质教育	"quality education," education that promotes well-rounded development to cultivate a desired creative and entrepreneurial population

tiaocao	跳槽	hop over / switch to another job
tongkao	统考	unified standardized test
tougao	投稿	contribute articles to newspapers or magazines for publication
tu	土	unfashionable, uncouth
tuifei	颓废	listless, decadent
waidi ban	外地班	"outsider class," a class filled with nonlocal students
waidiren	外地人	outsider, people from other provinces, nonlocal people
waidiren jiushi hui sheng	外地人就知道生	literally "outsiders just know how to breed"
wailai renkou suiqian zinü	外来人口随迁子女	children who move with the outsider population
waishengshi xuexi ban	外省市学习班	class composed of students from other provinces
wan xi shao	晚, 稀, 少	"Later, Longer, and Less," a family-planning campaign in the 1970s
weixin yuer gongzhonghao	微信育儿公众号	domestic WeChat accounts devoted to giving child-rearing advice
wenpinre	文凭热	"certification fever," the avid pursuit of educational qualifications
wenti xuesheng	问题学生	literally "problematic students," troublemakers
xian	县	county
xiangxia	乡下	the countryside
xiangxia ren	乡下人	people from the countryside, country bumpkin
xiaokai	小开	colloquial expression in the Shanghai dialect to refer to sons of rich men
xiaoqu	小区	neighborhood, housing compound
xinfang	新房	wedding room, newlyweds' apartment

xinshengdai nongmingong	新生代农民工	new generation of peasant workers
xin ye le	心野了	literally "the heart got wild," getting distracted and having a hard time refocusing on study or work
xueji	学籍	registration for school enrollment
xueli	学历	academic qualifications
yali shanda	压力山大	mountain-like pressure
yang er fang lao	养儿防老	raising children so that the children will care for their parents when they are old
yimin	移民	migrant, immigrant
yingbing	迎宾	to welcome guests
yingqin	迎亲	sending a party to escort the bride to the groom's house
yingshi jiaoyu	应试教育	examination-oriented education
ying zai qipaoxian	赢在起跑线	winning at the starting line
yinliao	饮料	beverage
yiri zhiji zaiyu chen	一日之计在于晨	morning hours are the best time of the day
youchulu	有出路	have good prospects
yousheng youyu	优生优育	bearing and rearing better children
yuanjiao	远郊	outer exurbia
yueguangzu	月光族	literally "moonlit tribe," people who save little from their monthly income
yue qiong yue sheng	越穷越生	"the poorer you get, the more you breed"
zang luan cha	脏乱差	dirty, chaotic, and inferior
zexiaore	择校热	school selection fever
zhaosheng jianzhang	招生简章	student recruiting brochure
zhaosheng jiuye bangongshi	招生就业办公室	student recruitment and placement office
zhifu guangrong	致富光荣	it is glorious to get rich
zhi sheng bu yang	只生不养	reproduction without cultivation

zhiqing	知青	sent-down youth during the Cultural Revolution
zhixiao	职校	professional school, one type of secondary vocational school
zhixiashi	直辖市	municipalities under the direct control of the central government (Beijing, Tianjin, Shanghai, Chongqing)
zhongdian	重点	literally "key or main point," elite
zhongdian xuexiao	重点学校	"key" or elite school
zhong nan qing nü	重男轻女	to prefer sons to daughters
zhongkao	中考	academic senior high school entrance examination (HSEE)
zhongzhuan	中专	specialist school, one type of secondary vocational school
zhuanshengben	专升本	an upgrade from a vocational college degree to a four-year university degree
zhuanye	专业	specializations in vocational school
zhuke	主课	major courses
zhunshengzheng	准生证	permission (from the government) to give birth
zizhu jiuye	自主就业	self-employed
zizhu zhaosheng	自主招生	schools that enroll students based on their own criteria and circumvent standardized enrollment processes administrated by education bureaus
zunji shoufa de xiandai hege gongmin	遵纪守法的现代合格公民	modern, qualified citizens who observe discipline and laws

REFERENCES

Adrian, Bonnie. 2003. *Framing the Bride: Globalizing Beauty and Romance in Taiwan's Bridal Industry*. Berkeley, CA: University of California Press.

Agamben, Giorgio. 2005. *State of Exception*. Translated by Kevin Attell. Chicago: University of Chicago Press.

Alberio, Marco. 2012. "Education and Social Inequalities in the Urban Space: A French Example." *Revue Interventions économiques* [En ligne] 45 (1). http://journals.openedition.org/interventionseconomiques/1547.

Anagnost, Ann. 1997. "The Child and National Transcendence in China." In *Constructing China: The Interaction of Culture and Economics*, edited by Ernest Young, 195–222. Ann Arbor: University of Michigan Center for Chinese Studies.

———. 2004. "The Corporeal Politics of Quality (Suzhi)." *Public Culture* 16 (2): 189–208.

Anagnost, Ann, Andrea Arai, and Hai Ren, eds. 2013. *Global Futures in East Asia: Youth, Nation, and the New Economy in Uncertain Times*. Stanford, CA: Stanford University Press.

Anderson, Benedict. 1983. *Imagined Communities: Reflections on the Rise and Spread of Nationalism*. New York: Verso.

Appadurai, Arjun. 1990. "Disjuncture and Difference in the Global Cultural Economy." *Theory Culture Society* 7: 295–310.

———. 1996. *Modernity at Large: Cultural Dimensions of Globalization*. Minneapolis: University of Minnesota Press.

Ariès, Philippe. 1962. *Centuries of Childhood: A Social History of Family Life*. Translated by Robert Baldick. New York: Vintage.

Bach, Jonathan. 2010. "'They Come in Peasants and Leave Citizens': Urban Villages and the Making of Shenzhen, China." *Cultural Anthropology* 25 (3): 421–458.

Barthes, Roland. 1972. *Mythologies*. Translated by Annette Lavers. New York: Hill and Wang.

Baudrillard, Jean. 1988. *Selected Writings*. Edited by Mark Poster. Cambridge: Polity.

Bergère, Marie-Claire. 2009. *Shanghai: China's Gateway to Modernity*. Stanford, CA: Stanford University Press.

Bian, Yanjie. 2002. "Chinese Social Stratification and Social Mobility." *Annual Review of Sociology* 28: 91–116.

Bonnin, Michel. 2013. *The Lost Generation: The Rustification of Chinese Youth, 1968–1980*. Translated by Krystyna Horko. Hong Kong: Chinese University Press.

Bourdieu, Pierre. 1984. *Distinction: A Social Critique of the Judgement of Taste*. Translated by Richard Nice. Cambridge, MA: Harvard University Press.

———. 1990. *The Logic of Practice*. Cambridge: Polity.

Bourdieu, Pierre, and Jean Claude Passeron. 1977. *Reproduction in Education, Society and Culture*. London: Sage.

Bourdieu, Pierre, and Loïc Wacquant. 2002. *An Invitation to Reflexive Sociology*. Cambridge: Polity.

Bourgois, Philippe. 1995. *In Search of Respect: Selling Crack in El Barrio*. Cambridge; New York: Cambridge University Press.

Bramall, C. 2001. "The Quality of China's Household Income Survey." *China Quarterly* 167: 689–705.

Burchell, Graham, Colin Gordon, and Peter Miller, eds. 1991. *The Foucault Effect: Studies in Governmentality*. Chicago: University of Chicago Press.

Butler, Judith. 1997. *The Psychic Life of Power: Theories in Subjection*. Stanford, CA: Stanford University Press.

Cai, Fang, Albert Park, and Yaohui Zhao. 2008. "The Chinese Labor Market in the Reform Era." In *China's Great Economic Transformation: Origins, Mechanism, and Consequences*, edited by Loren Brandt and Thomas Rawski, 167–214. Cambridge, UK: Cambridge University Press.

Chan, Anita. 2011. "Strikes in China's Export Industries in Comparative Perspective." *China Journal* 65: 27–51.

Chan, Chris King-Chi, and Pun Ngai. 2009. "The Making of a New Working Class? A Study of Collective Actions of Migrant Workers in South China." *China Quarterly* 198 (1): 287–303.

Chan, Jenny. 2017. "Intern Labor in China." *Rural China* 14 (1): 82–100.

Chan, Jenny, Pun Ngai, and Mark Selden. 2015. "Interns or Workers? China's Student Labor Regime." *Asia-Pacific Journal: Japan Focus* 13 (36).

Chan, Jenny, and Mark Selden. 2014. "China's Rural Migrant Workers, the State, and Labor Politics." *Critical Asian Studies* 46 (4): 599–620.

Chan, Kam Wing. 2010. "A China Paradox: Migrant Labor Shortage Amidst Rural Labor Supply Abundance." *Eurasian Geography and Economics* 51 (4): 513–530.

———. 2012. "Crossing the 50 Percent Population Rubicon: Can China Urbanize to Prosperity?" *Eurasian Geography and Economics* 53 (1): 63–86.

———. 2014. "China's Urbanization 2020: A New Blueprint and Direction." *Eurasian Geography and Economics* 55 (1): 1–9.

Chan, Kam Wing, and Will Buckingham. 2008. "Is China Abolishing the Hukou System?" *China Quarterly* 195 (1): 582–606.

Chan, Kam Wing, and Li Zhang. 1999. "The Hukou System and Rural-Urban Migration in China: Processes and Changes." *China Quarterly* 160: 818–55.

Chang, Leslie T. 2008. *Factory Girls: From Village to City in a Changing China*. New York: Spiegel & Grau.

Chatterjee, Partha. 2004. *The Politics of the Governed: Reflections on Popular Politics in Most of the World*. New York: Columbia University Press.

Chen, Chuanbo, and C. Cindy Fan. 2016. "China's Hukou Puzzle: Why Don't Rural Migrants Want Urban Hukou?" *China Review* 16 (3): 9–39.

Chen, Janet Y. 2012. *Guilty of Indigence: The Urban Poor in China, 1900–1953*. Princeton, NJ: Princeton University Press.

Chen, Y. P., and Zai Liang. 2007. "Educational Attainment of Migrant Children: The Forgotten Story of China's Urbanization." In *Education and Reform in China*, edited by Emily Hannum and Albert Park, 117–32. New York: Routledge.

Chen, Yu, and Caroline Hoy. 2008. "Rural Migrants, Urban Migrants and Local Workers in Shanghai: Segmented or Competitive Labour Markets?" *Built Environment* 34 (4): 499–516.

Chen, Yuanyuan, and Shuaizhang Feng. 2013. "Access to Public Schools and the Education of Migrant Children in China." *China Economic Review* 26: 75–88.

———. 2017. "Quality of Migrant Schools in China: Evidence from a Longitudinal Study in Shanghai." *Journal of Population Economics* 30 (3): 1007–1034.

China Family Planning Commission. 2010. *Zhongguo liudong renkou fazhan baogao* [Report on China's migrant population development]. Beijing: Zhongguo renkou chubanshu.

Chung, H. 2018. "Rural Migrants in Villages-in-the-City in Guangzhou, China: Multi-positionality and Negotiated Living Strategies." *Urban Studies* 55 (10): 2245–60.

Clifford, James. 1994. "Diasporas." *Cultural Anthropology* 9 (3): 302–38.

Cochran, Sherman, ed. 1999. *Inventing Nanjing Road: Commercial Culture in Shanghai, 1900–1945*. Ithaca, NY: East Asia Program, Cornell University.

Cockain, Alex. 2011. "Students' Ambivalence Toward Their Experiences in Secondary Education: Views from a Group of Young Chinese Studying on an International Foundation Program in Beijing." *China Journal* 65: 101–118.

Cohen, Myron L. 1993. "Cultural and Political Inventions in Modern China: The Case of the Chinese 'Peasant.'" *Daedalus* 122 (2): 151–70.

Cole, Jennifer, and Deborah Lynn Durham, eds. 2008. *Figuring the Future: Globalization and the Temporalities of Children and Youth*. Santa Fe: School for Advanced Research Press.

Collins, James. 2009. "Social Reproduction in Classrooms and Schools." *Annual Review of Anthropology* 38: 33–48.

Costello, Michael A. 1987. "Slums and Squatter Areas as Entrepots for Rural-Urban Migrants in a Less Developed Society." *Social Forces* 66 (2): 427–45.

Croll, Elisabeth J. 2006. *China's New Consumers: Social Development and Domestic Demand*. London: Routledge.

Davis, Deborah S. 2000. *The Consumer Revolution in Urban China*. Studies on China. Berkeley: University of California Press.

———. 2002. "When a House Becomes His Home." In *Popular China: Unofficial Culture in a Globalizing Society*, edited by E. Perry Link, Richard Madsen, and Paul Pickowicz, 231–50. Lanham, MD: Rowman & Littlefield.

———. 2005. "Urban Consumer Culture." *China Quarterly* 183: 692–709.

Davis, Deborah S., and Julia S. Sensenbrenner. 2000. "Commercializing Childhood: Parental Purchases for Shanghai's Only Child." In *The Consumer Revolution in Urban China*, edited by Deborah Davis, 54–79. Berkeley: University of California Press.

Davis, Deborah S., and Feng Wang. 2009. *Creating Wealth and Poverty in Postsocialist China*. Stanford, CA: Stanford University Press.

de Certeau, Michel. 1984. *The Practice of Everyday Life*. Berkeley: University of California Press.

Deleuze, Gilles, and Felix Guattari. 1987. *A Thousand Plateaus: Capitalism and Schizophrenia*. Translated by Brian Massumi. Minneapolis: University of Minnesota Press.

Ding, Xiaohao, and Yan Liang. 2012. "Changes in the Degree of Equalization in Opportunities for Entering Higher Education in China." *Chinese Education & Society* 45 (1): 22–30.

Douglas, Mary. 1996. *Thought Styles: Critical Essays on Good Taste*. London: Sage.

Downey, Douglas B., Paul T. von Hippel, and Melanie Hughes. 2008. "Are 'Failing' Schools Really Failing? Using Seasonal Comparison to Evaluate School Effectiveness." *Sociology of Education* 81 (3): 242–270.

Dutton, Michael Robert. 1999. "Street Scenes of Subalternity: China, Globalization, and Rights." *Social Text* 60: 63–86.

Eckholm, Erick. 2000. "China's Control on Rural Workers Stir Some Rarely Seen Heated Opposition." *New York Times*, March 10, 2000, A10.

Elman, Benjamin A. 1991. "Political, Social, and Cultural Reproduction via Civil Service Examinations in Late Imperial China." *Journal of Asian Studies* 50 (1): 7–28.

———. 2000. *A Cultural History of Civil Examinations in Late Imperial China*. Berkeley: University of California Press.

Escobar, Arturo. 2001. "Culture Sits in Places: Reflections on Globalism and Subaltern Strategies of Localization." *Political Geography* 20: 139–74.

———. 2008. *The Subject of Gender: Daughters and Mothers in Urban China*. Lanham, MD: Rowman & Littlefield.

———. 2010. "The Gender of Communication: Changing Expectations of Mothers and Daughters in Urban China." *China Quarterly* 204: 980–1000.

Fabian, Johannes. 1983. *Time and the Other: How Anthropology Makes Its Object*. New York: Columbia University Press.

Fan, Cindy C. 2002. "The Elite, the Natives, and the Outsiders: Migration and Labor Market Segmentation in Urban China." *Annals of the Association of American Geographers* 92 (1): 103–24.

———. 2008. "China on the Move: Migration, the State, and the Household." *China Quarterly* 196: 924–56.

———. 2011. "Settlement Intention and Split Households: Findings from a Survey of Migrants in Beijing's Urban Village." *China Review* 11: 11–41.

Fan, Jie, and Wolfgang Taubmann. 2002. "Migrant Enclaves in Large Chinese Cities." In *The New Chinese City: Globalization and Market Reform*, edited by John R. Logan, 183–97. Oxford: Blackwell.

Feldman, Marcus W, Shuzhuo Li, Xiaoyi Jin, and Nan Li. 2007. "Son Preference, Marriage, and Intergenerational Transfer in Rural China." In *Allocating Public and Private Resources Across Generations*, edited by Anne H. Gauthier, Cyrus C. Y. Chu, and Shripad Tuljapurkar, 139–62. Dordrecht, Netherlands: Springer.

Fleischer, Friederike. 2007. "To Choose a House Means to Choose a Lifestyle: The Consumption of Housing and Class-Structuration in Urban China." *City & Society* 19 (2): 287–311.

Flock, Ryanne, and Werner Breitung. 2016. "Migrant Street Vendors in Urban China and the Social Production of Public Space." *Population, Space and Place* 22 (2): 158–69.

Fong, Vanessa L. 2002. "China's One-Child Policy and the Empowerment of Urban Daughters." *American Anthropologist* 104 (4): 1098–109.

———. 2004. *Only Hope: Coming of Age Under China's One-Child Policy*. Stanford, CA: Stanford University Press.

———. 2011. *Paradise Redefined: Transnational Chinese Students and the Quest for Flexible Citizenship in the Developed World*. Stanford, CA: Stanford University Press.

Foucault, Michel. 1988. *Technologies of the Self: A Seminar with Michel Foucault*. Amherst: University of Massachusetts Press.

———. 2010. *The Government of Self and Others: Lectures at the College de France 1982–1983*. Basingstoke, UK: Palgrave Macmillan; New York: St. Martin's.

Friedman, Eli. 2014. *Insurgency Trap: Labor Politics in Postsocialist China*. Ithaca, NY: Cornell University Press.

———. 2018. "Just-in-Time Urbanization? Managing Migration, Citizenship, and Schooling in the Chinese City." *Critical Sociology* 44 (3): 504–18.

Friedman, Sara. 2006. *Intimate Politics: Marriage, the Market, and State Power in Southeastern China*. Cambridge, MA: Harvard University Asia Center, distributed by Harvard University Press.

Fu, Zhengji. 2002. "The State, Capital, and Urban Restructuring in Post-Reform Shanghai." In *The New Chinese City: Globalization and Market Reform*, edited by John R. Logan, 106–20. Oxford: Blackwell.

Gao, Qin. 2010. "Redistributive Nature of Chinese Social Benefit System." *China Quarterly* 201: 1–19.

Gerth, Karl. 2013. "Compromising with Consumerism in Socialist China: Transnational Flows and Internal Tensions in 'Socialist Advertising.'" *Past and Present* 218 (S8):S203–32.

Ghanem, Tania. 2003. *When Forced Migrants Return "Home": The Psychosocial Difficulties Returnees Encounter in the Reintegrating Process*. Oxford: Refugee Studies Centre.

Ghannam, Farha. 2002. *Remaking the Modern: Space, Relocation, and the Politics of Identity in a Global Cairo*. Berkeley: University of California Press.

Giddens, Anthony. 1991. *Modernity and Self-Identity: Self and Society in the Late Modern Age*. Cambridge: Polity.

Gmelch, George. 1980. "Return Migration." *Annual Review of Anthropology* 9: 135–59.

Goldman, Merle, and Elizabeth Perry. 2002. *Changing Meanings of Citizenship in Modern China*. Cambridge, MA: Harvard University Press.

Goodburn, Charlotte 2009. "Learning from Migrant Education: A Case Study of the Schooling of Rural Migrant Children in Beijing." *International Journal of Educational Development* 29 (5): 495–504.

———. 2014. "Rural-Urban Migration and Gender Disparities in Child Healthcare in China and India." *Development and Change* 45 (4): 631–55.

———. 2015. "Migrant Girls in Shenzhen: Gender, Education and the Urbanization of Aspiration." *China Quarterly* 222: 320–38.

Goodman, Bryna. 1995. *Native Place, City, and Nation: Regional Networks and Identities in Shanghai, 1853–1937*. Berkeley: University of California Press.

Goodman, David S. G. 2014. *Class in Contemporary China*. Cambridge: Polity.

Graham, Maureen J., Ulla Larsen, and Xiping Xu. 1998. "Son Preference in Anhui Province, China." *International Family Planning Perspectives* 24 (2): 72–77.

Gramsci, Antonio. 1991. *Prison Notebooks*. Translated by Joseph A. Buttigieg. European Perspectives. New York: Columbia University Press.

Greenhalgh, Susan. 2005. "Missile Science, Population Science: The Origins of China's One-Child Policy." *China Quarterly* 182: 253–76.

———. 2008. *Just One Child: Science and Policy in Deng's China*. Berkeley: University of California Press.

Greenhalgh, Susan, and Edwin A. Winckler. 2005. *Governing China's Population: From Leninist to Neoliberal Biopolitics*. Stanford, CA: Stanford University Press.

Guang, Lei. 2003. "Rural Taste, Urban Fashions: The Cultural Politics of Rural/Urban Difference in Contemporary China." *positions: asia critique* 11 (3): 613–46.

———. 2010. "Rural Prejudice and Gender Discrimination in China's Urban Job Market." In *One Country Two Societies*, edited by Martin King Whyte, 241–64. Cambridge, MA: Harvard University Press.

Gui, Tianhan. 2017. "'Devalued' Daughters Versus 'Appreciated' Sons: Gender Inequality in China's Parent-Organized Matchmaking Markets." *Journal of Family Issues* 38 (13): 1923–48.

Guo, Gang. 2007. "Persistent Inequalities in Funding for Rural Schooling in Contemporary China." *Asian Survey* 47 (2): 213–30.

Guo, Zhonghua, and Sujians Guo, eds. 2015. *Theorizing Chinese Citizenship*. Lanham, MD: Lexington.

Gupta, Akhil, and James Ferguson. 1992. "Beyond 'Culture': Space, Identity, and the Politics of Difference." *Cultural Anthropology* 7 (1): 6–23.

———, eds. 1997. *Culture, Power, Place: Explorations in Critical Anthropology*. Durham, NC: Duke University Press.

Han, Jialing. 2004. "Survey Report on the State of Compulsory Education Among Migrant Children in Beijing." *Chinese Education & Society* 37 (5): 29–55.

———. 2012. "Rapid Urbanization and the Aspiration and Challenge of Second-Generation Urban-Rural Migrants." *Chinese Education & Society* 45 (1): 77–83.

Hannerz, Ulf. 1996. "The Cultural Role of World Cities." In *Transnational Connections: Culture, People, Places*, 127–39. London: Routledge.

Hannum, Emily. 1999. "Political Change and the Urban-Rural Gap in Basic Education in China, 1949–1990." *Comparative Education Review* 43 (2): 193–211.

Hannum, Emily, and Albert Park, eds. 2007. *Education and Reform in China*. London: Routledge.

Hansen, Mette Halskov. 2015. *Educating the Chinese Individual: Life in a Rural Boarding School*. Seattle: University of Washington Press.

Harms, Erik. 2011. *Saigon's Edge: On the Margins of Ho Chi Minh City*. Minneapolis: University of Minnesota Press.

———. 2016a. *Luxury and Rubble: Civility and Dispossession in the New Saigon*. Berkeley: University of California Press.

———. 2016b. "Urban Space and Exclusion in Asia." *Annual Review of Anthropology* 45 (1): 45–61.

Harvey, David. 1990. *The Condition of Postmodernity: An Enquiry into the Origins of Cultural Change*. Cambridge, MA: Blackwell.

———. 2008. "The Right to the City." *New Left Review* 53: 23–40.

Hatfield, Madeleine E. 2010. "Children Moving 'Home'? Everyday Experiences of Return Migration in Highly Skilled Households." *Childhood* 17 (2): 243–57.

He, Shenjing. 2015. "Consuming Urban Living in 'Villages in the City': Studentification in Guangzhou, China." *Urban Studies* 52 (15): 2849–73.

Heimer, M., and S. Thøgersen. 2006. *Doing Fieldwork in China*. Honolulu, University of Hawaii Press.

Hershatter, Gail. 1989. "The Hierarchy of Shanghai Prostitution, 1870–1949." *Modern China* 15 (4): 463–98.

———. 1992. "Courtesans and Streetwalkers: The Changing Discourses on Shanghai Prostitution, 1890–1949." *Journal of the History of Sexuality* 3 (2): 245–69.

Herzfeld, Michael. 1987. *Anthropology Through the Looking-glass: Critical Ethnography in the Margins of Europe*. Cambridge: Cambridge University Press.

Ho, Karen Zouwen. 2009. *Liquidated: An Ethnography of Wall Street*. Durham, NC: Duke University Press.

Ho, Ping-Ti. 1962. *The Ladder of Success in Imperial China: Aspects of Social Mobility, 1368–1911*. New York: Basic.

Hoffman, Lisa M. 2010. *Patriotic Professionalism in Urban China: Fostering Talent*. Philadelphia: Temple University Press.

Holston, James, and Arjun Appadurai. 1999. "Cities and Citizenship." In *Cities and Citizenship*, edited by James Holston, 1–18. Durham, NC: Duke University Press.

Honig, Emily. 1989. "The Politics of Prejudice: Subei People in Republican-Era Shanghai." *Modern China* 15 (3): 243–74.

———. 1990. "Invisible Inequalities: The Status of Subei People in Contemporary Shanghai." *China Quarterly* 122: 273–92.

———. 1992. *Creating Chinese Ethnicity: Subei People in Shanghai, 1850–1980*. New Haven, CT: Yale University Press.

Horst, Heather A. 2011. "Reclaiming Place: The Architecture of Home, Family and Migration." *Anthropologica* 53 (1): 29–39.

Hsing, You-tien. 2006. "Land and Territorial Politics in Urban China." *China Quarterly* 187: 575–91.

———. 2010. *The Great Urban Transformation: Politics of Land and Property in China*. Oxford: Oxford University Press.

Hu, Feng. 2012. "Migration, Remittances, and Children's High School Attendance: The Case of Rural China." *International Journal of Educational Development* 32 (3): 401–11.

Huang, Y., and W. A. V. Clark. 2002. "Housing Tenure Choice in Transitional Urban China: A Multilevel Analysis." *Urban Studies* 39 (1): 7–32.

Huang, Yanzhong, and Dali L. Yang. 2006. "China's Unbalanced Sex Ratios: Politics and Policy Response." *Chinese Historical Review* 13 (1): 1–15.

Huang, Yasheng. 2008. *Capitalism with Chinese Characteristics: Entrepreneurship and the State*. Cambridge: Cambridge University Press.

Huang, Youqin, and L. Jiang. 2007. "Housing Inequality in Transitional Beijing." International Conference on China's Urban Transition and City Planning, Cardiff, UK, June 29–30, 2007.

Huddy, Leonie. 2001. "From Social to Political Identity: A Critical Examination of Social Identity Theory." *Political Psychology* 22 (1): 137–56.

Jacka, Tamara. 2009. "Cultivating Citizens: *Suzhi* (Quality) Discourse in the PRC." *positions: asia critique* 17 (3): 523–35.

Jacobs, Jane. 1961. *The Death and Life of Great American Cities*. New York: Vintage.

Jeong, Jong-Ho. 2011. "From Illegal Migrant Settlements to Central Business and Residential Districts: Restructuring of Urban Space in Beijing's Migrant Enclaves." *Habitat International* 35 (3): 508–13.

Jing, Jun, ed. 2000. *Feeding China's Little Emperors: Food, Children, and Social Change*. Stanford, CA: Stanford University Press.

Kipnis, Andrew B. 2001a. "Articulating School Countercultures." *Anthropology & Education Quarterly* 32 (4): 472–92.

———. 2001b. "The Disturbing Educational Discipline of 'Peasants.'" *China Journal* 46: 1–24.

———. 2007. "Neoliberalism Reified: Suzhi Discourse and Tropes of Neoliberalism in the People's Republic of China." *Journal of the Royal Anthropological Institute* 13 (2): 383–400.

———. 2011. *Governing Educational Desire: Culture, Politics, and Schooling in China*. Chicago: University of Chicago Press.

Kipnis, Andrew B., and Shanfeng Li. 2010. "Is Chinese Education Underfunded?" *China Quarterly* 202: 327–43.

Klimt, Andrea. 1989. "Returning 'Home': Portuguese Migrant Notions of Temporariness, Permanence and Commitment." *New German Critique* 16: 47–70.

Knörr, Jacqueline. 2005. "When German Children Come 'Home': Experiences of (Re-) migration to Germany and Some Remarks About the 'TICK'-Issue." In *Childhood and Migration: From Experience to Agency*, edited by Jacqueline Knörr, 51–76. Bielefeld, Germany: Bielefelder Verlag.

Koo, Anita. 2016. "Expansion of Vocational Education in Neoliberal China: Hope and Despair Among Rural Youth." *Journal of Education Policy*. 31 (1): 46–59.

Koo, Anita, Holly Ming, and Bill Tsang. 2014. "The Doubly Disadvantaged: How Return Migrant Students Fail to Access and Deploy Capitals for Academic Success in Rural Schools." *Sociology* 48 (4): 795–811.

Kuan, Teresa. 2015. *Love's Uncertainty: The Politics and Ethics of Child Rearing in Contemporary China*. Berkeley, CA: University of California Press.

Kwong, Julia. 2004. "Educating Migrant Children: Negotiations Between the State and Civil Society." *China Quarterly* 180: 1073–88.

———. 2011. "Education and Identity: The Marginalisation of Migrant Youths in Beijing." *Journal of Youth Studies* 14 (8): 871–83.

Lai, Lili. 2016. *Hygiene, Sociality, and Culture in Contemporary Rural China: The Uncanny New Village*. Amsterdam: Amsterdam University Press.

Lan, Pei-Chia. 2014. "Segmented Incorporation: The Second Generation of Rural Migrants in Shanghai." *China Quarterly* 217: 243–65.

Lareau, Annette. 2011. *Unequal Childhoods: Class, Race, and Family Life*. Berkeley: University of California Press.

Latham, Kevin. 2002. "Rethinking Chinese Consumption." In *Postsocialism*, edited by C. M. Hann, 227–28. London: Routledge.

Lee, Ching Kwan. 1998. *Gender and the South China Miracle: Two Worlds of Factory Women*. Berkeley: University of California Press.

———, ed. 2007. *Working in China: Ethnographies of Labor and Workplace Transformation*. Asia's Transformations. London: Routledge.

Lee, Leo Ou-fan. 1999. *Shanghai Modern: The Flowering of a New Urban Culture in China, 1930–1945*. Cambridge, MA: Harvard University Press.

Lefebvre, Henri. 1991. *The Production of Space*. Translated by Donald Nicholson-Smith. Malden, MA: Blackwell.

Leidner, Robin. 1993. *Fast Food, Fast Talk: Service Work and the Routinization of Everyday Life*. Berkeley, CA: University of California Press.

Leonard, Karen. 1992. "Finding One's Own Place: The Imposition of Asian Landscapes on Rural California." In *Culture, Power, Place: Explorations in Critical Anthropology*, edited by Akhil Gupta and James Ferguson, 118–36. Durham, NC: Duke University Press.

Leong, Solomon. 2006. "Who's the Fairest of Them All? Television Ads for Skin-Whitening Cosmetics in Hong Kong." *Asian Ethnicity* 7 (2): 167–181.

Li, Beibei. 2004. "Shanghai wailai mingong zinü yiwu jiaoyu diaoyan" [Investigation of compulsory education of migrant children in Shanghai]. *Lishi jiaoxue wenti* 6: 58–64.

Li, Bingqin, Mark Duda, and Xiangsheng An. 2009. "Drivers of Housing Choice Among Rural-to-Urban Migrants: Evidence from Taiyuan." *Journal of Asian Public Policy* 2 (2): 142–56.

Li, Bingqin, and Yongmei Zhang. 2011. "Housing Provision for Rural-Urban Migrant Workers in Chinese Cities: The Roles of the State, Employers and the Market." *Social Policy & Administration* 45 (6): 694–713.

Li, Chunling. 2012. "Sociopolitical Change and Inequality of Educational Opportunities." *Chinese Education & Society* 45 (1): 7–12.

Li, Jianghong, and William Lavely. 2003. "Village Context, Women's Status, and Son Preference Among Rural Chinese Women." *Rural Sociology* 68 (1): 87–108.

Li, Miao. 2015. *Citizenship Education and Migrant Youth in China: Pathways to the Urban Underclass.* New York: Routledge.

Li, Mingjiang. 2005. "The Rural-Urban Divide in Chinese Social Security: Political and Institutional Explanations." *Perspectives* 6 (4): 42–59.

Li, Na, Wei-Hsin Lin, and Xiaobing Wang. 2012. "From Rural Poverty to Urban Deprivation? The Plight of Chinese Rural-Urban Migrants Through the Lens of Last Train Home." *East Asia: An International Quarterly* 29 (2): 173–86.

Li, Shuzhuo, Yexia Zhang, and Marcus W. Feldman. 2010. "Birth Registration in China: Practices, Problems and Policies." *Population Research and Policy Review* 29 (3): 297–317.

Li, Tao, and Zhen Li, eds. 2005. *Nongmingong zai bianyuan* [Peasant worker: floating on the margin]. Beijing: Dangdai Zhongguo chubanshe.

Lian, Si, ed. 2009. *Yizu: Daxue biyesheng jujucun shilu* [Ant tribe: urban villages for college graduates]. Guilin: Guangxi shifandaxue chubanshe.

Liang, Chen, James Lee, Hao Zhang, Lan Li, Danqing Ruan, Wenlin Kang, and Shanhua Yang. 2012. "Wusheng de geming: Beijing Daxue yu Suzhou Daxue xuesheng shehui laiyuan yuanjiu 1952–2002" [A silent revolution: research on family backgrounds of students of Peking University and Soochow University 1952–2002]. *Zhongguo shehui kexue* 1: 98–118.

Liang, Zai, and Yiu Por Chen. 2007. "The Educational Consequences of Migration for Children in China." *Social Science Research* 6 (1): 28–47.

Liang, Zai, and Zhongdong Ma. 2004. "China's Floating Population: New Evidence from the 2000 Census." *Population and Development Review* 30 (3): 467–88.

Lin, George C. S., and Samuel P. S. Ho. 2005. "The State, Land System, and Land Development Processes in Contemporary China." *Annals of the Association of American Geographers* 95 (2): 411–36.

Ling, Minhua. 2015. ""Bad Students Go to Vocational Schools!": Education, Social Reproduction and Migrant Youth in Urban China." *China Journal* 73: 108–31.

———. 2017a. "Precious Son, Reliable Daughter: Redefining Son Preference and Parent-Child Relations in Migrant Households in Urban China." *China Quarterly* 229: 150–71.

———. 2017b. "Returning to No Home: Educational Remigration and Displacement in Rural China." *Anthropological Quarterly* 90 (3): 715–42.

Liu, Chengbin. 2008. *Liushou yu liudong: Nongmingong zinü de jiaoyu xuanze* [Staying behind and floating: educational choices of peasant workers' children]. Shanghai: Shanghai Jiaotong daxue chubanshe.

Liu, Xin. 1997. "Space, Mobility, and Flexibility: Chinese Villagers and Scholars Negotiate Power at Home and Abroad." In *Ungrounded Empires: The Cultural Politics of*

Modern Chinese Transnationalism, edited by Aihwa Ong and Donald M. Nonini, 91–114. New York: Routledge.

Liu, Zhijun. 2009. "*Liushou* Children in a Chinese Village: Childhood Apart from Parents." *Chinese Sociology & Anthropology* 41 (3): 71–89.

Lo, Celia C., Tyrone C. Cheng, Maggie Bohm, and Hua Zhong. 2018. "Rural-to-Urban Migration, Strain, and Juvenile Delinquency: A Study of Eighth-Grade Students in Guangzhou, China." *International Journal of Offender Therapy and Comparative Criminology* 62 (2): 334–59.

Loh, Charis, and Elizabeth J. Remick. 2015. "China's Skewed Sex Ratio and the One-Child Policy." *China Quarterly* 222: 295–319.

Long, Yingtai. 1998. *A, Shanghai nanren* [A, Shanghai men]. Shanghai: Xuelin.

Louie, Andrea. 2000. "Re-territorializing Transnationalism: Chinese Americans and the Chinese Motherland." *American Ethnologist* 27 (3): 645–69.

Lu, Hanchao. 1999. *Beyond the Neon Lights: Everyday Shanghai in the Early Twentieth Century*. Berkeley: University of California Press.

Lu, Jie, and Desheng Gao. 2004. "New Direction in the Moral Education Curriculum in Chinese Primary Schools." *Journal of Moral Education* 33 (4): 495–510.

Lü, Shaoqing. 2007. *Liushou haishi liudong: Mingongchao zhong de eryong yanjiu* [Staying behind or floating? An empirical study of peasant workers' children]. Beijing: Zhongguo nongye chubanshe.

Lu, Yao. 2012. "Education of Children Left Behind in Rural China." *Journal of Marriage and Family* 74 (2): 328–41.

Lu, Yao, and Ran Tao. 2015. "Female Migration, Cultural Context, and Son Preference in Rural China." *Population Research and Policy Review* 34 (5): 665–86.

Lu, Yao, and Hao Zhou. 2013. "Academic Achievement and Loneliness of Migrant Children in China: School Segregation and Segmented Assimilation." *Comparative Education Review* 57 (1): 85–116.

Ma, Li. 2010. "Internal Migration, Institutional Change and Social Inequality in Post-Communist Shanghai." PhD diss., Cornell University.

Malkki, Liisa H. 1992. "National Geographic: The Rooting of Peoples and the Territorialization of National Identity Among Scholars and Refugees." *Cultural Anthropology* 7 (1): 24–44.

———. 1995. "Refugees and Exile: From 'Refugee Studies' to the National Order of Things." *Annual Review of Anthropology* 24: 495–523.

Marshall, T. H. 1964. "Citizenship and Social Class." In *Class, Citizenship, and Social Development: Essays*. Garden City, NY: Doubleday.

Mbodj-Pouye, AÏSsatou. 2016. "Fixed Abodes: Urban Emplacement, Bureaucratic Requirements, and the Politics of Belonging Among West African Migrants in Paris." *American Ethnologist* 43 (2): 295–310.

Meng, Qingjie. 2009. *Shanghaishi wailai liudongrenkou de shenghuo fangshi yanjiu* [Study of the livelihood of Shanghai's floating population]. Shanghai: Shanghai shehuikexue chubanshe.

Miller, Daniel. 1995. *Acknowledging Consumption: A Review of New Studies*. London: Routledge.

Miller, Laura. 2006. *Beauty Up: Exploring Contemporary Japanese Body Aesthetics*. Berkeley, CA: University of California Press.

Mills, Mary Beth. 1999. *Thai Women in the Global Labor Force: Consuming Desires, Contested Selves*. New Brunswick, NJ: Rutgers University Press.

Milwertz, Cecilia N. 1997. *Accepting Population Control: Urban Chinese Women and the One-Child Family Policy*. Richmond, UK: Curzon.

Ming, Holly H. 2009. "Growing Up in the Urban Shadow: Realities and Dreams of Migrant Workers' Children in Beijing and Shanghai." PhD diss., Harvard University.

———. 2014. *The Education of Migrant Children and China's Future: The Urban Left Behind*. Abingdon, UK: Routledge.

Mok, Ka Ho, Yu Cheung Wong, and Xiulan Zhang. 2009. "When Marketisation and Privatisation Clash with Socialist Ideals: Educational Inequality in Urban China." *International Journal of Educational Development* 29 (5): 505–12.

Moore, Robert L. 2005. "Generation Ku: Individualism and China's Millennial Youth." *Ethnology* 44 (4): 357–76.

Murphy, Rachel. 2004. "Turning Peasants into Modern Chinese Citizens: 'Population Quality' Discourse, Demographic Transition and Primary Education." *China Quarterly* 177: 1–20.

———. 2006. *Domestic Migrant Remittances in China: Distribution, Channels, and Livelihoods*. IOM Migration Research Series. Geneva: International Organization for Migration.

———. 2014. "Study and School in the Lives of Children in Migrant Families: A View from Rural Jiangxi, China." *Development and Change* 45 (1): 29–51.

Murphy, Rachel, Ran Tao, and Xi Lu. 2011. "Son Preference in Rural China: Patrilineal Families and Socioeconomic Change." *Population and Development Review* 37 (4): 665–90.

Murphy, Rachel, Minhui Zhou, and Ran Tao. 2016. "Parents' Migration and Children's Subjective Well-Being and Health: Evidence from Rural China." *Population, Space and Place* 22 (8): 766–80.

Naftali, Orna. 2009. "Empowering the Child: Children's Rights, Citizenship, and the State in Contemporary China." *China Journal* 61: 79–103.

———. 2010. "Recovering Childhood: Play, Pedagogy, and the Rise of Psychological Knowledge in Contemporary Urban China." *Modern China* 36 (6): 589–616.

———. 2014. *Children, Rights and Modernity in China: Raising Self-Governing Citizens*. Basingstoke, UK: Palgrave Macmillan.

National Bureau of Statistics of China. 2012. *Zhongguo 2010 nian renkou pucha ziliao* [Tabulation on the 2010 Population Census of the People's Republic of China]. Beijing: Zhongguo tongji chubanshe.

Naughton, Barry. 2007. *The Chinese Economy: Transitions and Growth*. Cambridge, MA: MIT Press.

Newendorp, Nicole DeJong. 2008. *Uneasy Reunions: Immigration, Citizenship, and Family Life in Post-1997 Hong Kong*. Stanford, CA: Stanford University Press.

Ngai, Mae M. 2004. *Impossible Subjects: Illegal Aliens and the Making of Modern America.* Princeton, NJ: Princeton University Press.

Nie, Yilin, and Robert J. Wyman. 2005. "The One-Child Policy in Shanghai: Acceptance and Internalization." *Population and Development Review* 31 (2): 313–36.

O'Brien, Kevin, and Lianjiang Li. 2006. *Rightful Resistance in Rural China.* Cambridge: Cambridge University Press.

Ogbu, John U. 1978. *Minority Education and Caste: The American System in Cross-Cultural Perspective.* New York: Academic.

———. 1990. "Minority Education in Comparative Perspective." *Journal of Negro Education* 59 (1): 45–57.

Ogbu, John U., and Herbert D. Simons. 1998. "Voluntary and Involuntary Minorities: A Cultural-Ecological Theory of School Performance with Some Implications for Education." *Anthropology & Education Quarterly* 29 (2): 155–88.

Okano, Kaori, and Motonori Tsuchiya. 1999. *Education in Contemporary Japan: Inequality and Diversity.* Cambridge: Cambridge University Press.

Ong, Aihwa. 1999. *Flexible Citizenship: The Cultural Logics of Transnationality.* Durham, NC: Duke University Press.

———. 2006. "Mutations in Citizenship." *Theory Culture Society* 23 (2–3): 499–505.

Ong, Aihwa, and Donald Macon Nonini, eds. 1997. *Ungrounded Empires: The Cultural Politics of Modern Chinese Transnationalism.* New York: Routledge.

Otis, Eileen M. 2011. *Markets and Bodies: Women, Service Work, and the Making of Inequality in China.* Stanford, CA: Stanford University Press.

Pan, Xiaoling, Qianrong Shen, Qian Xia, Xing Liu, and Qian He. 2011. "Qionghaizi meiyou chuntian? Hanmen zidi weihe li yixian gaoxiao yuelai yueyuan" [Poor kids have no future? Why are children from poor families having less and less chance in getting into first-tier universities]. *Nanfang zhoumo,* August 4, 2011. http://www.infzm.com/content/61888.

Park, Albert, Fang Cai, and Yang Du. 2010. "Can China Meet Her Employment Challenges?" In *Growing Pains: Tensions and Opportunities in China's Transformation,* edited by Scott Rozelle Jean Oi, and Xuegang Zhou, 27–55. Stanford, CA: Stanford Asia-Pacific Research Center.

Piore, Michael J. 1979. *Birds of Passage: Migrant Labor and Industrial Societies.* Cambridge: Cambridge University Press.

Portes, Alejandro, and Rubén G. Rumbaut. 1990. *Immigrant America: A Portrait.* Berkeley: University of California Press.

———. 2001. *Legacies: The Story of the Immigrant Second Generation.* Berkeley: University of California Press; New York: Russell Sage Foundation.

Portes, Alejandro, and Min Zhou. 1993. "The New Second Generation: Segmented Assimilation and Its Variants." *Annals of the American Academy of Political and Social Science* 530: 74–96.

Potter, Robert B., Dennis Conway, and Joan Phillips. 2005. *The Experience of Return: Caribbean Perspectives.* Aldershot, UK: Ashgate.

Pufall, Peter B., and Richard P. Unsworth. 2004. *Rethinking Childhood*. New Brunswick, NJ: Rutgers University Press.

Pun, Ngai. 1999. "Becoming Dagongmei (Working Girls): The Politics of Identity and Difference in Reform China." *China Journal* 42: 1–18.

———. 2003. "Subsumption or Consumption? The Phantom of Consumer Revolution in 'Globalizing' China." *Cultural Anthropology* 18 (4): 469–92.

———. 2004. "Engendering Chinese Modernity: The Sexual Politics of Dagongmei in a Dormitory Labour Regime." *Asian Studies Review* 28 (2): 151–65.

———. 2005a. "Global Production, Company Codes of Conduct, and Labor Conditions in China: A Case Study of Two Factories." *China Journal* 54: 101–13.

———. 2005b. *Made in China: Women Factory Workers in a Global Workplace*. Durham, NC: Duke University Press.

Pun, Ngai, and Jenny Chan. 2012. "Global Capital, the State, and Chinese Workers: The Foxconn Experience." *Modern China* 38 (4): 383–410.

———. 2013. "The Spatial Politics of Labor in China: Life, Labor, and a New Generation of Migrant Workers." *South Atlantic Quarterly* 112 (1): 179–90.

Pun, Ngai, and Huilin Lu. 2010. "A Culture of Violence: The Labor Subcontracting System and Collective Action by Construction Workers in Post-Socialist China." *China Journal* 64: 143–58.

Purcell, Mark. 2003. "Citizenship and the Right to the Global City: Reimagining the Capitalist World Order." *International Journal of Urban and Regional Research* 27 (3): 564–90.

Rabinow, Paul, ed. 1984. *The Foucault Reader*. New York: Pantheon.

Ren, Hai. 2013. "The Middle-Class Norm and Responsible Consumption in China's Risk Society." In *Global Futures in East Asia: Youth, Nation, and the New Economy in Uncertain Times*, edited by Ann Anagnost, Andrea Arai, and Hai Ren, 29–52. Stanford, CA: Stanford University Press.

Rofel, Lisa. 2007. *Desiring China: Experiments in Neoliberalism, Sexuality, and Public Culture*. Durham, NC: Duke University Press.

Rong, Xue Lan, and Tianjian Shi. 2001. "Inequality in Chinese Education." *Journal of Contemporary China* 10 (26): 107–24.

Rose, Nikolas S. 1999. *Governing the Soul: The Shaping of the Private Self*. London: Free Association.

———. 2007. *The Politics of Life Itself: Biomedicine, Power, and Subjectivity in the Twenty-First Century*. Princeton, NJ: Princeton University Press.

Rosen, Stanley. 2004. "The Victory of Materialism: Aspirations to Join China's Urban Moneyed Classes and the Commercialization of Education." *China Journal* 51: 27–51.

Ruan, Danqing, ed. 2009. *Chongsu shanghairen* [Reconstructing Shanghainese]. Shanghai: Xuelin.

Santos, Gonçalo. 2016. "On Intimate Choices and Troubles in rural South China." *Modern Asian Studies* 54 (4): 1298–326.

Saunders, Doug. 2010. *Arrival City: How the Largest Migration in History is Reshaping Your World*. London: William Heinemann.

Schein, Louisa. 2001. "Urbanity, Cosmopolitanism, Consumption." In *China Urban*, edited by Nancy N. Chen, Constance D. Clark, Suzanne Z. Gottschang, and Lyn Jeffery, 225–41. Durham, NC: Duke University Press.

Selden, Mark, and Jieh-Min Wu. 2011. "The Chinese State, Incomplete Proletarianization, and Structure of Inequality in Two Epochs." *Asia Pacific Journal* 9 (5): 1–35.

Shanghai Bureau of Statistics. 2011. *Shanghaishi 2010 nian renkou pucha ziliao* [Tabulation on the 2010 Population Census of Shanghai Municipality]. Beijing: Zhongguo tongji chubanshe.

———. 2017. *2015 Shanghaishi 1% renkou chouyang diaocha ziliao* [2015 Shanghai 1% population sampling statistics]. Beijing: Zhongguo tongji chubanshe.

Shanghai Municipal Educational Commission. 2008. *Guanyu 2008 nian zai benshi bufen quanrizhi putong zhongdeng zhiye xuexiao shixing zizhu zhaoshou zaihu nongmingong zinü* [Announcement on selected full-time secondary vocational schools' experimental enrollment of peasant workers' children living in Shanghai in 2008]. Shanghai: Shanghai Municipal Educational Commission.

Shi, Bonian, ed. 2005. *Chengshi bianyuanren: Jincheng nongmingong jiating jiqi zinü wenti yanjiu* [The urban marginalized: research on migrant families and their children]. Beijing: Shehui kexue wenxian chubanshe.

Shi, Lihong. 2009. "'Little Quilted Vests to Warm Parents' Hearts': Redefining the Gendered Practice of Filial Piety in Rural North-Eastern China." *China Quarterly* 198 (1): 348–63.

———. 2017. *Choosing Daughters: Family Change in Rural China*. Stanford, CA: Stanford University Press.

Shi, Yaojiang, and John J. Kennedy. 2016. "Delayed Registration and Identifying the 'Missing Girls' in China." *China Quarterly* 228: 1018–38.

Sigley, Gary. 2009. "Suzhi, the Body, and the Fortunes of Technoscientific Reasoning in Contemporary China." *positions: asia critique* 17 (3): 537–66.

Siu, Helen F., ed. 1990. *Furrows: Peasants, Intellectuals, and the State: Stories and Histories from Modern China*. Stanford, CA: Stanford University Press.

———. 2007. "Grounding Displacement: Uncivil Urban Spaces in Postreform South China." *American Ethnologist* 34 (2): 329–50.

Skeldon, Ronald. 1977. "The Evolution of Migration Patterns During Urbanization in Peru." *Geographical Review* 67 (4): 394–411.

Skinner, G. William. 1964. "Marketing and Social Structure in Rural China: Part I." *Journal of Asian Studies* 24 (1): 3–43.

———. 1965a. "Marketing and Social Structure in Rural China: Part II." *Journal of Asian Studies* 24 (2): 195–228.

———. 1965b. "Marketing and Social Structure in Rural China: Part III." *Journal of Asian Studies* 24 (3): 363–99.

Slater, Don. 1997. *Consumer Culture and Modernity*. Oxford: Polity; Cambridge, MA: Blackwell.

Solinger, Dorothy J. 1995. "The Floating Population in the Cities: Chances for Assimilation?" In *Urban Spaces in Contemporary China: The Potential for Autonomy and*

Community in Post-Mao China, edited by Deborah S. Davis, Richard Curt Kraus, Barry Naughton, and Elizabeth J. Perry, 113–42. Washington, DC: Woodrow Wilson Center Press; Cambridge: Cambridge University Press.

———. 1999. *Contesting Citizenship in Urban China: Peasant Migrants, the State, and the Logic of the Market*. Berkeley: University of California Press.

Song, Geng. 2010. "Chinese Masculinities Revisited: Male Images in Contemporary Television Drama Serials." *Modern China* 36 (4): 404–34.

Spivak, Gayatri Chakravorty. 1988. "Can the Subaltern Speak?" In *Marxism and the Interpretation of Culture*, edited by Cary Nelson and Lawrence Grossberg, 66–111. Urbana: University of Illinois Press.

State Council. 2006. *Guowuyuan guanyu jiejue nongmingong wenti de ruogan yijian* [State Council's opinions on solving problems related to peasant workers]. Beijing: State Council.

Steffensmeier, Darrell, Hua Zhong, and Yunmei Lu. 2017. "Age and Its Relation to Crime in Taiwan and United States: Invariant, or Does Cultural Context Matter?" *Criminology* 55 (2): 377–404.

Suda, Kimiko. 2016. "A Room of One's Own: Highly Educated Migrants' Strategies for Creating a Home in Guangzhou." *Population, Space and Place* 22 (2): 146–57.

Sun, Wanning. 2009. "Suzhi on the Move: Body, Place, and Power." *positions: asia critique* 17 (3): 617–42.

Sun, Yuezhu. 2011. "Parenting Practices and Chinese Singleton Adults." *Ethnology* 50 (4): 333–50.

Swain, J. D. 2002. "The Right Stuff: Fashioning an Identity Through Clothing." *Gender and Education* 14: 53–69.

Swider, Sarah C. 2015. *Building China: Informal Work and the New Precariat*. Ithaca, NY: Cornell University Press.

Tam, Tony, and Jin Jiang. 2015. "Divergent Urban-Rural Trends in College Attendance: State Policy Bias and Structural Exclusion in China." *Sociology of Education* 88 (2): 160–80.

Tang, Wenfang, and Qing Yang. 2008. "The Chinese Urban Caste System in Transition." *China Quarterly* 196 (1): 759–79.

Thøgersen, Stig. 1990. *Secondary Education in China After Mao: Reform and Social Conflict*. Aarhus, Denmark: Aarhus University Press.

Tilly, Charles. 1965. *Migration to an American City*. Newark: Agricultural Experiment Station, University of Delaware.

———. 2006. "Migration in Modern European History." In *Human Migration: Patterns and Policies*, edited by William H. McNeill and Ruth S. Adams, 48–74. Bloomington: Indiana University Press.

Tomba, Luigi. 2004. "Creating an Urban Middle Class: Social Engineering in Beijing." *China Journal* 51: 1–26.

———. 2005. "Residential Space and Collective Interest Formation in Beijing's Housing Disputes." *China Quarterly* 184: 934–51.

———. 2009. "Of Quality, Harmony, and Community: Civilization and the Middle Class in Urban China." *positions: asia critique* 17 (3): 591–616.

Tsing, Anna Lowenhaupt. 2000. "The Global Situation." *Cultural Anthropology* 15 (3): 327–60.

Turner, Victor W. 1967. *The Forest of Symbols: Aspects of Ndembu Ritual*. Ithaca, NY: Cornell University Press.

———. 1969. *The Ritual Process: Structure and Anti-Structure*. Chicago: Aldine.

Unger, Jonathan. 1982. *Education Under Mao: Class and Competition in Canton Schools, 1960–1980*. New York: Columbia University Press.

Urry, John. 2004. "The 'System' of Automobility." *Theory, Culture & Society* 21 (4–5): 25–39.

Wallace, Jeremy L. 2014. *Cities and Stability: Urbanization, Redistribution, and Regime Survival in China*. Oxford: Oxford University Press.

Wang, Fei-Ling. 2004. "Reformed Migration Control and New Targeted People: China's Hukou System in the 2000s." *China Quarterly* 177: 115–32.

———. 2005. *Organizing Through Division and Exclusion: China's Hukou System*. Stanford, CA: Stanford University Press.

Wang, Feng. 2008. *Boundaries and Categories: Rising Inequality in Post-Socialist Urban China*. Stanford, CA: Stanford University Press.

Wang, Feng, Xuejin Zuo, and Danching Ruan. 2002. "Rural Migrants in Shanghai: Living under the Shadow of Socialism." *International Migration Review* 36 (2): 520–45.

Wang, Jing. 2005. *Locating China: Space, Place, and Popular Culture*. London: Routledge.

Wang, Kaiyu, ed. 2007. *Buyiyang de tongnian: Zhongguo nongmingong zinü diaocha* [Unusual childhood: an investigation of Chinese peasant workers' children]. Hefei: Hefei gongyedaxue chubanshe.

Wang, Leslie. 2010. "Importing Western Childhoods into a Chinese State-Run Orphanage." *Qualitative Sociology* 33 (2): 137–59.

Wang, Liping, ed. 2002. *Shanghai renkou yu fazhan luntan: Renkou yu fazhan luntan wenji* [Shanghai Population and Development Forum: Population and Development journal compilation]. Shanghai: Shanghai kexuejishu chubanshe.

Wang, Lu. 2008. "The Marginality of Migrant Children in the Urban Chinese Educational System." *British Journal of Sociology of Education* 29 (6): 691–703.

Wang, Shaoguang, Deborah Davis, and Yanjie Bian. 2006. "The Uneven Distribution of Cultural Capital: Book Reading in Urban China." *Modern China* 32 (3): 315–48.

Wang, Yijie, and Yan Gao, eds. 2010. *Liudongertong yu chengshi shehui ronghe* [Floating children and urban social integration]. Beijing: Zhongguo shehuiwenxian chubanshe.

Wang, Ying, and Vanessa L. Fong. 2009. "Little Emperors and the 4:2:1 Generation: China's Singletons." *Journal of the American Academy of Child & Adolescent Psychiatry* 48 (12): 1137–39.

Wasserstrom, Jeffrey N. 2009. *Global Shanghai, 1850–2010: A History in Fragments*. London: Routledge.

Weber, Max. 1930. *The Protestant Ethic and the Spirit of Capitalism*. New York: Scribner.

———. 1978. *Economy and Society: An Outline of Interpretive Sociology*. Berkeley: University of California Press.

White, Tyrene. 1994. "The Origins of China's Birth Planning Policy." In *Engendering China: Women, Culture, and the State*, edited by Christina K. Gilmartin, Gail Hershatter, Lisa Rofel, and Tyrene White, 250–78. Cambridge, MA: Harvard University Press.

———. 2006. *China's Longest Campaign: Birth Planning in the People's Republic, 1949–2005*. Ithaca, NY: Cornell University Press.

Whyte, Martin King. 1995. *City Versus Countryside in China's Development*. The Fifty-Sixth George Ernest Morrison Lecture in Ethnology, 1995. Canberra: Australian National University Press.

———. 2005. "Continuity and Change in Urban Chinese Family Life." *China Journal* 53: 9–33.

———. 2010. *One Country, Two Societies: Rural-Urban Inequality in Contemporary China*. Cambridge, MA: Harvard University Press.

Whyte, Martin King, Wang Feng, and Yong Cai. 2015. "Challenging Myths About China's One-Child Policy." *China Journal* 74 (1): 144–59.

Whyte, Martin King, and S. Z. Gu. 1987. "Popular Response to China's Fertility Transition." *Population and Development Review* 13 (3): 471–93.

Williams, Raymond. 1973. *The Country and the City*. New York: Oxford University Press.

Willis, Paul. 1981. *Learning to Labor: How Working Class Kids Get Working Class Jobs*. New York: Columbia University Press.

Wilson, Brian, and Robert Sparks. 1996. "'It's Gotta Be the Shoes': Youth, Race, and Sneaker Commercials." *Sociology of Sport Journal* 13 (4): 398–427.

Windle, Joel. 2015. *Making Sense of School Choice: Politics, Policies, and Practice Under Conditions of Cultural Diversity*. New York: Palgrave.

Wong, Jocelyn Lai-Ngok. 2004. "School Autonomy in China: A Comparison Between Government and Private Schools Within the Context of Decentralization." *International Studies in Educational Administration* 32 (3): 58–73.

Woronov, T. E. 2004. "In the Eye of the Chicken: Hierarchy and Marginality Among Beijing's Migrant Schoolchildren." *Ethnography* 5 (3): 289–313.

———. 2007. "Chinese Children, American Education: Gloablizing Child Rearing in Contemporary China." In *Generations and Globalization: Youth, Age, and the Family in the New World Economy*, edited by Jennifer Cole and Deborah Durham, 29–51. Bloomington: Indiana University Press.

———. 2008. "Raising Quality, Fostering 'Creativity': Ideologies and Practices of Education Reform in Beijing." *Anthropology & Education Quarterly* 39 (4): 401–22.

———. 2009. "Governing China's Children: Governmentality and 'Education for Quality.'" *Positions: asia critique* 17 (3): 567–89.

———. 2011. "Learning to Serve: Urban Youth, Vocational Schools and New Class Formations in China." *China Journal* 66: 77–99.

———. 2015. *Class Work: Vocational Schools and China's Urban Youth*. Stanford, CA: Stanford University Press.

Wu, Haixia, Marcus W. Feldman, Xiaoyi Jin, and Shuzhuo Li. 2007. "Social Networks and Son Preference Among Rural-Urban Migrants in China: A Study in Shenzhen." In *Watering the Neighbor's Garden: The Growing Demographic Female Deficit in Asia*, edited by Isabelle Attane and Christophe Z. Guilmoto, 229–46. Paris: Committee for International Cooperation in National Research in Demography.

Wu, Haixia, Shuzhuo Li, and Xusong Yang. 2005. "Zhongguo xiangcheng liudong yu chengzhen chusheng renkou xingbiebi" [Rural-urban migration and the sex ratio at birth in urban regions in China: analysis based on the fifth population census]. *Renkou yanjiu* 25 (6): 11–18.

Wu, Jinting. 2012. "Disenchantment and Participatory Limits of Compulsory Education: Lessons from Southwest China." *Compare: A Journal of Comparative and International Education* 42 (4): 621–45.

———. 2016. *Fabricating an Educational Miracle: Compulsory Schooling Meets Ethnic Rural Development in Southwest China*. Albany: State University of New York Press.

Wu, Ka-Ming. 2018. "Elegant and Militarized: Ceremonial Volunteers and the Making of New Women Citizens in China." *Journal of Asian Studies* 77 (1): 205–23.

Wu, Ka-Ming, and Jieying Zhang. 2016. *Feiping Shenghuo: Lajichang de Jingji, Shequn Yu Kongjian* [Living with waste: economies, communities and spaces of waste collectors in China]. Bordertown Thinker Series. Hong Kong: Chinese University Press.

Xiang, Biao. 2005. *Transcending Boundaries Zhejiangcun: The Story of a Migrant Village in Beijing*. Leiden, Netherlands: Brill.

———. 2007. "How Far Are the Left-Behind Left Behind? A Preliminary Study in Rural China." *Population, Space and Place* 13 (3): 179–91.

Xie, Yu, and Haiyan Zhu. 2009. "Do Sons or Daughters Give More Money to Parents in Urban China?" *Journal of Marriage and Family* 71 (1): 174–86.

Xiong, Yihan. 2010a. *Chengshihua de haizi: nongmingong zinü de shenfen shengchan yu zhengzhi shehuihua* [Urbanized kids: identification and political socialization among migrant workers' children]. Shanghai: Shanghai shijie chuban jituan.

———. 2010b. "Diceng, xuexiao yu jieji zaishengchan" [Social underclass, school and class reproduction]. *Kaifang shidai* 1: 94–110.

———. 2015. "The Broken Ladder: Why Education Provides No Upward Mobility for Migrant Children in China." *China Quarterly* 21: 161–84.

Xu, Feng. 2000. *Women Migrant Workers in China's Economic Reform*. International Political Economy Series. Basingstoke, UK: Macmillan; New York: St. Martin's.

Xu, Jing. 2017. *The Good Child: Moral Development in a Chinese Preschool*. Stanford, CA: Stanford University Press.

Yan, Hairong. 2002. "Xiandaihua de huanying: xiaofei he shengchan de shuangrenwu" [Mirage of modernity: pas de deux of consumption and production]. *Taiwan shehui yanjiu jikan* 48: 95–134.

———. 2003. "Neoliberal Governmentality and Neohumanism: Organizing Suzhi Value Flow Through Labor Recruitment Networks." *Cultural Anthropology* 18 (4): 493–523.

———. 2005. "Refusing Success, Refusing 'Voice': The Other Story of Accumulation." Global Field Notes No. 8. eScholarship Repository, University of California, http://repositories.cdlib.org/ucias/gfn/8.

———. 2007. "Rurality and Labor Process Autonomy." In *Working in China: Ethnographies of Labor and Workplace Transformation*, edited by Ching Kwan Lee, 145–65. New York: Routledge.

———. 2008. *New Masters, New Servants: Migration, Development, and Women Workers in China*. Durham, NC: Duke University Press.

Yan, Yunxiang. 2006. "Little Emperors or Frail Pragmatists? China's '80ers Generation." *Current History* 105 (692): 255–62.

———. 2009. *The Individualization of Chinese Society*. English ed. Oxford: Berg.

———. 2010. "The Chinese path to individualization." *The British Journal of Sociology* 61 (3): 489–512.

Ye, Jingzhong. 2010. *Liushou Zhongguo: Nongcun liushou renkou yanjiu* [Left-behind China: a study of left-behind population in rural China]. Beijing: Shehui kexue wenxian chubanshe.

Ye, Jingzhong, and Lu Pan, eds. 2008. *Bieyang tongnian: Zhongguo nongcun liushou ertong* [Differentiated childhoods: children left behind in rural China]. Beijing: Shehuikexue wenxian chubanshe.

Yeh, Wen-hsin. 1997. "Shanghai Modernity: Commerce and Culture in a Republican City," in *Reappraising Republic China*, special issue, *China Quarterly* 150: 375–94.

———. 2007. *Shanghai Splendor: Economic Sentiments and the Making of Modern China, 1843–1949*. Berkeley: University of California Press.

Yi, Lin. 2008. *Cultural Exclusion in China: State Education, Social Mobility and Cultural Difference*. London: Routledge.

———. 2011. "Turning Rurality into Modernity: Suzhi Education in a Suburban Public School of Migrant Children in Xiamen." *China Quarterly* 206: 313–30.

Yiu, Lisa. 2016. "The Dilemma of Care: A Theory and Praxis of Citizenship-Based Care for China's Rural Migrant Youth." *Harvard Educational Review* 86 (2): 261–88.

Yu, LiAnne. 2014. *Consumption in China: How China's New Consumer Ideology Is Shaping the Nation*. Cambridge, UK: Polity.

Yuan, Zhenguo, ed. 2010. *Zhongguo jincheng wugong nongmin suiqianzinü jiaoyu yanjiu* [Study of the education of migrant workers' children living in Chinese cities]. Beijing: Jiaoyu kexue chubanshe.

Zanten, Agnes van. 1997. "Schooling Immigrants in France in the 1990s: Success or Failure of the Republican Model of Integration?" *Anthropology & Education Quarterly* 28 (3): 351–74.

———. 2003. "Middle-Class Parents and Social Mix in French Urban Schools: Reproduction and Transformation of Class Relations in Education." *International Studies in Sociology of Education* 13 (2): 107–23.

———. 2005. "New Modes of Reproducing Social Inequality in Education: The Changing Role of Parents, Teachers, Schools and Educational Policies." *European Educational Research Journal* 4 (1): 155–69.

Zavoretti, Roberta. 2017. *Rural Origins, City Lives: Class and Place in Contemporary China*. Seattle: University of Washington Press.

Zelizer, Viviana A. 1985. *Pricing the Priceless Child: The Changing Social Value of Children*. New York: Basic.

Zhan, Yang. 2015. "'My Life Is Elsewhere': Social Exclusion, Stratified Urban Space and Rural Migrant Consumption of Homeownership." *Dialectical Anthropology* 39 (4): 405–22.

Zhang, Jun. 2009. "Driving Toward Modernity: An Ethnography of Automobiles in Contemporary South China." PhD diss., Yale University.

———. 2019. *Driving Toward Modernity: Cars and Lives of the Middle Class in Contemporary China*. Ithaca, NY: Cornell University Press.

Zhang, Li. 2001a. "Contesting Crime, Order, and Migrant Spaces in Beijing." In *China Urban: Ethnographies of Contemporary Culture*, edited by Nancy N. Chen, Constance D. Clark, Suzanne Z. Gottschang, and Lyn Jeffery, 201–22. Durham, NC: Duke University Press.

———. 2001b. "Migration and Privatization of Space and Power in Late Socialist China." *American Ethnologist* 28 (1): 179–205.

———. 2001c. *Strangers in the City: Reconfigurations of Space, Power, and Social Networks Within China's Floating Population*. Stanford, CA: Stanford University Press.

———. 2002a. "Spatiality and Urban Citizenship in Late Socialist China." *Public Culture* 14 (2): 311–34.

———. 2002b. "Urban Experiences and Social Belonging Among Chinese Rural Migrants." In *Popular China: Unofficial Culture in a Globalizing Society*, edited by E. Perry Link, Richard Madsen, and Paul Pickowicz, 275–300. Lanham, MD: Rowman & Littlefield.

———. 2008. "Private Homes, Distinct Lifestyles: Performing a New Middle Class." In *Privatizing China: Socialism from Afar*, edited by Li Zhang and Aihwa Ong, 23–40. Ithaca, NY: Cornell University Press.

———. 2010. *In Search of Paradise: Middle-Class Living in a Chinese Metropolis*. Ithaca, NY: Cornell University Press.

———. 2012. "Economic Migration and Urban Citizenship in China: The Role of Points Systems." *Population and Development Review* 38 (3): 503–33.

Zhang, Tiedao, and Minxia Zhao. 2006. "Universalizing Nine-Year Compulsory Education for Poverty Reduction in Rural China." *International Review of Education* 52 (3–4): 261–86.

Zhao, Shukai. 2000. "Bianyuanhua de jichujiaoyu: Beijing wailairenkou zidixuexiao de chubudiaocha" [Marginalized basic education: preliminary investigation of migrant children schools in Beijing]. *Guanli shijie* 5: 70–78.

Zheng, Tiantian. 2007. "From Peasant Women to Bar Hostesses: An Ethnography of China's Karaoke Sex Industry." In *Working in China: Ethnographies of Labor and Workplace Transformation*, edited by Ching Kwan Lee, 125–43. New York: Routledge.

———. 2009. *Red Lights: The Lives of Sex Workers in Postsocialist China*. Minneapolis: University of Minnesota Press.

Zhong, Minghua, and Jian Zhang. 2015. "Analysis of the Citizenship Education of China's Junior High School Stage." *Asian Education and Development Studies* 4 (2): 190–203.

Zhu, Meihua. 2001. "The Education Problems of Migrant Children in Shanghai." *Child Welfare* 80 (5): 563–69.

INDEX

Page numbers in italics refer to figures, map, and tables.

civil service examination system, 132, 226n3

class reproduction, 107–9, 127

concept city, vs. pedestrian city, 40–41

consumer revolution, 21, 151–74; cars, 170–73, 227nn5–6; childhood discourses and, 158–59; citizenship and, 154; fair skin, 162–65; fashion, 165–70; freedom and, 166, 227n4; hierarchy of consumer markets, 159–61, 168–69, 227n2; *hukou* status and, 161, 174; identity formation and, 153–54; migrants and, 152–53; migrant youth and, 154; pocket money and consumption expectations, 155–59; return migration and, 151–52

continuing education, 191–93

Cultural Revolution, 59, 71, 148, 224n6

dagong (working for others), 178, 179–80

danwei (work unit) system, 6, 58, 68, 117

dating. *See* marriage and dating

Davis, Deborah, 153–54

de Certeau, Michel, 40

Deng Xiaoping, 178

detention and deportation system, 9, 220n12

dibao welfare, 119, 225n6

"eating bitterness" (*chiku*), 190, 228n4

edge, 29. *See also* social edginess

education: accessibility of, 7, 83–84, 223n1; attainment expectations, 225n5; bonding through complaints about exam preparation, 115; citizenship curriculum, 62–63; citizenship debate and high school entrance exams, 61–64; civil service examination system, 132, 226n3; continuing education, 191–93; costs, 135, 226n8; disillusionment with, 192, 193;

dropouts, 100; elite public schools in Shanghai, 89, 224n8; exam-oriented education (*yingshi jiaoyu*), 75–76, 94, 98, 116, 139, 140; exclusion of migrant students from high school entrance exams, 82, 84, 87, 88–89, 104–5, 115, 134; extracurricular activities, 75–76; *gongzhu minban xuexiao* (publicly sponsored, privately run schools), 84, 223n3; government funding, 224n7; homeroom system, 97, 221n1; home visits by teachers, 25, 221n2; *hukou* status and, 83, 133, 224n6, 225n4; junior college, 124, 192–93; migrant schools, 1–2, 3, 83–84, 139, 223n3; quality education reform (*suzhi jiaoyu*), 98–99, 140; relations between local and nonlocal students, 221n20; school selection fever (*zexiaore*), 89; seat assignment, 224n12; segmented inclusion of migrant students, 14, 82–83, 201–3; study abroad, 140–41, 204, 227n11; troublemakers and underperforming students, 85–86; upward mobility through, 14, 75, 79, 131–33, 226n4. *See also* high school; middle school; return migration; university education; vocational school

Elman, Benjamin, 132

employment prospects, 21, 175–98; adulthood pressures, 193–97; continuing education, 191–93; entrepreneurship vs. *dagong* (working for others), 178–80, 228n2; frustration over prospects, 175–76; income expectations, 176–78; job hunting, 184–86; labor market segmentation and discrimination, 188–90; office work vs. manual labor, 186–88; on-the-job training and internships, 158, 181–84

entrepreneurship, 20, 178–79, 228n2